ROYAL BOROUGH C

Follow us on twitter

Please return by the last date shown

12/18		

Thank you! To renew, please contact any
Royal Greenwich library or renew online or by phone
www.better.org.uk/greenwichlibraries
24hr renewal line 01527 852384

Martin Robison Delany

The Making of an Afro-American

Martin Robison Delany
1812–1885

by DOROTHY STERLING

DA CAPO PRESS

Library of Congress Cataloging in Publication Data

Sterling, Dorothy, 1913–
　　The making of an Afro-American: Martin Robison Delany, 1812–1885 /
by Dorothy Sterling.—1st Da Capo Press ed.
　　　p.　　cm.
　　Originally published: Garden City, N.Y.: Doubleday, 1971.
　　Includes bibliographical references (p.　　) and index.
　　ISBN 0-306-80721-1 (alk. paper)
　　1. Delany, Martin Robison, 1812–1885. 2. Soldiers—United States—
Biography. 3. Afro-American soldiers—Biography. 4. Abolitionists—United
States—Biography. 5. Afro-American abolitionists—Biography. I. Title.
E185.97.D458　1996
973.7′092—dc20　　　　　　　　　　　　　　　　　　　　　96-7781
[B]　　　　　　　　　　　　　　　　　　　　　　　　　　　CIP

First Da Capo Press edition 1996

This Da Capo Press paperback edition of *The Making of an
Afro-American* is an unabridged republication of the edition first
published in New York in 1971. It is reprinted by arrangement
with the author.

10　9　8　7　6　5　4

Published by Da Capo Press
A Member of the Perseus Books Group
http://www.dacapopress.com

CONTENTS

One ever feels his twoness–an American, a Negro; two souls, two thoughts, two unreconciled strivings; two warring ideals in one dark body, whose dogged strength alone keeps it from being torn asunder. The history of the American Negro is the history of this strife.

W. E. B. Du Bois, *1903*

What is Africa to me:
Copper sun or scarlet sea,
Jungle star or jungle track,
Strong bronzed men, or regal black,
Women from whose loins I sprang
When the birds of Eden sang?
—COUNTEE CULLEN

1

THE RAIN AND THE THUNDER

Graci Peace sat at her spinning wheel in front of the open
fire. Her foot rocked up and down on the treadle to the beat
of the rain on the roof. Listening to the wheel's quiet *hmm-
mm-mm, hmm*-mm-mm, she joined her own humming to it.
The humming became a song: *Oja pa, batta, batta . . .*
Young Martin left off staring through the window to look at
her. His grandmother's head was raised and her eyes were
narrowed as though seeking some point far beyond the walls
of their house. The rain drummed, the wheel hummed, and
his grandmother sang:

> *Oja pa, batta, batta,*
> *Oja pa, batta, batta,*
> *Lori apatta, lode ajalubatta*

The song was African. She had learned it when she was a
little girl. Martin, who had heard it before, knew what the
words meant:

> The rain beats, patter, patter
> The rain beats, patter, patter,
> On the rock in the drummer's yard.

His grandmother had often talked about the land, farther away than he could imagine, where she had been born. On such rainy afternoons as this she told him of trees bright with birds and ripe with fruit, of chattering monkeys and elephants that crashed through the bush to bathe in the great river that her people called "Yolla Ba." To Martin, listening wide-eyed, Africa sounded like the Garden of Eden that the minister spoke of on Sundays.

Grandma Graci was a Mandingo. A hundred and fifty years before the discovery of America her people had ruled the richest empire in West Africa. Although invading armies had destroyed their power, they remained a proud people, noted throughout the African world as craftsmen and traders.

While the rain drummed on the roof and thunder split the sky, Graci told Martin about Shango, the powerful storm god of her people. He hurled thunderbolts at the wicked and brought life to the fields with his rains. His wives were the lakes and the rivers. His sons were the kings of Africa.

Martin's grandfather, named Shango in honor of the storm god, had been a prince of the walled city in which he and Graci had lived, and Graci was his promised bride. Before they could marry, men from central Africa made war on their city. The young couple were captured and sold to slave traders.

A sailing ship crammed full of black captives carried them across the Atlantic to the colony of Virginia. They were sold at auction to the owner of a plantation near Richmond. There Shango set out tobacco plants each spring, hoed and suckered them during the long summer days and hung the broad leaves in the drying barn in the fall. Graci, who had learned the art of weaving from her mother, made the coarse cloth that her master supplied to his slaves. Both learned the King's English and became practicing Christians. Neither gave up the dream of returning to Africa one day.

Somehow—Martin never learned how—Shango and Graci won their freedom. Probably it was at this time too that they acquired a last name. Most slaves were known by their master's surname, but Shango wanted nothing to remind him of the years of bondage. One name had been sufficient for a man in the land of his fathers; if two were needed now he would select his own. Perhaps he recalled the talk he had heard in church about the Prince of Peace. At any rate, Shango and his wife, Graci, became Shango and Graci Peace.

Making their way to Norfolk, the colony's port city, they hunted for a ship that would carry them home. Vessels from all over the world were tied up at the wharves, but it cost ten pounds just to travel up the coast to New York and the couple owned nothing but the clothes on their backs. When the captain of a ship heading for the West Indies offered to sign Shango on as a sailor, he jumped at the chance. In the islands he could surely find another vessel and work his way to Africa. Once he reached the valley of the Yolla Ba, family and friends would help him. In a year—two at the most— he would be back to fetch Graci and their baby daughter, Pati.

A year passed, two years, three, but Shango did not return. Was he drowned at sea? Did he die of the fever? Graci never knew. While waiting she worked to support herself and her baby.

According to the laws of the colony, a child born of a free mother was also free. So Pati Peace was a free black Virginian, and a subject of His Majesty King George III of England.

Pati was seven when Patrick Henry took the floor at a convention in Richmond to say "Give me liberty or give me death!" Less than a year later, Norfolk was in flames, caught in a cross fire between British and American troops. With two thirds of the city burned to the ground, Graci and Pati joined the throng of refugees who fled up the coast.

All during the Revolution, Graci and Pati cooked, sewed, scrubbed other people's floors, washed other people's clothes, and saved their pennies. The end of the war brought no change in their lives. Despite the fine speeches about liberty and equality, Virginia was still a slave state. Hearing of lands to the west where life could be better for people who were not afraid of hard work, the two women sold their few belongings and set out on a long journey over the Blue Ridge Mountains. They traveled on horseback and on foot until they reached a settlement near the Shenandoah River where Charles Washington, youngest brother of the President, had set aside eighty acres of land for a town. Called "Charles Town" in his honor, its principal streets were named "George," "Samuel," "Lawrence," "Mildred" after members of the Washington family. Graci and Pati bought a half-acre lot on Lawrence Street and built a small house there.

Soon after they settled in Charles Town, Pati met Samuel Delany. Samuel's parents, too, had been captured in Africa and carried across the ocean into bondage. His father, a village chief in his homeland, had hated slavery as heartily as had Shango. He had run away when Samuel was small, taking his wife and two sons all the way to Canada before his master caught up with him.

Samuel was still a slave, working as a carpenter in Martinsburg, fourteen miles away. He was better off than many slaves, however, because his master allowed him to hire his time. This meant that Samuel collected his own wages and fed and clothed himself, paying his owner a weekly sum for the privilege. Anything he could save, he put aside to buy his freedom. He had already made a down payment on himself.

In the last years of the eighteenth century Pati Peace married Samuel Delany. They had five sons and daughters. Their youngest, Martin Robison Delany, was born in Charles Town on May 6, 1812.

Thus Martin, grandson of Shango the African, whose forefathers had been rulers in the valley of the Yolla Ba, began life in the valley of the Shenandoah, in the United States of America.

I am in a great degree principled against increasing my number of slaves by purchase. . . . Yet if you are not disposed to buy the bricklayer which is advertised for sale . . . and his price does not exceed one hundred, or a few more pounds, I should be glad if you should buy him for me. I have much work in this way to do this summer. If he has a family, with which he is to be sold; or from whom he would reluctantly part, I decline the purchase; his feelings I would not be the means of hurting in the latter case, nor at any rate be incumbered with the former.

—GEORGE WASHINGTON *to Henry Lee,*
1787

2

MR. CHARLES WASHINGTON'S
TOWN

Charles Town in the first decades of the nineteenth century was no longer a frontier town. Other well-to-do families like the Washingtons had left their worn-out tobacco plantations along the coast and had crossed the mountains with livestock and slaves. On the rich rolling lands of the valley the slaves planted wheat and corn and set out rows of apple trees. The Virginians were joined by Scotch-Irish and German immigrants who came down from Pennsylvania to farm. Although there were still bears on the mountain slopes and wolves in the woods, the settlers lived in comfortable brick houses and stored their grain in barns of stone. Jefferson County became the wealthiest county west of the Blue Ridge Mountains and Charles Town was its business and social center.

Stagecoaches clattered through town, following the turn-Pike from Harper's Ferry to Winchester. Farm wagons carried corn to the mill and crops to the market house. Gentlemen drove in from the country to transact their business over bottles of wine at the taverns or to attend the sessions of the circuit court which met on the second Tuesday of the month in the new brick courthouse at the corner of George and Washington streets. Charles Town's weekly paper carried advertisements for "a good assortment of cutlery, gentlemen's fashions and best spurs" and offered "For hire on first day of January next, a negro woman aged about 26 years and a boy aged about 11."

Charles Town had less than a thousand residents when Martin was born. They were the blacksmiths, saddlers, wagoners, shoemakers, storekeepers who supplied goods and services to the surrounding countryside. Although slaves made up almost a third of the population of Jefferson County, the townspeople seldom owned more than a servant or two. The third United States Census, taken in 1810, found only twenty-nine free black people in Charles Town. The largest family in this list of "Other Free Persons, except Indians" was the household headed by Graci Peace.

Graci, her back bent and her fingers knotted with age, looked after the children while their mother went out to work. Pati was probably a seamstress, going from home to home to cut cloth for a coat for the miller's wife, to fit dresses in a back room at the blacksmith's or shoemaker's house. Her earnings supplied food and clothing for her youngsters and paid the taxes on their home. Samuel's wages were put aside, penny after penny, for the day when he would be able to buy his freedom.

The children worked too—cutting wood for the fire, helping to make candles and soap, weeding the family vegetable garden. As the baby of the family, Martin was his grandmother's errand boy. He filled the woodbin and cleared the ashes from the fireplace, fed the chickens and gathered their eggs. Fetching water from the pump down the street, he tried to carry the bucket on his head, African style. When the water sloshed over, drenching his shirt, Graci laughed.

The woods around Charles Town abounded with small game. Although it was against the law for a black man to own a gun, laws were not always strictly enforced in the western counties. Samuel Jr., Martin's oldest brother, went hunting regularly, bringing back squirrels and rabbits for stew. One fall he shot a wild turkey and Martin helped his grandmother pluck the bird and roast it over the fire.

Indians had hunted in these woods not long before. When Sam Jr. found one of the sharp-edged triangular stones that they used as arrowheads, he gave it to Martin. Grandma, reaching for it eagerly, called it a thunderbolt. Although Sam laughed, she insisted that it was one of Shango's thunderbolts, like those her mother had kept when she was small, to protect their home from lightning.

Martin thought about the conversation the next day when he went out to play. Mr. Downey, a gentleman who owned eight slaves, lived across the street. Not long before, he had had a metal lightning rod, the first in town, installed on the roof of his house. People said it had been invented by a man named Benjamin Franklin, from up north in Philadelphia.

Fingering the stone that Sam had given him, Martin squinted up at the metal rod fastened to the Downeys' chimney. Thunderbolt or lightning rod? Shango or Franklin? Who was he to believe in?

After Graci's death in 1817, Martin thought less about Africa, more about America. He was old enough now to tag after his brothers and to play with the neighborhood children, all of whom were white. Samuel Offutt, a baker, and Nathaniel Offutt, a saddler, lived next door. Martin played with the Offutt boys, but his closest friend was John Avis, son of a cooper. When their chores were done the boys wandered out of town along the wagon roads. In summer they filled baskets with raspberries, blueberries, wild grapes. In fall they tossed sticks up at the trees, scrambling after the walnuts and hickories that pattered down. Sometimes they walked to the banks of the Shenandoah to fish, stopping on the way to explore a cave that George Washington had visited when he was a young man.

No one could live in Charles Town without learning about General Washington, who had led the colonists in their war against the British and had become the first President of the United States. Dozens of Washingtons were buried in the graveyard on Mildred Street. Dozens more—grandnieces and grandnephews—lived in white-pillared mansions on the outskirts of town.

Besides, there was that other Washington, the capital city, less than fifty miles away. During the second war against the British, which had started a month after Martin's birth, volunteers from Charles Town had taken arms from the government arsenal at Harper's Ferry and had sailed down the Potomac to defend Washington. Weeks later, when the British attacked Baltimore, Francis Scott Key wrote "The Star-Spangled Banner." Set to the tune of a drinking song, it was still the musical hit of the day.

As Martin walked down Liberty Street or stared at the

flag in front of the courthouse, he seldom doubted that "the land of the free and the home of the brave" was his land, his home. Still, there were big questions to puzzle over about white and black, slave and free.

Boylike, he swapped dreams with John Avis about the future. When John announced that he was going to be a soldier, Martin said, "Me too." He frowned when John informed him that it was against the law for blacks to join the militia.

Could that be true? His mother had said that he could be a carpenter, a blacksmith, or whatever he wanted when he grew up. What was a law? Were there separate laws for black and white? He knew that slaves had to obey their masters. Men and women who worked on the near-by farms occasionally visited the Delanys. They couldn't come to Charles Town unless they carried a piece of paper called a "pass." But *he* didn't have to carry a pass. Wasn't he as free as John?

Slowly Martin learned that being free and black was not the same as being free and white. Back in 1800 Gabriel Prosser, a slave, had led an army of blacks against the city of Richmond. Like George Washington's soldiers in the Revolution, they were seeking their freedom. But their rebellion had been put down and Gabriel and his lieutenants hanged.

Because free blacks had aided the Rebels, the Virginia legislature declared them "obnoxious to the laws and dangerous to the peace" of the state. Even before Gabriel's rebellion, free Negroes had been required to register at their county courthouse and to carry certified copies of the court register —known as "free papers"—to prove that they were not slaves. Now they were forbidden to move from town to town without the court's permission. Free blacks from other states were no longer allowed to enter Virginia, and slaves who won their freedom had to leave within a year after emancipation.

Once when Martin was a baby, Pati had had an argument with a storekeeper who had threatened to sell "them brats of yours" into slavery. Pati had neglected to register her two youngest children. If the storekeeper found this out, he could indeed sell them to the slave traders.

She flew home. With her little girl strapped to her back and Martin in her arms she walked to Winchester where the circuit court was sitting. Days later she returned to Charles Town, tired but triumphant, with free papers for both children.

Martin had been too young to remember the trip to Winchester, but he never forgot the night that his father failed to arrive home. Sunday was usually a day off for slaves. Whenever he could get a pass, Samuel trudged the fourteen miles from Martinsburg after work on Saturday to spend his free day with his family.

On this particular Saturday Martin had begged to stay up until his father arrived. When it grew late his mother sent him off to bed. In the middle of the night the sound of voices awakened him. From the attic where he and his brothers slept he could hear their neighbor, James Hogan, talking. Something about a fight, the sheriff, jail.

"A mercy they didn't kill him, Pati."

Kill who? Scrambling down the steps, Martin ran to his mother. As the grownups talked, he pieced together the story. His father, his quiet father who never lost his temper, had fought with his employer, a man named Violet, because Violet had threatened to whip him.

"Violet kept coming at him with the whip and Samuel kept shoving him off. Said he didn't want to hurt him but he wouldn't stand to be whipped by nobody," Mr. Hogan said. "Violet ran for help. Sheriff and a bunch of his deputies happened to be near by."

By the time the sheriff and his men caught up with him, Samuel had fortified himself behind a wagon, in a narrow lane. Armed with a swingletree—a heavy wooden crossbar from the wagon—he warned them to keep back. No one dared to approach him until a rock thrown by one of the deputies struck him in the face and knocked him senseless. Now he was lying in a cell in Charles Town's jail.

What would they do to him? Hang him? Whip him? Sell him south so he would never see his family again? A slave had no rights before the court. He could not testify in his own defense, hire a lawyer, ask for bail.

With the children in tow, Pati knocked on the sheriff's door the next morning. The jail was a two-story brick building at the corner of George and Washington streets. The sheriff and his family lived at one end of the building, the prisoners at the other. Martin, his eyes red-rimmed from lack of sleep, shivered as he looked up at the barred windows of the cells.

"What do you want?" the sheriff asked.

"To see Samuel Delany."

"Can't see him now. You'll see him tomorrow—in court." And he slammed the door.

The Delanys stood outside the jail all morning, hoping that Samuel would see or hear them, would somehow know they were there. Before long the street was crowded with churchgoers. The Offutts passed and then the Avises. John waved a cheerful hello, but Martin turned his face away. Suddenly he felt angry at John and all the other white people who were free to go to church or wherever they wanted, while his father was in jail. John might be his friend, but he could never understand how it felt to be a black Virginian with a father who was a slave.

The long day passed and then it was Monday. From the

back of the courtroom Martin tried to follow the proceedings. His father was standing in front of the judge's bench with the sheriff on one side and Mr. Violet on the other.

"Got to make an example of him," the sheriff said. "The law don't allow——."

"Devil with the law," Violet interrupted. "He's the best carpenter in Martinsburg. If he'll work straight through, Sundays, holidays, rain, shine, till he finishes my house I won't press charges—this time."

"You hear that, boy?" The judge crooked a finger at Samuel. "Think you can behave yourself?"

Samuel Delany, who hadn't been a boy for thirty years, nodded, his face expressionless.

"Speak up," the judge commanded. "Your master's being mighty nice. Another man might have sold you to the traders without thinking twice. You going to behave?"

In a voice so strained that Martin scarcely recognized it, Samuel replied: "Yes, sir. Thank you, sir. I'll behave."

Violet hustled him from the courtroom. As she watched them drive up the street, Pati sighed with relief. "If only he can stay out of trouble two-three more years, till he can buy himself free. Then we'll leave Virginia so fast they won't see us for our dust."

But the Delanys were to leave sooner than Pati anticipated —all because Martin wanted to go to school.

> These blacks who are free obtain a knowledge of facts by passing from place to place in society; they can thus organize insurrection. . . . It may be proven that it is the free blacks who instill into the slaves ideas hostile to our peace.
> —*Virginia Argus, January 17, 1806*

3

THE PEDDLER
SELLS A PRIMER

When Martin was a boy, free public schools did not exist in Virginia or in most parts of the United States. The prosperous planters around Charles Town sent their sons to the Charles Town Academy on South Lawrence Street and their daughters to the Female Academy across the way. After the young gentlemen studied Greek and Latin, French and geography at the Academy, they completed their educations at the College of William and Mary in Williamsburg or went abroad to the great universities of England and Germany.

There were no regular schools for the sons of working people, who were considered well enough educated if they learned a trade. Most could "figger" a little, enough to count and make change. Some could write their own names, but many Virginians still made an "X" as their mark when they agreed to a contract or recorded a deed for a piece of land.

In answer to a growing demand for tax-supported schools, the Virginia legislature in 1818 set aside $45,000 for "the education of the poor." While farmers built field schools— log buildings with dirt floors—in the country districts, Charles Town's citizens opened a school in one of the public rooms of Captain Cherry's tavern, the Old Ordinary.

The tavern was at the corner of North and West streets, less than two blocks from the Delanys' home. On the first day of school Martin followed the other youngsters, hoping against hope that he would be allowed in.

The schoolmaster frowned when he saw him. "You know better than to come here. Now run along and don't bother me again."

Martin's shoulders sagged as he walked back home. His brothers were at the market house, looking for odd jobs; his sisters were helping Mama with her sewing. The day seemed endless. He ate a piece of corn bread that his mother had left for his lunch, climbed a tree, chopped some wood, tossed sticks for his dog to retrieve. Nothing helped. He was too young to work—and too old to play when everyone else was in school.

Irresistibly, as if a magnet were pulling him, he found himself walking up North Street toward the Old Ordinary. Once there he circled the tavern warily, making sure that no one was watching. From an open window he could hear children's voices. The school was what was known as a "blab school" because all lessons were recited out loud.

> A-E-I-O-U
> Ba-be-bi-bo-bu
> Ca-ce-ci-co-cu
> Da-de-di-do-du

the children were chanting. Without a book or teacher's pointer in front of him the sounds were gibberish to Martin. Nevertheless he pursed his lips and silently repeated them.

Without telling anyone what he was doing, he went back to the tavern the next day and the day after. Sitting cross-legged under the window, half hidden by a bush, he followed the class recitations.

> Bad bed bid
> Bob fob job
> Mob rob sob

Sometimes they did arithmetic, learning to count in a chorus of "one-two-three-fours" and progressing to "one-and-one-are-two, two-and-one-are-three, three-and-one-are-four." Martin was so absorbed in the recitation that he forgot where he was and began to do his addition out loud.

A man's voice brought him back to reality. "What in tarnation are you saying?"

Martin jumped up guiltily.

"Didn't mean to startle you, son. Just couldn't figure out what you was talking about." The man smiled.

The boy was silent. The man—tall, thin, white—looked to be a stranger. Something about his speech, the way he snapped out the words, sounded different from the slow drawl of Virginians.

"Well, if you can't say, let me guess. Them children up there"—the man jerked his head toward the window—"are studying their lessons. You don't like being indoors on such a fine day, so you're having your own class out here. Right?"

Behind the stranger, Martin could see a horse and wagon tied to a hitching post. From a boxlike framework on top of the wagon hung rows of shiny tin pots and pans.

"You must be a Yankee peddler!" he guessed.

"Jonathan Dwight of Connecticut, at your service." The man bowed. "Need any wooden nutmegs? Oak cheeses? Solid birch hams? Or I have a fine assortment of pins—brass pins, sheet pins, lace pins, rolling pins, clothespins, tenpins."

Martin understood that Mr. Dwight was joking. The peddlers who came from New England were reputed to be sharp traders who sold wooden nutmegs instead of genuine East India spices and tried to talk housewives into buying realistically carved wooden hams. Actually, people welcomed the peddlers whose wagons were stocked with all sorts of goods—tinware, needles, buttons, calicoes—which were not manufactured in the South.

"Maybe my mother would like some pins," he timidly suggested.

"At your service," Mr. Dwight repeated. "But you ain't told me what you're doing out here, hiding behind the bushes."

"They won't let me go to school. Because I'm black."

"You a slave?"

The boy shook his head.

"And you think you've as much right to learn to read as they have?"

Martin knew better than to answer. Black boys didn't talk to white men about "rights"—not in Charles Town.

Mr. Dwight's voice dropped to a whisper. "*I* think you've as much right to learn to read as they have. And there's spelling books in my wagon. I'll trade one to your mother for rags or old pewter."

The peddler pulled a watch from his pocket and consulted it. "I've some goods to deliver out in the country. Then I'm putting up here at the tavern for the night. You tell me where you live and I'll be by after supper."

Martin spent the afternoon ransacking the house for things to trade. As the others returned they caught his excitement.

"No, you can't have my good pewter pitcher," Pati protested, "but they's a basket of linen scraps out back that I was saving for patches. Likely he can sell them to a paper mill up North."

In return for the linen scraps, bent spoons, blunt knives, and dented pewter plates that Martin had collected, Mr. Dwight gave him *The New York Primer and Spelling Book.*

Martin opened the book confidently, but his face fell as he turned the pages. Which was a-e-i and ba-be-bi? Nothing in the lines of print seemed familiar.

Mr. Dwight laughed when he noticed Martin's dismay. "Can't read yet, sonny? You're too impatient." He looked at his watch again. "I've a snigger of time left. If you like I'll stay and give you a lesson."

Everyone crowded around as he pointed out the letters. "This here's 'a' . . . Them's the vowels. . . . Now 'ba,be' . . ."

With mounting excitement, Martin began to recognize some of the syllables he had been sing-songing. So that was what "bad" looked like. Three separate letters and when you put them together they made a word. Before the evening was over he had learned "bed" and "bid," "bob" and "boy." When the peddler dropped by a week later all the Delanys knew the alphabet and were tackling sentences like "A bad man is a foe to God" and "Do as you are bid, but if you are bid, do no ill."

For Martin the days sped by. When his chores were done he pored over the primer, puzzling out the lessons. Each errand that he ran became a voyage of discovery. There were words to be deciphered everywhere. T-A-V-E-R-N. B-L-A-C-K-S-M-I-T-H. W-H-E-E-L-W-R-I-G-H-T. In the window of a shop on Washington Street he found easy words like SHOE BLACK-ING that he could read right off and hard ones like CUTLERY and COUGH MEDICINE that called for careful studying out.

After supper, the whole family pooled their knowledge. In the winter they read in front of the fire or spread out papers to practice writing with goose-quill pens and ink that they made from pokeberries. By spring they had finished the last lessons in the primer and were hungry for fresh reading matter. Martin found a crumpled poster on the street announcing a new stagecoach line. Sam Jr. contributed a copy of the *Farmers Repository,* a weekly paper, and Samuel brought them a Bible that a black preacher in Martinsburg had given him.

By common consent the family kept its studies a secret. A year earlier Quakers in a near-by town had been prosecuted for opening a school for black children. So it seemed best to the Delanys not to take any chances. Nevertheless the news got around.

The slaves were the first to hear it. In church on Sundays slaves and free blacks sat side by side in the gallery, while the whites worshiped in their high-backed pews on the main floor. A slave next to Sam Jr. noticed that he was following the words in the hymn book as the choir sang.

"You c'n read?" he whispered.

Sam nodded.

"Write too?"

"Uh huh."

"Will you write me a pass so's I c'n go see my wife next weekend? Hear she 'n the baby's sick but master won't let me off till the harvest's in."

Without saying anything to the others, Sam wrote a pass for the man with a sick wife. Before long he was writing passes for other slaves in the neighborhood. Pati was angry when she discovered this.

"They find out who's writing them passes, we'll be in trouble."

The trouble came from another source. On summer days the younger Delany children often congregated in their back yard. When it was too hot for strenuous games, they found a shady spot under the grape arbor and played school. Hidden from view by the tangle of leaves and vines, they took turns acting as schoolmaster and pupil.

One warm August afternoon Martin was reading the story of Adam and Eve from the Bible. Absorbed in the book, he failed to notice that two men had entered the yard. A booming voice interrupted him.

"You really readin' that, boy, or you know it by heart?"

Martin looked up to see Mr. Downey and another white man. "I'm reading," he replied.

The stranger took the book, turned the pages, and handed it back to Martin. "Now read here," he ordered.

"And-the-Lord-said-unto-Moses, Go-in-unto—" Martin hesitated over a word he had never seen before.

"'Pharaoh,'" Mr. Downey prompted.

"Pharaoh-for-I-have-hardened-his-heart—"

The stranger took the book again and turned to a new place. "Now here."

"And-the-Lord-said-unto-Moses-depart—"

"Amazing!" the stranger said. "A nigger boy reading like a preacher. Never would have believed it if I hadn't seen it with my own eyes. How old are you?"

"Ten." The boy smiled, flattered by the attention.

"Who taught you to read?"

"Taught myself mostly." Then pride overcame caution and Martin volunteered, "I can write too. And spell."

"Me too," his sister chimed in.

The man lifted his eyebrows, looking questioningly at Mr. Downey. As they walked away Martin had an uneasy feeling. Had he said the wrong thing? His mother sighed when he told her what had happened.

"You fool!" Sam Jr. said. "Haven't you any sense?"

Martin turned to his mother for comfort, but she shook her head. "I'm afraid he's right," she said.

Her fears were realized a day later when the sheriff knocked at their door. "I have here a summons calling on you to appear at the next sitting of the circuit court," he informed Mrs. Delany. "You're charged with having your children taught to read, in violation of the law."

Pati started to protest.

"You give the court the name of the person who taught them," the sheriff cut her off. "Maybe the judge'll go easy on you. Now if you'll just hand over them books you have, I'll be leaving."

He stalked from the house with their primer and Bible under his arm. Martin bit his lip to keep from crying. Now what would happen?

"Looks bad," James Hogan stopped by to tell them. "Everybody's talking all over town, saying the free colored is a problem. They'd as lief get rid of us all. They ain't going to believe these children taught themselves. Won't give 'em credit for having that much sense."

"I was listening to some men in the market house," Sam agreed. "Said Mama always was too proud, forgetting that she was black and brought us up the same way. Time she was taught a lesson, they said."

Even the people Pati sewed for began to recall times when she had been "uppity." "Jus' the way she holds her head, like she thinks she's as good as we," the blacksmith's wife said. "Serves her right," the storekeeper's daughter agreed.

Only one white person, Randall Brown, the banker, remained friendly and his advice was "Get out of town!"

"But what can they do to me?" Pati asked him.

"Send you to jail."

"And the children?"

"Declare them vagrants without means of support and hire them out till they're twenty-one."

That was all she needed to hear. When Samuel came from Martinsburg for his week-end visit, they arrived at a decision.

"We're leaving," Mrs. Delany told the children the next day.

"Leaving Charles Town?"

"Leaving Virginia," she corrected them.

After a moment of stunned silence, everyone had questions.

"Where'll we go?"

"What about Daddy?"

To travel south was unthinkable. Since the nearby states of Maryland and Delaware forbade the settlement of free blacks from other places, Pati and the children would go to Pennsylvania. They would stay in Chambersburg, sixteen miles from the southern border of the state, until Samuel was free to join them. Their father explained how they would go about it.

"Tomorrow, or the next day, your mama'll let it be known she's going to Martinsburg to see a lawyer. You young ones'll go with her. That's all anyone's to know, no matter who tries to sweet-talk you."

Martin flushed as his father continued. "Means no good-bys, not even to James Hogan—or John Avis. Later maybe you could write. But now you're going to Martinsburg *for a visit! Understand?*"

By midweek they were ready. Pati wandered through the house and out to the yard for a last glimpse at the place she had called "home" for more than twenty years. They were leaving with nothing but the clothes on their backs and the few possessions they could stuff in their pockets. No one looked back as they turned the corner of Lawrence Street heading north.

In Martinsburg, Samuel had arranged for a free man who owned a cart to drive them to Chambersburg. Twice they were stopped by patrollers. Twice they showed their free papers and were waved on.

At last, on a bright September morning in 1822, they crossed the border. Martin took a deep breath, exhaling slowly. He was in the free state of Pennsylvania.

That the coloured man is clothed
with the political rights and
privileges of the white man is an
opinion which . . . at no period
generally prevailed in Pennsylvania.
On the contrary he has always been
viewed as a *quasi* freeman, only—
deriving his imperfect freedom from
the will of the white community, and
enjoying it under their government
rather by *toleration* than *right*. His
occupation is usually menial; his social
and civil grade below that of the
meanest white man.

> —*"An Essay on the Political Grade
of the Free Coloured Population,"
published in Chambersburg,
Pennsylvania, 1836*

4

SCHOOL DAYS

The cart jounced along on the final lap of the journey. The
valley of the Shenandoah led into the Cumberland Valley—
the same gently rolling land, walled in by mountains. As the
road followed the corkscrew curves of Conococheague Creek,
forests of walnut and oak gave way to well-tilled fields, green
pastures, red barns.

Turning his head from side to side, Martin tried to take in
everything at once. He could see vineyards on the mountain
slopes, then orchards of apple and peach, with cherry trees

planted along the fence rows. The land was the same, but there were differences. Instead of slaves toiling in the fields, white men and women were harvesting corn while their children filled baskets with ripe apples. Unlike the plantations around Charles Town, these were family farms owned and worked by the German immigrants whom everyone called "Pennsylvania Dutch."

Chambersburg was not originally a German settlement. In 1730 a Scotch-Irishman named Benjamin Chambers had built a gristmill on the eastern branch of Conococheague Creek where the waters of Falling Spring provided power for his mill wheel. He laid out a town on both sides of the creek after the French and Indian War. Placing advertisements in newspapers as far away as Germany, he invited settlers to join him. They came—Germans, Swiss, Scotch-Irish, English— to farm in the valley and to build taverns, markets, shops around the Diamond, the eight-sided public square in the center of town.

By the 1820s Chambersburg was a thriving community with eight churches and three weekly newspapers for its population of three thousand. The old Indian trail that Benjamin Chambers had followed had become a turnpike, and Chambersburg was a stopping-off place on the main highway from Philadelphia to the West.

At a crossing on the outskirts of town, the Delanys' cart pulled to the side of the road to let a wagon train pass by. Martin counted thirty of the huge Conestoga wagons, admiring their boat-shaped, bright blue bodies and their tightly stretched canvas tops. Pulled by powerful six-horse teams whose jingling harness bells echoed across the valley, they covered fifteen miles in a day. Some of them were loaded to their wheel hubs with sugar, salt, iron, and whiskey for the western counties. Others were piled high with the household goods of German immigrant families. Men and women wearing wooden shoes walked alongside these wagons while towhaired children ran to the doors of farmhouses to ask for a "shtick brode"—a piece of bread.

To the ten-year-old boy from Virginia, the wagon train and the strange-speaking people who accompanied it were an impressive sight. For the first time he realized that he was living in a big country in a big world. He continued to be impressed by his new home in the months that followed. Compared to the slow pace of Charles Town, everything in Chambersburg was busy, noisy, exciting. The waters of Falling Spring turned the wheels of a paper mill, a sawmill, and a factory where tools were made. In a forge at the edge of town he could watch iron ore being smelted. The rough ore, looking like ordinary rock from the mountains was transformed into smooth pig-iron bars or cast into flat sheets for stoves.

In Virginia, people depended on fireplaces to heat their homes. Here almost everyone had a "Franklin stove" in his parlor. The big cast-iron stoves which kept houses warm even in zero weather had been developed by the same Benjamin Franklin who invented lightning rods. In Pennsylvania, Franklin's name was as familiar as the name of Washington in Virginia. Chambersburg, which was the seat of Franklin County, had a Franklin Road and a Franklin Street.

When Martin found a shop on the Diamond that had copies of Franklin's autobiography, he made up his mind to buy one some day. No one here objected to a black boy's owning a book—if he had the money to pay for it.

Money was not easy to come by. Although blacks were free in Pennsylvania, they were barred from most trades and professions. They could perform the hot and heavy work in a forge or sawmill, but they could not be wagoners, stagecoach drivers, stone masons, or clerks. Sam Jr. had hoped to apprentice himself to a blacksmith. Instead he helped to support the family by digging cellars, sawing wood, repairing roads. Pati was a skilled seamstress, but the thrifty housewives of Chambersburg made their own clothing and the few wealthy families in town preferred to hire German girls. She was forced to turn to the most menial kind of domestic work, scrubbing floors and scouring pots in a tavern for long hours and low pay.

The family's prospects improved when Samuel joined them, a free man at last. But the man who had been the best carpenter in Martinsburg could no longer work at his trade. "I've no objection to hiring you," one builder explained, "but my men'd walk out in a minute if they had to work 'long side a black." After months of doing odd jobs, he finally found employment in the paper mill.

Once again Martin was discovering that being free and black was not the same as being free and white. In theory, blacks could live and work and worship wherever they wanted to. In practice, Chambersburg's small black community was confined to the southwestern part of town, close to the mills and factory. In this section, known as Kerrstown, two or three black families had managed to build brick houses. The others lived in small story-and-a-half log cabins.

Black people had always been accepted in Chambersburg's churches. As slaves they had sat apart from their masters, in the balcony or on separate "Negro benches." When this custom was continued after Pennsylvania freed its slaves, black worshipers left the white churches and formed a congregation of their own. In 1812 they had bought a log building and moved it to Kerrstown. Their log church became a part of the growing African Methodist Episcopal Church, which had branches in cities all over the North.

Martin attended the African Church on Sundays, but on

weekdays he went to school with white children. Like Virginia, Pennsylvania had no public schools. Parents who were unable to pay for private schools could have their children admitted free if they declared themselves paupers. Since most were unwilling to do this, three quarters of the children in the state received little or no schooling. The Delanys were one of the few Kerrstown families who managed to scrape together money for tuition. It was hard going. Martin's older brothers and sisters soon dropped out and went to work, but they were all determined to see that Martin got an education.

School was drill, drill, drill. Memorize the grammar rules. Copy long lists of words for spelling. Add endless columns of figures. When pupils were letter-perfect in the fundamentals, they advanced to English readers designed, one title page said, "to establish a Taste for Just and Accurate Composition and to Promote the interests of Piety and Virtue."

Martin read Aesop's fables, the story of George Washington and the cherry tree, Socrates' defense before his judges, and the purported writings of Ossian, a third-century Gaelic poet.

In the higher grades he was taught public speaking. He learned to recite Hamlet's "To be or not to be" and *On the Death of Benjamin Franklin* with the proper pauses, changes of pitch, and expressive gestures.

In his last year in school, the brand-new subject of geography was introduced. First Pennsylvania—mountains, rivers, principal products. Then the boundaries and chief towns of the other twenty-three states. After that, the world.

"Europe is the abode of civilization, refinement, science, learning, and the arts," his teacher read aloud. "Europe has numerous universities which frequently contain two to three thousand students . . . Great Britain, France, and Germany excel in the number of their scientific and learned men. . . .

The French are gay, lively, impetuous . . . polite and amiable in their manner. . . . The Irish are robust, active, healthy, and brave. They make fine soldiers."

Martin had already located Africa on the globe in front of the room, but he was not prepared for the lesson that followed. "Western Africa is inhabited chiefly by various tribes of Negroes who go almost naked, lead a barbarous life, and are an ignorant and warlike race . . . The people are generally pagans and show little signs of intelligence. They believe in witchcraft and offer sacrifices to the devil."

Martin's cheeks flamed as everyone in the room turned to look at him. Most of his classmates were Pennsylvania Dutch youngsters who spoke English with a foreign accent and said "brode" and "kuchen" when they meant bread and cake. Their parents painted hex signs on their barns to keep witches away and consulted powwow doctors who used charms and amulets to cure them when they were sick. Yet *they* were descended from scientific and learned men while *his* ancestors were naked devil-worshipers.

Another geography described Africans as "rude and extremely stupid . . . The people are cannibals. They kill and eat their first-born children and their friends who die are eaten by their relations . . . There is a market where human flesh is sold. . . . They esteem it a luxury and it is said that a hundred prisoners or slaves are daily killed for the king's table."

Martin recalled Grandma Graci's stories of the market place in her village and of Shango, the king's son. Flesh-eaters? Cannibals? No!

He walked home in a daze. Could the geographies be wrong?

Although Chambersburg had no public library, several prominent men had taken an interest in Martin and had offered to lend him books. At the homes of Dr. Andrew McDowell and William Elder, a medical student, he hunted for answers to his questions. Africans, the travel books on their shelves reported, were "ill made," "savage," "filthy," "indolent," acquainted with but few of the arts of civilized life. And their continent, which his grandmother had described so glowingly, was a land of noxious fevers, man-eating beasts, venomous snakes.

Martin was deeply dissatisfied. This could not be the whole truth. These books did not explain his grandmother or why she yearned to return to her homeland. And the questions he had started out with led to others.

Why did some people have black skins while others were white? Did a man's color have anything to do with his ability?

Scientists knew little about the subject. No one had actually looked through a microscope and seen what a man's skin was made of. Indeed, a microscope powerful enough to do this had not yet been invented. Some scientists theorized that a Negro's skin contained a black liquid called "bile." Dr. Samuel Stanhope Smith, president of the College of New Jersey (later Princeton), had written "An Essay on the Causes of the Variety of Complexion and Figure in the Human Species," in which he concluded that color was the effect of climate. Everyone knew that the sun caused freckles. In the same way, excessive heat produced "a redundancy of bile." Thus a dark skin, he summed up, might "be justly considered as a universal freckle."

Not so, said Dr. Benjamin Rush, the most respected doctor in the country and a founder of the nation's first anti-slavery society. "The black color of the Negro is derived from leprosy," he reported to a meeting of the American Philosophical Society. Therefore, Rush urged, "Let science and humanity combine their efforts and endeavor to discover a remedy for it."

Most people, however, were content to turn to the Bible where the chapters of Genesis told the story of man's origins. Adam and Eve, everyone agreed, were white. So were their descendants until after the Flood when Ham incurred Noah's wrath. Then Noah pronounced a curse on Canaan, son of Ham, saying "a servant of servants shall he be unto his brethren" (Genesis 9:25). Biblical scholars interpreted this to mean that the sons of Ham were condemned by Noah's curse to have black skins and to be slaves.

Alongside the Bible in Dr. McDowell's library, Martin discovered Thomas Jefferson's *Notes on the State of Virginia*, published in 1784. Blacks were ill-formed and unattractive, the noted statesman wrote. "Are not the fine mixtures of red and white (in white skins) . . . preferable to that immovable veil of black which covers . . . the other race? Add to these, flowing hair, a more elegant symmetry of form, and their own judgment in favour of the whites, declared by their preference of them, as uniformly as is the preference of the Oran-ootan for the black women over those of his own species. The circumstance of superior beauty, is thought worthy of attention in the propagation of our horses, dogs, and other domestic animals; why not in that of man?"

Martin had to read and re-read the passage to be sure that he understood it. Was Thomas Jefferson, scientist and philosopher, actually saying that black women mated with *apes?* He read on.

"Comparing them by their faculties of memory, reason, and imagination, it appears to me, that in memory they are equal to the whites; in reason much inferior . . . and that in imagination they are dull, tasteless, and anomalous. . . . I advance it therefore as a suspicion only, that the blacks . . . are inferior to the whites in the endowments both of body and mind."

Martin closed the book. This, then, was the judgment of his white fellow countrymen—not the meanest of them, but the most generous and learned of their day. Blackness was a curse, a loathsome disease. American blacks as well as Africans were physically repellent, mentally inferior, doomed always to take second place.

Was it true? He walked home along the muddy streets of Kerrstown. Some boys were playing ball, tossing it high in the air and running with deerlike grace to catch it as it fell. A group of girls stood near by, talking, laughing. Monotonous faces? Inelegant forms? Martin, who was beginning to look at girls appraisingly, thought they had a beauty and sparkle that made the white girls in school seem pale and dull.

Catching a glimpse of himself in a shop window he paused to look at the reflection. He smirked, frowned, smiled, trying to guess what others saw when they looked at him. Close-cropped hair, tightly curled . . . dark eyes that were almost almond-shaped . . . straight high-bridged nose . . . shiny black skin . . .

Grandma Graci had once told him that his skin was like the polished ebony that African villagers used for carving. When Kerrstown neighbors called him handsome, his mother always said "handsome is as handsome does." But he could tell from her tone that she agreed with their estimate.

He stared at the reflection for a long time, thinking of his family and friends. After the long years of working to buy his freedom, his father had accepted what Chambersburg offered him—the log house, the Negro church, the dead-end factory job. Even his brother Sam, whom Martin had always looked up to, had given up the struggle. Married now, he no longer dreamed of becoming more than a common laborer—

living in the Negro section of a Northern town. Along with most of Kerrstown, Sam and his father were defeated not only by the white man's laws and customs, but by his estimate of their abilities.

They were wrong. All of them. His father and Thomas Jefferson and the ministers who said, "It's God's will that you are black. Walk humbly in the sight of the Lord." Martin didn't *feel* humble. Deep within himself was a pride in his blackness. In a hundred classroom contests he had proved that he was not inferior. Someday, somehow, he would prove this to the world.

He finished his last school term in the spring of 1829. Although he was already better educated than most of his contemporaries, he would need far more learning if he were to compete in the white world. The only high school in Chambersburg, the Academy, was both exclusive and expensive. His friends the McDowells and the Elders gave him the same advice that Charles Town's banker had given his mother: "Get out of town!"

For two years he worked his way up the Cumberland Valley to Carlisle, where he dreamed of attending Dickinson College, and to Harrisburg, the state capital. As hired hand on a farm, errand boy in shops, pick-and-shovel worker on the Pennsylvania Canal, he earned enough to feed and clothe himself, but had nothing to put by for tuition or books. Disappointed, he returned home to tell his parents that he was going to join the emigrant tide to the West.

On July 29, 1831—a date he never forgot—Martin Delany said good-by to his family and set out on the 150-mile journey over the Alleghenies that would bring him to Pittsburgh. The turnpike, completed a dozen years earlier, was a winding road—up mountain, down valley, up mountain again. Stagecoaches and wagon trains passed him by. Farmers gave him rides in their carts for short distances. Most of the time he was alone and on foot. The weather was warm and he slept in the woods at night, building a fire to ward off wolves and wildcats. Mornings he bathed in the cold clear water of mountain streams.

His money ran out when he had traveled only a third of the way. For a month he stayed in Bedford, helping a farmer bring in his harvest. In September he started out again.

Travelers who caught a glimpse of him through the curtained windows of a stagecoach saw a black teenager in rumpled clothes, worn carpetbag in hand. They could not know the mood of exultation that was building up inside him. Ordinarily, Martin was more interested in people than in scenery. But the days and nights alone and the grandeur of the view from the mountain peaks were a soul-expanding experience. Years later, after he had crossed the Alleghenies many times, he wrote a letter describing his emotions:

"It is only in the mountains that I can fully appreciate my existence as a man in America, my own native land. It is there my soul is lifted up, and I am lost in wonder at the dignity of my own nature. I see in the works of nature around me, the wisdom and goodness of God. I contemplate them, and conscious that He has endowed me with faculties to comprehend them, I then perceive the likeness I bear to Him. What a being is man—of how much importance!"

We can, if we will, arise and distinguish ourselves as well as other men,
by mental improvement. That man
whose complexion is white, and who
climbs the hill of science with un-
wearied zeal, knows to absolute
certainty that such a step opens his
way to the first honor of a nation
and will not fail to repute him one
among the most excellent of this earth.
But does such an expectation excite
men of our colour? We may hope, but
our expectations shall be disappointed.
—REVEREND JOHN GLOUCESTER,
January 1, 1830, Philadelphia

5

THE SMOKY CITY

He was almost there now. Following a road that snaked
steadily downward from the hills to the river, he could see
thin columns of black smoke rising from Pittsburgh's chim-
neys. He crossed the Allegheny River through the sudden
darkness of a wooden bridge, emerged into daylight again,
and looked . . . and looked.

Pittsburgh was built on a triangle of land between the Allegheny and Monongahela rivers. At the tip of the triangle,
which pointed westward like an arrow, the two rivers met to
form the broad Ohio. From Pittsburgh's docks a boat could
sail south and west for a thousand winding miles, into the

Mississippi, and a thousand more to New Orleans and the Gulf of Mexico.

Pittsburgh's strategic location at the head of the Ohio had made it the nation's busiest inland port. It was also the largest manufacturing center in the United States. Soft coal, lying close to the surface of the near-by hills supplied fuel for rolling mills, cotton factories, salt works, glass works, breweries. Clouds of smoke billowing from their smokestacks cast a pall over the city even at midday.

"Pittsburgh is the blackest place which I ever saw," an English traveler reported. "The tops of the churches are visible and some of the larger buildings may be partially traced through the thick brown settled smoke. But the city itself is buried in a dense fog."

English travelers tended to exaggerate conditions in the States. Pittsburghers cheerfully accepted the nickname of "Smoky City" and argued that the smoke and carbon dust protected them from the fevers that were prevalent elsewhere. "It is not improbable that the presence of iodine or some other element in our smoke has had a salutary effect. Strangers with weak lungs for a while find their coughs aggravated by the smoke, but asthmatic patients have found relief in breathing it. On the whole it may be said that no city in the union is more healthy," one Pittsburgh booster wrote.

Martin walked along Water Street which bordered the Monongahela, fascinated by the river traffic. At every wharf, keelboats, canalboats, flatboats, side-wheelers were taking on cargoes and passengers.

Near the Point, where the two rivers met, fleets of Conestoga wagons jammed the side streets. This was the end of the line for wagon trains and stagecoaches from Philadelphia and Baltimore. Here emigrants transferred from the "land schooners" to the river boats that would carry them down the Ohio to Kentucky, Indiana, Illinois.

Streets and wharves were a noisy confusion of people, horses, dogs, and pigs. Stagecoach drivers, coming to a halt with creaking brakes, blew bugles to announce their arrival. Drays and carts rattled over the cobblestones and steamboat whistles tooted "All aboard!" warnings.

Turning from the waterfront, Martin headed for the center of town. Pittsburgh, too, had its Diamond, with a brick courthouse and a large semicircular market house at one end. The sight of the market reminded him that he was hungry. Feeling in his pocket for one of his few remaining coins, he may well have thought of his hero, Benjamin Franklin. On just such a day as this, with the same feeling of discovery, young Ben had arrived in Philadelphia. Travel-stained, hungry, almost penniless, Ben had bought three penny rolls and had walked through the streets eating them.

Martin bought a sack of rolls and walked on. The streets leading from the Diamond were lined with hotels, taverns, homes with soot-blackened walls. More than half of the city was built of wood—built hastily, cheaply, and with no pretense at architectural style. Martin recalled the fine brick homes and well-kept gardens of Charles Town. By Charles Town's standards, Pittsburgh was ugly. But Pittsburgh, raw and new, seemed to promise more freedom than Charles Town had been willing to give Martin. Perhaps here in this frontier metropolis a man would not be judged by the color of his skin.

That remained to be seen, of course. Right now, he needed a place to sleep and a job. Young Franklin had put up in a tavern on his first night in Philadelphia and had gone to work in a print shop the next day. Martin knew that his own path would not be as easy.

Where was the black section of Pittsburgh? Two years of traveling through Pennsylvania had taught him to expect it at the outskirts of town, in the poorest, meanest section of a city. But he had followed Water Street to the Point and had doubled back along the Allegheny waterfront without seeing the familiar shacks and shanties where he might find supper and a bed. Now, like a scout lost in the woods, he hunted for another landmark.

His footsteps quickened as he turned down Third Street. A few doors from the corner he saw what he was looking for—a barber pole. Barbering was almost the only trade open to a black man, one of the few where he could earn more than a bare minimum. For blacks away from home, the red-and-white-striped pole which was a barber's insignia meant "Welcome, stranger!"

The sign in front of the shop said:

JOHN B. VASHON
BARBER & HAIRDRESSER
A SHAVING SALOON

Martin opened the door—and entered a new world.

The slender light-skinned man who greeted him was John Boyer Vashon. Son of a black woman and a white man—his father an Indian agent who represented the government in its dealings with the Cherokees—Vashon had grown up in Virginia and had fought in the War of 1812. After the war, the restrictions placed on free blacks drove him from his native state. With his wife and children he had settled first in Carlisle and then in Pittsburgh. Although he had only been in the city two years, he owned a well-furnished barber shop and a comfortable home next door.

The Vashons invited Martin to lodge with them. He could

shared a bed with their son, George, until he was able to find a room of his own. In their front parlor after supper they talked—as black men everywhere were talking in that fall of 1831—of Nat Turner, a fellow Virginian, who had led a slave revolt late in August. His band of slaves had killed sixty white people before state and federal troops arrived to crush the rebellion. But Turner was still at large.

Vashon brought out the latest copy of *The Liberator,* a new antislavery paper edited by William Lloyd Garrison. He was a friend of Garrison's and agent for the paper in Pittsburgh. Martin hunted through its columns for news of Turner.

"Have they caught him yet?" a booming voice interrupted.

A tall, heavy-set man stood in the doorway. Six years older than Martin, Lewis Woodson was the son of Virginia slaves who had bought their freedom and moved to Ohio. Educated by Quakers, he was a minister and teacher. A few weeks earlier he had come to Pittsburgh to open a school—for black children during the day and for adults at night.

The discussion shifted from Turner to a convention of colored men held in Philadelphia earlier in the year. The delegates to the convention were raising money for a college where black students could receive a classical education as well as training in "the mechanic arts." The college was to be located in New Haven, Connecticut, near Yale.

John Vashon frowned as he read them an account of a meeting in New Haven at which the mayor, common council, and freemen of the city had resolved that "the founding of colleges for educating colored people is an unwarrantable and dangerous interference with the concerns of other states. . . . We will resist the establishment of the proposed college in this place by every lawful means."

"The vote," he added angrily "was 700 to 4."

School, college, convention of colored men . . . Martin sat

in silence, drinking it all in. Vashon and Woodson were widely read, widely traveled. They were in touch with black men across the North, from Boston to Baltimore to the new settlements on the Western Reserve.

The Liberator was not the only paper in the parlor. On the bottom shelf of a crowded bookcase, Martin saw back issues of *The Rights of All,* a weekly published in 1829 by a black New Yorker. And in the place of honor on a table by the fireplace lay David Walker's "Appeal to the Colored Citizens of the World." Walker's pamphlet, issued two years earlier, called on slaves to fight for their freedom—"to kill or be killed." Turning its pages, Martin saw blunt and angry answers to questions about slavery and race prejudice that he had scarcely dared to ask of himself.

Martin came to Pittsburgh at a time of unprecedented activity in black circles. In the years after the Revolution most Americans believed that slavery would slowly disappear. Congress passed a law abolishing the African slave trade. The Northern states, one by one, were freeing their slaves. Patience and time would do the rest.

But a half century had gone by and a new generation of blacks was losing faith in patience and time. The slave system was stronger than ever. Its defenders were now saying, "God intended Negroes to be slaves. To give them freedom would be a curse instead of a blessing."

While men like Nat Turner plotted rebellions in the slave states, free blacks were also organizing. First had come the African churches, which were meeting houses and social centers as well as places of worship. Then came mutual benefit societies. Blacks could not be buried in "white" cemeteries? They chipped in a penny a week, a dollar a year, and formed their own burial societies. Blacks were shiftless and improvident? They established funds for their sick and their poor. Blacks were ignorant? They opened libraries and raised money for schools.

In black neighborhoods in the free states, the mouth-filling magic words were "Self Elevation," "Mental Improvement," "Moral Reform." By working hard, saving money, studying at night, free blacks could make better lives for themselves. And they could also help the slaves. Slaveowners claimed that blacks were an inferior people who could not take care of themselves. The achievements of free blacks were the best answer to this argument. If they were respectable and industrious then prejudice would fade away—and so would slavery.

Boston had an African Society, an Afric-American Female Intelligence Society, and an African Lodge of the Masons that dated back to the eighteenth century. In Providence, blacks organized an African Educational and Benevolent Society. In New Haven, a Peace and Benevolent Society of Afric-Americans was formed. Black New Yorkers established an African Improvement Society, a Philomathean Society "devoted to literature and useful knowledge," and a Library for the People of Color. There was a Union Society for the Improvement of the Colored People in Morals, Education and Mechanic Arts in Albany and a Mental and Moral Improvement Association in Troy. Philadelphians supported a Library Company of Colored Persons, a Female Literary Association, and more than forty charitable organizations for "the relief of our distressed brethren."

Three months after Martin's arrival in Pittsburgh, the city's black people organized an African Education Society. At a meeting in John Vashon's house, Martin cast his vote in favor of a constitution which explained "that ignorance is the sole cause of the present degradation and bondage of the people of color in these United States; that the intellectual capacity of the black man is equal to that of the white, and that he is equally susceptible of improvement."

The black movement found allies after the American Anti-Slavery Society was formed in 1833. Started by William Lloyd Garrison and a group of liberal whites, it was the first national organization to demand "freedom now" for the slaves. Its members planned to end slavery by non-violent means— "the destruction of error by the potency of truth; the overthrow of prejudice by the power of love," they said. Through lectures, newspaper articles, books, they would hammer away at slavery's evils, until they had changed the minds and hearts of the slaveowners.

Pittsburgh's Anti-Slavery Society was also organized in the Vashons' front parlor. With a white minister as president and Lewis Woodson as secretary, it brought antislavery lecturers to the city and sparked other state and local abolitionist groups.

Over the next years, Martin threw himself into the movement, heart and soul. Any black man who drank too much damaged the fight for freedom everywhere. Martin signed a "cold-water" pledge and became recording secretary of the Temperance Society of the People of Color. He helped to start a Philanthropic Society, which took on the double job of raising money for the black poor and assisting the runaway slaves who flocked to the city from Virginia and Maryland. He joined the Young Men's Bible Society, the Young Men's Anti-Slavery and Literary Society, and became a manager of the Moral Reform Society whose aim was "the moral and intellectual improvement of our race."

Although the meetings of these groups were earnest, they did not seem dull to Martin and his contemporaries. The lectures and discussions were stimulating and the gatherings offered a chance to meet people and make friends. Tem-

perance meetings might be enlivened by the testimony of a
reformed drunkard who summed up his bouts with "the
Demon Rum" by singing:

> And then I had nothing but rags to my back.
> My boots would not hide my toes.
> The crown of my hat went flip, flip, flip
> And you could tweak my rum-blossom nose.

Topics for debates at the Literary Society ranged from "Was
Brutus justified in taking the life of Caesar?" to "Is the
human mind limited?" Antislavery meetings opened with a
rousing hymn that Garrison had written:

> I am an Abolitionist,
> I glory in the name

and ended with toasts like

> Success to the lover
> Honor to the brave
> Health to the sick
> Freedom to the slave.

Refreshments were simple—often no more than biscuits and
water—but the participants felt that they were taking part in
"mental feasts."

During these years, Martin also struggled to complete his
education. By day he worked on the waterfront, loading coal
and pig iron on barges. At night he enrolled in Lewis Woodson's school. The school was located in the basement of the
African Methodist Episcopal Church in Miltenberger's Alley,
a few squares from the Diamond. Classes were informal.

Woodson taught the ABCs to ex-slaves and laid out a course of reading for his advanced students. Martin read—history, geography, ethics, metaphysics, natural philosophy (which was the early nineteenth-century phrase for science)—and reported back to his teacher whenever Woodson could spare time for him. But the school lasted only a short while. Few of his pupils were able to pay tuition and Woodson, who was newly married, turned to barbering to support his family.

Martin found another teacher in the person of Molliston Madison Clark, a twenty-five-year-old student at Jefferson College in nearby Canonsburg. Molliston Clark was a rare find indeed. In 1833 he was probably the only black college student in all of the United States. Perhaps because he was studying for the ministry, he had been admitted to the regular course of studies at Jefferson. Between semesters and during his seven-week summer vacations, he came to Pittsburgh to work. Martin, who rented a room on Fourth Street, gladly shared it with Clark in exchange for tutoring.

Lewis Woodson had the equivalent of a high school education, but Clark was a classical scholar and a linguist. He taught Martin a smattering of Latin and Greek and started him on the study of Spanish. Together they pursued history, searching for their past—their African past—in accounts of ancient times.

Americans had recently "discovered" Egypt. Some ten years earlier a French scholar had learned to decipher the hieroglyphics on Egyptian monuments. His studies had touched off a widespread interest in Egyptian history and art. Wealthy Americans traveled to Africa to see the Sphinx and the Pyramids at first hand, while those who could not afford the trip learned about the tombs and their mummified occupants from an outpouring of books and magazine articles.

Historians and popular writers hailed Egypt as "the parent of civilization, the cradle of the arts, the land of mystery"— and at the same time insisted that the Pyramid builders were not a colored people but were white. Where, then were black Africans at this time? Why, they were slaves of course, just as they are today, the experts explained. Egyptian civilization had in fact collapsed because the Egyptians later intermarried with "inferior tribes." It was this dilution of their "white blood" that supposedly accounted for the sorry state of Egypt in the nineteenth century. So the discovery of a great civilization in Africa had been turned into another "proof" of Negro inferiority and a justification of slavery in the United States!

Neither Molliston Clark nor Martin Delany could accept this. Turning to the Old Testament, which was still the authoritative source on ancient history, they dug up chapter and verse to show the relationship between the Ethiopians and other black peoples and the ancient Jews and Egyptians.

As others became involved in their nightly discussion, Martin and Molliston formed a club for young men who wanted to study and debate. The club was patterned on the Junto, organized by Benjamin Franklin and his friends a century earlier. But Martin named it the Theban Literary Society, after the ancient Egyptian city of Thebes.

Reading travelers' accounts of Central and South America and the black republic of Haiti, Martin became the club's expert on geography. When he learned that black freedmen were granted equal status in Spanish-speaking lands, he proposed that club members take up the regular study of Spanish. His proposal was voted down. Although the talk bounced back and forth from ancient Egypt to modern Mexico, it always returned to the topic that concerned them most—the position of the black man in Pittsburgh.

The Theban Literary Society later became the Young Men's

Literary and Moral Reform Society. The L. and M. R. Society, as its members called it, aimed "to let the world see and know that we are the offspring of that noble race of people who were once in possession of the arts and sciences and who delivered them down to a people illiterate as many of us are at this time." To combat illiteracy, they pooled their dues of 12½ cents a month and started a library with Martin Delany as librarian. When the society held a contest to see who could write the Lord's Prayer in the smallest possible space, it was Martin who won the prize. He had written it on a piece of paper the size of a quarter!

After Molliston Clark completed his studies at Jefferson College, he stopped in Pittsburgh to say good-by before leaving for a pastorate in Ohio. The hour grew late, and the talk turned as it had so many times before to Africa. In a burst of enthusiasm Molliston proposed that he and Martin go to Africa one day. He as a clergyman and Martin—what *was* Martin going to do when he tired of pushing barrowloads of coal along Water Street?

The oil lamp sputtered and died. Martin sat in silence in the dark room, thinking about the future. Africa, yes. He must go there some day. But first he wanted to prove that a black man could succeed in the United States.

What *was* he going to do? John Vashon now owned a public bathhouse for ladies and gentlemen, the first one west of the Alleghenies, as well as his barber shop. Lewis Woodson operated barber shops in the city's leading hotels. John Peck, who had recently come to Pittsburgh, was also a barber and wigmaker. All of them had offered to hire Martin, but he had shied away. Although he was as interested in making money as the next man, shaving a stranger's face, brushing off his coat, waiting with hand extended for a tip, seemed too servile. No, barbering was a "Negro job" and he wanted something more challenging.

From the days when he had borrowed books from the McDowells and William Elder he had cherished a secret dream—to become a doctor. Both Dr. McDowell and Dr. Elder now lived in Pittsburgh. Elder had switched to the practice of law and was to become a well-known writer and lecturer, while McDowell was one of the city's leading physicians.

Martin straightened up in his chair as he blurted out the words: "I'm going to be a doctor."

The day after Molliston Clark took passage on a steamboat for the West, Martin knocked on the door of Dr. Andrew McDowell's dispensary.

Medicine appropriates everything from every source that can be the slightest use to anybody who is ailing. It learned from a monk how to use antimony, from a sailor how to keep off scurvy, from a dairy-maid how to prevent smallpox. It borrowed acupuncture from the Japanese heathen, and was taught the use of lobelia by the American savage.

—DR. OLIVER WENDELL HOLMES

6

DR. MCDOWELL'S APPRENTICE

Puffing on his pipe, Dr. McDowell studied his visitor. He remembered Martin Delany as an awkward teenager with compelling dark eyes and a fiercely intelligent face. The young man seated across the desk from him had filled out. He was chunkily built, his broad, muscled shoulders telling of long hours of labor on the waterfront. Yet even in his workingman's clothes, there was something about him that inspired confidence.

If not for his color, McDowell thought, he might have made a doctor at that. Good hands. An energetic way of walking and talking. But a black doctor! Where would he study? What patients would trust him? In the whole history of North America, there had never been a black doctor.

True, there were herb doctors on plantations in the South.

And slaves whose masters had taught them to compound medicines and administer simple treatments. Benjamin Rush had written about one who had lived in Philadelphia. Durham? Derham?

"James Derham"—Martin was talking again—"bought his freedom and practiced medicine successfully in New Orleans. With white as well as Negro patients. Dr. Rush thought highly of him."

McDowell's eyebrows shot up. So he'd been reading Rush? This was not a man who could be dismissed easily. Somehow he would have to make him see that his dream was impossible.

Laying his pipe on the desk, McDowell outlined the training needed. Two years of reading medicine with a reputable physician. A year or two attending lectures at a medical school in the East. After that—

"If I had a son I'd send him to Paris for a year. Best doctors in the world work there now."

Martin nodded gravely, as if a trip to Paris was an everyday event in his life.

"Then back home to open an office. Equipment, books. Need a horse and buggy to make calls. And doctors' bills are the last ones people pay.

"Of course there are short-cuts." He was watching Martin's face. "There are men on the frontier calling themselves doctors that I wouldn't trust with a sick chicken. There's nothing to stop anyone from hanging out a shingle, but to be a trained physician takes time and money as well as work. Medical education is expensive. Don't suppose I could have done it if my father hadn't been a doctor with a practice I could walk into."

"I have some money saved," Martin said. "Figure I can always take on odd jobs when that runs out."

McDowell sighed. Didn't this man realize what he was up against? He'd have to spell it out for him.

"More than half the medical students in Philadelphia come from the South. They won't accept you in a college there—not in a thousand years. And even in Pittsburgh, what doctor's going to take you on as an apprentice?"

"I thought *you* might."

McDowell's jaw dropped. He had never interested himself in helping the Negro. He was not an abolitionist—didn't in fact approve of meddling in other people's business. But he admired a fighter.

Why not?

There were compelling answers to that question. Patients who would object to a black man in their sick rooms . . . his colleagues in the Medical Society . . . Besides, did a black have the ability to master anatomy and physiology, chemistry, pharmacology? Most people would say no. Might be interesting to find out.

"I'll gamble." Dr. McDowell slowly nodded. "Be here at seven sharp tomorrow morning. You'll have a long day ahead of you."

Martin walked home whistling. One hurdle had been overcome.

For more than a year he turned up at the doctor's office every morning. He pounded drugs into powders with pestle and mortar, mixed soothing syrups and strong-smelling emetics. He folded bandages, prepared mustard plasters and helped to apply them to aching chests. He scrubbed the doctor's lancet, polished his stethoscope, and carried his bag when he went on rounds. And after the McDowells had retired for the night, he swept the office before settling down to study Wistar's *System of Anatomy*.

There had been startling advances in technology since Martin had come to Pittsburgh. Steam ferries now puffed across the Monongahela River and steam engines hauled cars over the Alleghenies on a series of inclined planes. A traveler could go from Pittsburgh to Philadelphia in three days. Or if he had a mind to, he could sail straight up in the air in a basket suspended from a balloon.

A year earlier Martin had watched a balloonist take off from Penn Street to land in a field twenty miles away. This year gas lights were being installed on Pittsburgh's street corners and there was talk of a new invention called the "telegraph."

But medicine had made no comparable advances. Doctors were still practicing much as their forebears had done centuries earlier. They carried stethoscopes but not thermometers. They had no knowledge of antiseptics or anaesthetics. A few eastern cities had hospitals, but in Pittsburgh surgery was still performed at home. Instruments were not sterilized and the death rate from infection after surgery was high.

Microscopes had been invented, but were not yet used to study diseased tissues. Medicine was practiced mostly by educated guesswork. Doctors diagnosed an "inflammation of the chest," but could not tell if it was bronchitis, pleurisy, or pneumonia. And they were a long way from knowing its cause or cure. Even broken bones had to be set by guesswork because nothing was known about X-rays.

Most illnesses were described as "fevers," which came from "noxious emanations from swamps," "bad air," or "general debility." The treatment for them was "puke, purge, and bleed." Patients were given massive doses of physics, such as calomel, "to clean them out." After this, they were relieved of "bad blood." One doctor boasted that he had "dispensed enough calomel to load a paddle steamer and cupped enough blood to float it."

Although blood-letting had been practiced since the days of Hippocrates, the father of medicine, its widespread use in the first half of the nineteenth century stemmed from the theories of Dr. Benjamin Rush. Dr. Rush traced all diseases to the same cause—"excessive action" in the walls of the blood vessels. Anyone could see that a sick person had a flushed face and rapid pulse. The way to cure him was to take blood from him until he "relaxed." Then his pulse "softened," his face grew pale, and he would—or would not—get well.

One of Martin's first assignments as Dr. McDowell's assistant was to master the techniques of blood-letting. In the case of serious illness, the doctor opened a vein in the patient's arm and allowed as much as a pint of blood to flow into a basin. If the symptoms returned, so did the doctor—to draw more. Strange as this sounds today, it was widely accepted in the 1830s. People still recalled that when George Washington fell ill, he insisted that his doctors bleed him. What was good enough for the Father of his Country was good enough for them. The fact that Washington died a day after the bleeding did not lead many to question the remedy.

For minor ailments doctors resorted to cupping and leeching. Martin learned to tear small holes in a sick person's skin with an instrument known as a "scarificator." When a glass cup was placed over these holes in such a way as to create a vacuum, the cup filled with blood. Leeching was even simpler. To relieve a toothache or localized infection, two or three—or eight or ten—leeches were put on the infected area. Newspapers carried advertisements for "LEECHES! By the Dozen, Hundred & Thousand! Fresh and Warranted to Bite Quick" and jars of these blood-sucking aquatic relatives of the earthworm were standard equipment in every doctor's kit.

After Martin became adept at carrying out these procedures, Dr. McDowell asked him to take some of his night calls.

The first time he entered a sick room alone, he braced himself for a rebuff. Suppose the patient objected to black hands tending him? But the man who looked up at him from his pillow murmured, "Glad you got here so fast. I feel awful. Ain't you going to bleed me, Doc?"

Doc! How good that title sounded—even though he hadn't earned it yet. No patient ever received more loving care than Martin gave that night. He bled the man until the fever subsided, brewed him tea, and sat alongside his bed while he fell into a restless sleep.

Blood-letting was not the only skill that Martin mastered. Dr. McDowell taught him how to sew up wounds, set broken legs, deliver babies. Diphtheria was then the commonest cause of children's deaths. Although doctors could not cure the disease, they saved lives by cutting into the windpipe of a choking child so that he could breathe again. After Martin assisted at a number of these tracheostomies, McDowell permitted him to perform them on his own.

The doctor was no longer concerned about his pupil's ability to master the work. However, as time passed, he was aware that something was troubling Martin. That something was money. His savings were gone. He had been subsisting on the meal a day that Mrs. McDowell gave him, piecing it out with suppers of beans and an occasional Sunday dinner with his parents.

The older Delanys and Sam Jr. and his family had moved to Pittsburgh and were living across the river in Allegheny. They had arrived during boom times when factories were expanding and jobs were plentiful. But the boom had been quickly followed by a bust. Some said that too many railroads and turnpikes had been built too fast, others that there had been too much speculation in the western lands sold by the government to settlers. Whatever the reason, 1837 was a depression year all over the United States.

In Pittsburgh, factories shut down, businesses failed, and thousands were thrown out of work. As newcomers, Martin's father and brother were among the first to lose their jobs. Pati could no longer serve big Sunday dinners. Some days there were no dinners at all.

Martin found himself faced with a painful decision. He could scrape along as he had been doing, tightening his belt. But could he allow his parents and Sam's children to go hungry?

Pacing his room at night he concluded that studying to be a doctor was a luxury he could no longer afford. He would have to say good-by to Dr. McDowell and look for work.

The doctor's disappointment came close to matching Martin's. "Wish I could offer to pay you a salary. But I'm having the devil's own time collecting bills. What will you do?"

Martin shrugged. "I'll find something—maybe ship out on a river boat."

"Wait!" McDowell had an idea. There was a shortage of doctors in Pittsburgh. Why couldn't Martin set himself up as a doctor's assistant—a cupper and bleeder? "I'd send you out on cases and I'll wager Joe Gazzam would too."

Martin's gloom began to lift. Dr. Gazzam was a vice-president of the Pittsburgh Anti-Slavery Society as well as a member of the City Council. If he and McDowell would recommend him, it just might work. And maybe he could do dentistry too. The first dental college was yet to be organized. Doctors pulled teeth, and so did barbers—or anyone with self-confidence and a pair of suitable pincers.

McDowell's suggestion proved a wise one. Pittsburgh's overworked doctors were glad to have someone to take over routine work. Before long Martin was answering so many calls that he gave up all thoughts of dentistry. When the *Pittsburgh Business Directory* for 1837 was issued, it listed, after the names of the city's physicians, "DELANY, MARTIN R. Cupping, Leeching and bleeding."

All too frequently, many young, middle-class, white Americans, have wanted to "come alive" through the black community. . . . Many have come seeing "no difference in color," they have come "color blind." But at this time and in this land, color *is* a factor and we should not overlook or deny this.

—STOKELEY CARMICHAEL AND CHARLES HAMILTON *in* Black Power, *1967*

7

THE SEARCH FOR A PLACE

In 1836 Martin Delany and Lewis Woodson had been chosen as Pittsburgh's delegates to the annual Convention of Colored Men in New York. They had traveled across the mountains on the new Portage Railroad and then by canalboat to Philadelphia. When they reached New York after another two days on the road, they learned that the convention had been postponed indefinitely.

Talking to men in the East, Martin found that many were questioning the need for separate black organizations. Abolitionists were urging blacks to give up their "Colored Conventions" and their "African" churches and social groups. In the antislavery movement whites and blacks could work together for the good of all mankind. Some men even objected to words like "black," "colored," "Negro," "sons of Africa" and suggested as a substitute a phrase like "oppressed Americans."

Were they right? Martin puzzled over the question after he returned to Pittsburgh. Even if *he* could forget his dark skin, would white men be willing to do so?

The antislavery movement had grown swiftly. Abolitionists were holding meetings, distributing pamphlets, collecting signatures on petitions in every city in the North. Tens of thousands of people were reading *The Liberator, The Anti-Slavery Standard, The Emancipator,* and even a magazine for children called *The Slave's Friend.*

But were the slaves any closer to freedom? Had the situation improved for free blacks?

Blacks were accepted in the antislavery societies, but few were chosen as officers. Fewer still were employed as speakers or as reporters for the antislavery papers. It was as if the white abolitionists were saying, "We know what's best. We'll fight your battles for you."

The battles seemed to grow more intense with each passing year. Sometimes Martin felt that black people were losing ground in their struggle for equality. After the Revolution black men had been allowed to vote in most northern cities and towns. Now state after state was passing laws to disfranchise them. Despite strenuous opposition by abolitionists, Pennsylvania had just revised its constitution to limit the ballot to white men.

The legislature had also passed a Common School Bill to establish free public schools throughout the state. But Pittsburgh's African School was located in a damp church basement and was supported largely through the efforts of the black community.

Along with this there had been a frightening increase in mob violence. Returning from a trip to Boston, John B.

Vashon described how a crowd of respectable citizens had broken up an antislavery meeting and had dragged William Lloyd Garrison through the streets with a rope around his neck. Garrison had escaped lynching, but Elijah Lovejoy, editor of an abolitionist paper in Illinois, was killed by a proslavery mob. His death sent shock waves across the North. In Pittsburgh, abolitionists wore black arm bands and went to a meeting at a downtown church to protest "the atrocious murder of our revered brother."

Few wore crepe, however, to mourn the blacks who were killed in race riots. Year after year, white mobs invaded the black sections of northern cities. Homes, churches, shops were burned; men, women, and children were forced to flee for their lives. Even in Pittsburgh, where relations between the races were better than in most communities, Martin was awakened one evening by the news of a mob attack on John B. Vashon's house. The militia dispersed the rioters before they could do much damage. For many weeks afterward Martin patrolled the streets at night as a member of a volunteer police force appointed by the mayor. During a second outbreak in Pittsburgh several years later, a black child was killed and three black homes destroyed.

More often than not these attacks were led by unemployed whites who hoped that if they drove away the blacks, especially those who had achieved some success, they would open up jobs for themselves. Native workingmen and Irish immigrants who had only been in the United States for a few months joined forces to shout "Down with the niggers! Send them back to Africa where they belong."

Workingmen did not originate the back-to-Africa slogan, however. Martin had been a boy in Charles Town when a group of prominent citizens organized the American Colonization Society. Most of the society's supporters were slaveholders who believed that whites and blacks could not live side by side except as master and slave. They considered free blacks to be dangerous people whose presence threatened the slave system. With semiofficial backing from the government, the Society established the colony of Liberia on Africa's West Coast as a "homeland" for American blacks. Although the Society offered to pay the passage of all who wished to emigrate, only a small number of free blacks and slaves freed expressly for this purpose took advantage of the offer.

The vast majority of free blacks looked on the Colonization Society as their enemy. "African colonization is a scheme to drain the better-informed part of the colored people out of the United States, so that the chain of slavery may be riveted more tightly," a meeting of Pittsburgh blacks declared. "We consider every colored man who allows himself to be colonized in Africa a traitor to our cause."

No one was louder than Martin Delany in denouncing the American Colonization Society. However, when he read of new antiblack outrages he sometimes wondered if blacks and whites *could* ever live in harmony. Perhaps there really was an impassable barrier between the races, "a mutual repellency" as the colonizationists said. Maybe black people should set up their own communities, not in Africa but in the United States.

"Where would we go?" a friend challenged him when he brought up the subject at a Moral Reform meeting. "White men can take up homesteads all over the West. Government sells 'em cheap land. But us? Ohio won't even let us settle in the state unless we put up a $500 bond. Who's got that kind of money?"

"Same with Illinois, Indiana, Michigan," another man took up the argument. "They all got black laws. Negro can't enter.

Negro can't farm. Can't vote, can't send his kids to school. They got us hemmed in."

Martin knew all this. "I'm thinking of the Southwest. Texas for a start."

Texas was very much in the news. In 1836 American settlers had wrested the territory from Mexico. Under the leadership of General Sam Houston they had established the independent Republic of Texas. Slaveowners from the South, Yankee businessmen, adventurers from as far away as England were streaming to the new nation which many expected would soon be annexed to the United States. The republic's blue flag floated over a vast territory that could be carved into four or five separate states. Abolitionists opposed annexation because they feared that these would all become slave states.

But suppose that thousands of black men joined this exodus to the Southwest and took up land for themselves? When annexation came, they would be able to determine the fate of their own region.

Martin didn't know whether this was practical, but he made up his mind to find out. He decided to take a trip through the South. To see slaves and slavery at first hand. To visit Texas, the new state of Arkansas, and the Indian Territory that bordered it. Somewhere on this vast continent there had to be a place for black men.

Many states in the deep South had laws forbidding free blacks to cross their borders. Others required them to show their free papers on demand or be subject to arrest and sale as slaves.

Pati cried when Martin asked for the certificate of freedom that she had obtained from the court in Winchester so long before.

"You crazy?" Sam Jr. asked. "Those southerners'll sell you into slavery—if they don't hang you first."

But nothing could dissuade Martin from leaving. On a late fall day in 1839 he locked the door and shuttered the window of his office on Fifth Street. He walked briskly to the Point where the steamer *Buckeye State* was taking on passengers. Pati had come over from Allegheny to say good-by. Her face creased with anxiety, she watched him walk up the gangplank. He turned to wave before climbing the ladder to the upper deck. Would she ever see him again?

8

WHITE MAN'S COUNTRY

Martin stood at the rail until the houses and factories of
Pittsburgh were hidden by a bend in the river. The *Buckeye
State* was in midstream now, following the winding course of
the Ohio. On either side the banks were steep and tree-cov-
ered. Here and there a single log cabin stood on a patch of
cleared ground. Otherwise the woods looked as they had a
century earlier when they were Indian hunting grounds.

On the lower deck, well-to-do ladies and gentlemen were
making themselves comfortable in their staterooms, resting on
curtained bunks until a bell called them to the main saloon
for dinner. Martin was a deck passenger. For three dollars,
paid in advance at the shipping office in Pittsburgh, he was
entitled to passage to Cincinnati. His "stateroom" was any
space he could find on the open deck that was not occupied
by cargo—or other deck passengers. A plank of wood covered

with a gunny sack served as bunk, and it was up to him to provide his own food.

Most of his traveling companions were Irish or German immigrants. Mothers, fathers, and a brood of children huddled around an old sea chest, a high-backed chair, a stack of pots and pans. They had opened sacks of sausage and dried herring and were passing them from hand to hand. Tired from months of travel, they stared with only a faint stirring of curiosity as Martin walked by. No one offered him food, nor did he expect them to. He was looking for the crew's quarters.

The firemen who stoked the furnace, the cook in the galley below, the waiters, stewards, and the roustabouts who carried freight up the gangplank were all black men. Most spent time in Pittsburgh between voyages. Martin knew several from his waterfront days. After the cabin passengers dined, pans heaped high with leftovers were brought on deck. When a steward cried, "Grub pile!" the crew assembled for their meal. Dining was not elegant. The deck served as table and fingers took the place of forks. But Martin was glad to be asked to join them.

He joined them again when the boat made its twice-daily stop for fuel. Its boiler consumed from two to three dozen cords of wood a day. When river bank farmers cleared their fields, they cut up the felled trees and stockpiled them along the shore. As soon as the boat tied up at one of these wood yards, all hands turned out to bring the logs aboard. By working alongside the roustabouts, Martin earned a rebate on his fare.

From the boatmen he learned the gossip of the river towns. "Cincinnati can be a rough place for colored, less'n you know where to go . . . Louisville's pretty good for a slave city, but stick close to the levee. Out in the country they don't care for free blacks. 'Fraid we'll stir up the slaves . . ."

Three days and two nights brought him to Cincinnati where he transferred to the *Telegraph No. 2* for Louisville. He spent long lazy hours on deck. The rocky bluffs had given way to low banks with great stretches of fields behind them. Fields cultivated by slaves. Slavery became a familiar fact of life beyond Louisville. There, after traversing the Falls of the Ohio, a series of rapids, on a small steamer, he boarded the *Queen of the West*.

The immigrant families were gone. They had been put ashore—chairs, chests, and children—at landings in Indiana and Illinois. "Them foreigners'll do all right," a steward commented bitterly. "Five years from now they'll be voting their own men into the legislature and passing laws to keep the niggers out."

Their places on deck were taken by slaves. Men with clanking chains around their ankles, women nursing babies, frightened-looking girls and boys. Bought by traders in Virginia and Maryland, they were being carried down-river to the sugar and cotton plantations in the deep South. Slaves were dirt-cheap in Richmond. They would fetch big prices in Natchez and New Orleans.

Martin's heart sank when he saw them. He had known runaways in Pittsburgh, eagerly embarking on new lives. Even the slaves he remembered from Charles Town had had hopes and dreams to sustain them. But these men and women had been sold from family, friends, and everything dear to them. They lay on the deck, limp and dispirited, except when the trader who owned them came up to see that they exercised.

"Shake a leg now," he ordered. "Can't have you getting sick on me."

They obeyed listlessly, walking bow-to-stern, stern-to-bow

with expressionless faces. Occasionally, at night when the trader was drinking in the saloon, they seemed to come alive. Then one of the men might strike up a song:

> See wives and husbands torn apart,
> Their children's screams,
> They grieve my heart.
> They are torn away to Georgia!

The others joined in a mournful chorus:

> Come and go along with me—
> They are torn away to Georgia!

Martin thought it was the saddest song he had ever heard. Something about the tune reminded him of songs that Grandma Graci used to sing. He caught tantalizingly familiar notes again several days later. The *Queen of the West* had left the Ohio behind and was plowing through the murky waters of the Mississippi. As she approached the wharf boat at the Natchez landing, the black firemen began to sing "Natchez-Under-the-Hill."

Natchez was a major port on the Mississippi and a way point on the road to the Southwest. Planters lived in stately houses on a high bluff overlooking the river. Below, on a narrow stretch of muddy ground, was Natchez-Under-the-Hill. There slaves were traded and gamblers and prostitutes hung out. The firemen's dirgelike song reminded listeners of the slave marts where their brethren were sold.

The melody captivated Martin. Was it possible that these songs derived from African music? He hummed a few bars, trying to memorize them, so that he could ask his mother about them when he returned home.

"If you return home," a boatman grimly reminded him. Martin had planned to leave the *Queen of the West* at Natchez and travel to Louisiana on foot. The boatmen warned of the dangers of his undertaking.

"Don't go waving around them free papers of yours. A free black coming from the North! They'll nab you soon's you set foot on a plantation. Wasn't but two years ago they strung up a parcel of free blacks around here. Claimed they was planning to kill the whites and run the slaves off to Mexico."

Martin weighed their advice carefully. Before leaving the *Queen* he hid his free papers and money in a belt around his waist. The clean clothes he had worn when he left Pittsburgh were rumpled and dirty. Meeting him on the road, who could say whether he was slave or free? White people never looked closely at blacks anyway.

A roustabout shook his head. "It's the way you talk. You sound *educated.* You don't sound Mississippi or black."

Seventeen years in Pennsylvania had given his speech a northern, almost a nasal, ring. But he still retained traces of the softer slower speech of his childhood. Many of the slaves of Mississippi—and the masters too—had come from Virginia as he had. If he could remember to talk as his parents did, he would be all right.

"You gotta remember," the roustabout counseled. "And no big words—or reading and writing neither."

After an anxious day or two, Martin fell into the patterns of southern ways. Posing as a slave was easier than he had expected it to be. Occasionally a white man stopped to ask who he was and where he was going. As long as he kept his voice low, his manner respectful, his explanation that he was "a new boy goin' down the road a piece" on an errand for his master was readily accepted.

The main danger came at night when a strict curfew for

slaves was enforced. Armed men on horseback patrolled the roads. Any slave without a pass was thrown into jail. Martin avoided the patrollers by cutting across the fields to the slave cabins before dusk. There people willingly shared their meager rations and made a place for him to sleep on a cabin floor. He repaid them sometimes with money, always with a report of what life was like in the North.

But he did more listening than talking. From Natchez he crossed into Louisiana. Not daring to make notes, he stored facts and figures in his memory and wrote them down later. Natchez planters gave their slaves three pounds of bacon and a peck of corn meal a week. No coffee, no tea, no sugar . . . Along the Little River in Louisiana, the women who worked in the fields were given one dress a year. No underclothes, no shoes . . . In the Red River country ("the water red as if colored by iron rust") slaves worked all day including Sundays "till we can't see to pick no more." At harvest time they were required to pick 225 pounds of cotton a day, "else we get 30 lashes" . . . A slave born without arms learned to pick cotton with his toes. Because of his handicap, his task was only one hundred pounds daily . . . On the bayous near Baton Rouge, free blacks owned sugar plantations and slaves. "An' they beat us for little an' nothin' just like the white masters do."

At a plantation landing on the Mississippi, Martin hailed a steamboat again. It was February 1840, still winter in Pittsburgh. Here the trees were green, and bright-colored warblers and tanagers were feeding along the marshy shore. A day's sail brought him to New Orleans. As the boat nosed in to the dock, Martin listened to the songs of the slaves on the levee. "Men of sorrow" he later described them. Their songs "are apparently cheerful but are in reality wailing lamentations."

New Orleans was different from any city he had ever visited. Although it had been a part of the United States since 1803, its buildings, its people, its cookery retained the flavor of France. France and Africa.

On the crowded streets black *marchande* women balanced baskets on their heads as they cried out their wares: *"Belles des figues! . . . Bons petits calas! . . . Pralines, Pistache! . . ."* From the doorways of shops brown-skinned saleswomen curtsied and smiled, inviting *m'sieu* to walk in and buy a present *pour votre aimée.* Even the city's renowned gumbo soup had taken its name from *ngombo,* an African word for okra, its main ingredient.

Martin walked through the Lower Faubourg admiring the open courtyards and gardens, the well-stocked market—and the girls. He recalled the words of a popular song:

> I suppose you've heard how New Orleans
> Is famed for wealth and beauty.
> There's girls of every hue it seems
> From snowy white to sooty.

It was true. He had never seen so many beautiful women. Not only fashionable white ladies, he noted, but "handsome maidens of African origin, mulatto, quadroon, or sterling black." And the dark-skinned Creoles dressed as elegantly as their white counterparts. A law forbade black women to wear jewels or feathers in their hair. They got around this by wearing bright *tignons,* or bandannas, tying them in a dashing style that only added to their attractiveness.

New Orleans had a large class of free blacks—*gens de couleur libres*—who had acquired education and property during the decades of French rule. Although the colony's *Code Noir* forbade intermarriage between black and white, planters had taken slave women as their mistresses. During the course of these relationships, which were often life-long, the planters had freed their brown-skinned children. Once they were free, the *gens de couleur libres* were granted the same rights and privileges as white men. They operated businesses, owned homes, and, for more than a century, had their own militia company.

In 1815 the Battalion of Free Men of Color had helped to win the Battle of New Orleans and were commended for their "courage and perseverance" by General Andrew Jackson. Martin had often heard the details of the battle from a member of the battalion who had moved to Pittsburgh. Jules Bennoit, his name anglicized to John Julius, had become the proprietor of a concert hall and café that was a favorite night spot of Pittsburgh society. He described the battle to everyone who talked with him, "not so much for his own notoriety," Martin explained "as for the purpose of exposing the wrongs done to him and hundreds of his fellows."

Because, as New Orleans became Americanized, life changed drastically for the free blacks. They could no longer vote or bear arms. Schools for their children were forbidden and in 1834 their militia company was disbanded. Perhaps most humiliating was the curfew. At dusk each day the cannon at the old fort in the Lower Faubourg sounded a warning to all black people, free as well as slave, to get off the streets until morning.

Martin arrived in New Orleans on the eve of Mardi Gras. The curfew was lifted during the celebrations. Although the cannon boomed, blacks continued to promenade on the streets, exchanging greetings with each other and with white passers-by. Martin found it hard to believe that he was in a southern city. "The night was beautiful," he wrote. "Freedom seemed for once to go forth untrammeled through the highways of the town."

Like Cinderella after the ball, New Orleans returned to normal when the Mardi Gras was over. Chains and whips were the rule in the slave pens where new cargoes from Baltimore and Washington arrived daily. Martin attended a slave auction, remembering forever after the peals of laughter that greeted the auctioneer as, rawhide in hand, he made heartless jokes about the trembling men and women on the block alongside him.

The free blacks Martin talked with were bitter about the rigid regulations that were "almost destroying their self-respect and manhood, and certainly impairing their usefulness." Yet he left the city with a feeling of optimism. Despite the restrictions, a century of near-freedom had allowed the *gens de couleur libres* to achieve positions in the community that their brothers in Pittsburgh and New York might well envy. In stores on the main business streets he had seen black salesmen and saleswomen—a sight that was unheard of in any city in the North. "On the arrival of steamers at the Levees, among the first to board them and take down the Manifestos are colored Clerks," he wrote. "One of the most respectable Brokers and Bankers of the city was a black gentleman . . . Certainly, there need be no farther proofs required to show the claims of colored people as citizen members of society."

After New Orleans, a river boat carried him upstream to Alexandria on the Red River where the Texas Road led to the West. The road was little more than a trail through a pine forest. Stopping in Alexandria to fill a pouch with provisions, Martin had a strange experience.

Two soldiers were brawling in the street. When one was stabbed by his drunken comrade, Martin somewhat hesitantly volunteered to dress the wound. After watching him bandage the wounded man, the soldiers' leader offered him the post of surgeon with his troops.

The tall, sandy-haired man introduced himself as General Felix Huston, former commander of the army of the Texas Republic. A distant kinsman of Texas' President, Sam Houston, he was in the United States to raise an army of adventurers for further conquest in Mexico.

Huston stood for everything Delany was opposed to. The Mexicans were a colored people who had abolished slavery after winning their freedom from Spain. Their country was a haven for American runaway slaves. Its conquest would only strengthen the southern planters who dreamed of a great slaveholding empire that some day might include all of Central America and the West Indies as well. Yet Huston, a Mississippi slaveowner, was asking black Martin Delany to take part in his scheme and was offering him protection and a share of the spoils if he joined him.

Delany quickly turned down Huston's offer. As he followed the Texas Road the next morning, he wondered if he would ever understand Southerners. They were unbelievably callous and brutal toward their slaves. Yet Huston had treated him with a courtesy and respect that he seldom received in the North.

Any kindly feelings he held toward Southerners were dispelled when he entered Texas. The country was sparsely settled, the fertile rolling land a pleasant contrast to the flat, marshy plains of Louisiana. But the people he encountered were for the most part hard-drinking, trigger-happy gamblers and land speculators. Gun fights were frequent. In one eastern county he witnessed a pitched battle involving hundreds of men.

"They'd as lief kill you as not," a slave told him. "And they feels the same way about Mexicans and Indians."

Clearly the Texas Republic was no place for a black settlement. Martin headed north for the Indian Territory. The territory had been organized after 1830 when Congress passed an Indian Removal Bill that required the tribes of the Southeast to move west of the Mississippi. Tens of thousands of Indians—Choctaws, Creeks, Chickasaws, Cherokees, Seminoles—were being driven from their ancestral lands to the grass-covered prairies of the territory, which would later become Oklahoma. Some went peacefully, if reluctantly. Others were forcibly moved by United States troops.

Crossing the Texas border, Martin passed Fort Towson, an army outpost of log buildings, and entered the Choctaw Nation. The Choctaws were the first of the tribes to have been moved. In the nine years since their uprooting, they had cleared land for farms, built mills and trading posts along the north bank of the Red River. Although most were miserably poor, a few owned cotton plantations which were worked by Negro slaves.

Despite the fact that they were slaveowners, Martin was welcomed by the Choctaws who considered blacks as their allies in a common struggle against the whites. "Indian work side by side with black man," an old chief explained. "Eat with him, drink with him, and both lay down in the shade together. Not like white man who won't talk to us."

Riding through the Choctaw and Chickasaw Nations on a pony that the chief loaned him, Martin visited farmers, hunters, members of the tribal councils. Although the Choctaws had been driven from their homes, they were still a nation with a common language, a shared history and culture. Even in exile, they made their own laws, chose their own lawmakers. Offenders were tried in Indian courts. Children were schooled in Indian ways. Their chiefs were recognized by the United States as the representatives of a separate people who

could sign treaties and collect reparations—however inade-
quate—for the land that had been taken from them. The
Choctaws hoped that the Indian Territory would become an
Indian state with its own congressmen in Washington.

Martin was struck by the difference between the Indians
and his own people. The sons of Africa were also in exile.
But they were scattered across the continent, their culture
lost, their language forgotten, without a voice in their own
destiny.

From the Indian Territory, Martin traveled through Arkansas which he found "the roughest of all the states. Armed
with bowie knives and revolvers, he who displays the greatest
number of deadly weapons seems to be considered the
greatest man." It was midsummer when he reached the Mississippi again and boarded a steamboat bound for Pittsburgh.

Stretched out on the deck, with a bale of cotton for back
rest, he sorted out his impressions. Like many black Northerners, he had started his trip with mixed feelings of sympathy
and contempt for the slaves. If they had any manhood, why
didn't they resist, run away, kill their masters?

Now he saw the problem more clearly. With the whole
machinery of government against them—laws, guns, dogs
trained to track runaways—the wonder was not that so few
rebelled, but that so many tried.

Another important weapon in the slaveowners' arsenal was
religion. Masters had erased the slaves' memories of ancestral
gods, substituting instead a Christianity that said, "Obey. Be
patient. Trust in the Lord for salvation." The slaves' willingness to accept this had sometimes driven Martin to angry
outbursts.

"You've put your trust in the Lord for sixty years. What
good has it done you?" he shouted at one old woman. "Your

master uses the Bible to make you obey. You have to learn to use it in your own interests."

More often he had been lost in admiration of the slaves' strength of body and spirit. After deadening hours of toil, they still had the energy and imagination to create their own expressions of humanity—music, dances, word-of-mouth literature—and their own dreams of freedom.

The moon rose. Martin paced the deck, still thinking of the plight of black men and women in the United States. In the North where they were a tiny minority, they struggled to prove that they could take care of themselves. In the South, they were not only taking care of themselves, but of white people as well.

Black hands built the pillared big houses of Natchez. Black hands fashioned the wrought-iron balconies of New Orleans. Slaves cleared the land, planted the crops, ginned the cotton, boiled the sugar cane. And baked the bricks, wove the cloth, cobbled the shoes, cooked, sewed, and raised generations of their masters' children.

And there were *three million* slaves in the South.

Many years passed before Martin Delany wrote a detailed account of his southern trip. Then he cast it in the form of a novel which he called *Blake; or The Huts of America.* His hero was a black man—"handsome, manly and intelligent"—who traveled from Natchez to New Orleans to Texas to Arkansas organizing a general insurrection of the slaves.

9

THE MYSTERY

Banners waved, drums boomed as the procession marched from the Point. Hauling a log cabin mounted on wheels, the paraders chanted:

Tippecanoe and Tyler too!
Tippecanoe and Tyler too!

Martin had returned to Pittsburgh at the height of the 1840 election campaign. Following the crowd to the Diamond he listened to speakers proclaim the virtues of William Henry Harrison and his running mate, John Tyler. Harrison, who had defeated the Indians at the Battle of Tippecanoe almost thirty years earlier was the Whig candidate for President, opposing Martin Van Buren, running for re-election on the Democratic ticket.

Martin watched the hoopla thoughtfully. His months in

the South had made him question the abolitionists' plan to end slavery through moral suasion. Slaveowners, he felt sure, would never voluntarily give up their slaves. But perhaps they could be forced to do so through the machinery of government. If enough antislavery men were elected to Congress, they could change the laws, amend the Constitution. Black men would have to learn the great American game of politics.

While he had been away, a small group of abolitionists had organized a new political party, the Liberty Party. He liked the sound of its name. Its candidates were pledged to abolish slavery in the District of Columbia and to prevent its spread to new states and territories.

In 1841 the Liberty men in Pennsylvania nominated Dr. Francis J. LeMoyne as their candidate for governor. Here was the opportunity Martin had been waiting for. LeMoyne, a doctor from near-by Washington, Pennsylvania, was an outspoken abolitionist who had helped found the state antislavery society and was active in Underground Railroad work. No one expected the Liberty Party to win the election, but a large vote for LeMoyne would strengthen the freedom movement throughout the state.

Martin threw himself into the campaign, distributing handbills, knocking on doors, urging people to turn out for rallies. But it was difficult to interest Pittsburgh's black community.

"Why should I go to a rally," a friend asked, "when I can't vote?"

Martin was hard put to answer the question. For four years, black Pennsylvanians had been petitioning the legislature to restore their voting rights, without success. If politics was the key to freedom, the vote was the key to politics. Without it black men were dependent on their white friends. They had no political power of their own.

Although he continued to campaign for LeMoyne, he also joined in organizing a Convention of the Colored Freemen of Pennsylvania to consider anew "the present disfranchisement of the colored people of the Commonwealth." As a member of the Corresponding Committee he helped write the call to convention, which explained in 1-2-3 fashion the reasons for meeting:

"It is hardly to be expected that the Constitution will be altered and the right of voting granted to colored persons unless at least a majority of them in the whole state desire it. If a majority desire this right, they must in some way or other show it. The general way of showing the popular will in the United States in favor of any great measure is holding a Convention."

The convention was scheduled to meet in Pittsburgh in late August—"because immediately after harvest will best enable the farmers to attend." As the day for the meeting drew near, Pittsburgh officials were apprehensive. Did the delegates plan to parade through the streets as Harrison's supporters had done a year earlier? The presence of so many blacks might stir up trouble, perhaps touch off a riot. So much concern was expressed that Lewis Woodson wrote a soothing letter to the Pittsburgh *Gazette,* promising "a lawful and peaceable meeting . . . Such a thing as marching through the streets was never dreamed of."

With a police officer in attendance "to keep order," the convention held its morning and afternoon sessions at the African Methodist Episcopal Church on Front Street. Once more the delegates petitioned the legislature, asking that the word "white" be removed from the article in the state constitution that said "Every white freeman of the age of twenty-one . . . shall enjoy the rights of an elector." Their main business accomplished, they turned to other matters—schools for black youngsters, self-elevation, farming versus city life.

Martin was particularly interested in a discussion that took place on the convention's third day. Unanimously agreeing that "a newspaper conducted by the colored people and adapted to their wants is much needed in this state," the delegates called on black Pennsylvanians, particularly in the East, to co-operate in establishing such a paper. Until their own could be started, they accepted *The Colored American* which was published in New York as "our general public organ."

Before adjourning, the delegates agreed to meet again the following summer. A final resolution thanked "the gentlemanly and accomplished police officer who has waited upon us during our sitting, to preserve order among spectators and others" and presented him with a gift of five dollars.

If nothing else had been accomplished, the convention gave Martin Delany the germ of an idea—a newspaper for black Pennsylvanians. A paper was another way of showing the popular will, of organizing and unifying people. The idea grew as he watched his white neighbors going to the polls on election day. Black men were powerless, but there were all kinds of power. There was the power in the vote, power in the muzzle of a gun—and there was power in the printed word.

The idea became a conviction when *The Colored American* ceased publication in 1842. That meant that there was no Negro newspaper in all of the United States.

As Martin studied Pittsburgh's daily and weekly papers, the conviction gradually became an obsession. The white papers seldom printed news about blacks. When stories did appear, they were often derogatory. Once or twice he had tried to answer an article in Pittsburgh's *Chronicle* or *Gazette,* only to be told that his letter to the editor could not be published because it was "impolitic."

Delany was working as a cupper and bleeder, with an office on Third Street not far from John Vashon's barber shop. As he walked home after answering a sick call, he found himself calculating costs, counting up possible subscribers . . . Need from five to seven hundred dollars for a printing press . . . Figure expenses of $35 to $40 a week for a four-page paper . . . Fifty thousand black people in Pennsylvania. Say, two thousand paid a dollar a year. Or should it be one thousand at $2.00? . . . Then there were out-of-state subscribers. With headquarters in Pittsburgh, a paper could cover not only Pennsylvania, but also Ohio, Indiana, Michigan. . . . And income from advertising . . .

By the winter of 1843 a newspaper began to seem feasible —but there was a new complication. Martin Delany had fallen in love. Pati was pleased when he brought the young lady to Allegheny to meet his family. Slender, of medium height, Catherine Richards had glossy black hair and a complexion the color of an Indian's. Although she had just turned twenty-one, there was a set to her head and shoulders that suggested strength and determination. And Lord knew she would need it, Pati thought, because Martin was off on one of his crazy schemes again.

Even by a fond mother's standards, Catherine Richards was a good catch. She came from the wealthiest black family in Pittsburgh. Benjamin Richards, her grandfather, who was known to everyone as "Daddy Ben," had crossed the Alleghenies when Pittsburgh was a village. A butcher by trade, he bought up droves of cattle that farmers brought to market and supplied U. S. Army posts along the frontier with meat. With the profits from his butcher shop he bought land on the

Point, land that increased rapidly in value. At one time his holdings were estimated at a quarter of a million dollars.

Both Daddy Ben and his son Charles had married Irish immigrant girls. Although Charles was also a butcher, he was not as wealthy as his father. White businessmen, resenting the fact that a black man owned so much property, had hired lawyers to prove that the deeds to Daddy Ben's land were not properly drawn. Much of Ben's estate had been lost in court actions.

On the 15th of March, 1843, Pati and Samuel Delany sat alongside the Richards in the first pew of the African Methodist Episcopal Church on Front Street and saw Martin and Catherine married.

Martin brought his bride to his combined home and office, now on Third Street, and continued to make plans for his newspaper, which he decided to call *The Mystery*. For a motto to print below the masthead he chose a phrase from the Bible: "And Moses was learned in all the wisdom of the Egyptians." The mottoes of other antislavery papers quoted from the Declaration of Independence or paraphrased Thomas Paine. His would remind readers of the dependence of the West on Africa's ancient culture.

In 1843 there was no Associated Press or other wire service. A newspaper editor obtained his out-of-town news from correspondents and from a system of "exchanges." These were newspapers sent to him in exchange for his own publication. He was free to reprint articles from the exchanges as long as he credited the source.

The newlyweds spent their spare time that spring arranging for exchanges and finding men in other towns who would sell subscriptions for *The Mystery*. By summer they had lined up forty agents in Pennsylvania and Ohio, with another half dozen in scattered localities as far west as Iowa Territory.

On Wednesday morning, August 30, Martin handed a stack of folded papers to a newsboy. From the doorway of the print shop he watched the boy walk down the street shouting, "Get your copy of *The Mystery!* Only two cents! Read *The Mystery!*" At the corner a man stopped the boy and bought a paper.

The Mystery was launched.

Like most antislavery weeklies, it was a four-page paper. A prospectus explained that its purpose was to give "news both foreign and domestic as well as to make something of a literary paper . . . it shall aim at the Moral Elevation of the Africo-American and African race, civilly, politically, religiously . . . We shall also aim at the different branches of Literary Sciences, the Mechanic Arts, Agriculture and the elevation of labor." It was a big order.

The front page was given over to speeches and essays, most of them taken from exchange papers. "The Doctrine of Equality vs Slavery" might be followed by "The Niggers Can't Learn," an account of a slave blacksmith in Mississippi who had taught himself Latin and Greek. Inside pages carried editorials, letters to the editor, reports from correspondents in other cities, as well as announcements of meetings, birth and marriage notices, and obituaries.

Martin planned to encourage the "Literary Sciences" by publishing stories and poems from his readers. Not many suitable compositions were submitted, however. Some were such obvious copies of other people's work that he later made a stern announcement:

"Henceforth no *literary contribution* will be admitted excepting they are *really* the *productions* of the person's head and hand who sends them. This provision is made to put a stop to the continual custom of getting *others* to write poetry and literary articles for them, and sending them in as their own—even those whom it is known *cannot* READ! As you have a mind and talents, we wish you to improve them and thereby do your own work."

Most of the ads in *The Mystery* were placed by black businessmen and women. John Peck announced "a large assortment of Ladies Wigs, Curls, Gentlemen's Wigs, Topees, Scalps all made in the best and most fashionable style." Miss Vashon offered to instruct the ladies of Pittsburgh in "French Raised Work" and Mrs. Parker called their attention to her "Bonnets, Flowers, Feathers, and Fancy Trimmings."

An innkeeper in Ohio advertised rooms "for respectable colored citizens," while the proprietor of the Great Western Eating House in Pittsburgh assured readers that "Ladies and Gentlemen of my own color can be accommodated with OYSTERS done up in every variety of style."

John Templeton, the teacher of Pittsburgh's only colored school, announced the opening of an evening school for adults and offered to sell copies of "An Address to All the Colored Citizens of the United States." And Editor Delany advertised *A General View of the World*—"An excellent and superior Historical Geography"—as well as "well-executed Lithograph portraits" of outstanding black men. *The Mystery* also carried a weekly reminder that "M. R. Delany will always have on hand good, active, healthy Leeches and the best of Cupping instruments and will attend calls at all hours, day and night."

The paper was well received. A thousand copies of the first issue were sold in Pittsburgh alone. The *Pennsylvania Freeman* described it as "a spirited anti-slavery newspaper. The paper is conducted with ability and tact, and deserves the patronage of all interested in its noble objects." The editor of Pittsburgh's annual *Business Directory* praised "the talented editor of *The Mystery*. The ability and propriety with which this paper is conducted has raised the magnanimous editor high in the good opinion of the whole community."

But praise did not pay the printer. After months of digging down into his own pocket to meet a deficit, Delany called for help. A Publishing Committee headed by John Peck and John Templeton took over the business side of *The Mystery* in May 1844, leaving Martin as its editor.

Pittsburgh's black community joined in to keep the paper afloat. Each winter the ladies held a soiree for the benefit of *The Mystery*. In summer they organized picnics and festivals. "Had it not been for the generosity of Pittsburghers, particularly the ladies, in holding First of August levees, the paper would have long since stopped," Martin later wrote.

The Fourth of July was the nation's big summer holiday, but abolitionists, both black and white, boycotted it. How could anyone cheer Independence Day when millions of Americans were in bondage? Instead, they celebrated August 1, the anniversary of the abolition of slavery in the British West Indies.

Black Pittsburgh's annual First of August festival was held in Arthur's Grove, on the outskirts of the city. A reporter for the *Chronicle* described "a large concourse of the better class of our colored people and a good sprinkling of whites . . . The tables fairly groaned under the weight of good things with which they were covered. The speeches were animated and to the point . . . We particularly admired the singing . . . No doubt *The Mystery* will be able to keep on its legs without difficulty hereafter."

Even with this backing, Delany found it necessary to make trips away from home to build up his readership. Twice in 1844 he visited Ohio, traveling as far west as Cincinnati to lecture on the moral elevation of free black people. In those premicrophone days the first requisite of a public speaker was volume. A man who heard him in a crowded church in Zanesville wrote enthusiastically:

"His voice was both full and clear, his lowest whisper was distinctly heard; his middle tones were sweet, rich and beautifully varied; when he elevated his voice to its highest pitch the house was completely filled with the volumes of the sound . . . He spoke near three hours but nobody seemed fatigued . . . We believe his discourses had a good effect upon our citizens."

After giving three lectures in Columbus, Delany boarded a stagecoach to return home. Before he could sit down, the driver barked a command that was all too familiar to black travelers.

"Get down! We don't take colored passengers."

Describing the incident, the Pittsburgh *Chronicle* said, "Mr. Delany, although a colored man, is a gentleman of talent and ability. His name will long be remembered as a benefactor of his race, after the contemptible puppy who refused him a seat in the stagecoach on account of his color shall have gone down 'to the base earth whence he sprung, unwept, unhonored and unsung.'"

In the summer of 1846 young George Vashon accompanied him to Philadelphia. The first black man to graduate from Oberlin College, Vashon was then reading law in the office of a Pittsburgh attorney. After they gave a series of "able, eloquent and instructive lectures," a group of Philadelphians declared that *The Mystery* was a "powerful instrument in effecting the social and political disenthralment of our people" and pledged themselves "to improve every opportunity to extend its circulation and influence."

As *The Mystery*'s circulation grew, Martin renewed some old friendships. The paper had only been in existence a few months when he heard from Molliston Clark who was now pastor of a church in Cincinnati. Clark became a regular contributor of letters to the editor. Soon after the Mexican War started, *The Spirit of Jefferson*, an exchange paper, reported that a company of volunteers was leaving Charles Town, Virginia, for the front. One of its officers was Lieutenant John Avis.

John Avis! Thirty years had gone by and at last John was a soldier. Martin leaned back in his chair, recalling their boyhood discussions. Now John was fighting for the extension of slave territory, while Martin, in *The Mystery*, was calling for an end to the war.

On an impulse he mailed a letter and a *Mystery* subscription to John. When John's answer came, months later, it was guardedly friendly. Certainly he remembered Martin and was glad to hear what he was doing. Only, he sheepishly asked, would Martin please stop sending him the paper? *The Mystery*'s antiwar and antislavery stand had already attracted attention at the post office. A lieutenant in the U. S. Army couldn't be too careful.

Martin smiled grimly as he drew a line through "Avis, John" on his subscription list. He and John were on opposing sides in a conflict that would last much longer than the Mexican War. Yet they were tied by a common bond of humanity. Perhaps their paths would cross again.

Throughout these years Editor Delany continued to work as a cupper and bleeder in order to support his growing family. His first child died in infancy, but a second was born on February 28, 1846. For months beforehand he and Catherine played the game of prospective parents everywhere: What shall we name the baby?

The Vashons, the Pecks, the Woodsons had given their children familiar English names—George and David, Mary and Harriet, John, Thomas, Emma. Martin had always dis-

liked the name "Delany." Bestowed on his father's father by
a Scotch-Irish master, it was a reminder of the years of
servitude. He wanted his children to have names that would
make them proud of their race and color.

As he watched the tiny brown-skinned boy whose balled
fists and flailing feet were striking the sides of the cradle, he
decided to call him Toussaint L'Ouverture Delany, after the
heroic slave who had liberated Haiti. There was a name to
grow by!

Martin and Catherine had nine more children, six of whom
survived. Charles Lenox Remond Delany, born in 1850, was
named for a black American abolitionist. He was followed by
Alexander Dumas, after the French author whose grandmother had been African. Then came Saint Cyprian, named
for a third-century black bishop, and Faustin Soulouque,
namesake of a Haitian emperor. Their sixth son, born during
the Civil War, was called Rameses Placido, in honor of an
Egyptian king and a Cuban revolutionary poet. To their
youngest child and only daughter, they gave the proud name
of Ethiopia.

Before Toussaint's birth they had moved to larger quarters
on Hand Street near the Allegheny waterfront. They had
only been in their new house five days when they heard the
dreaded cry of "FIRE!" A washerwoman had been heating
water in a back yard on Ferry Street. A gust of wind carried
embers from her fire to the frame house next door. The blaze
spread down Second Street, Third Street, Market Street, with
unbelievable speed. Hotels, homes, churches, even the bridge
across the Monongahela were in flames.

Delany hurried Catherine to his parents' home across the
Allegheny, then returned to the Point to join the volunteer
bucket brigade. "Never did any event appear more like Judgment Day," he wrote in *The Mystery*. "People running, some

screaming, others hallowing, warning people to fly for their lives. Carts, drays, furniture wagons, omnibuses, horses and all and every kind of vehicle crowded the streets. May we never again witness such a scene, until the last great conflagration of this terrestrial globe!"

By evening when the wind and flames died down, a third of the city was in ruins and twelve thousand people were homeless. The AME church on Front Street was a mass of rubble. So was John Vashon's home and barber shop and the building the Delanys had lived in a week earlier. Although a pall of smoke hung over Hand Street, their new home had escaped the blaze.

While Catherine helped to feed homeless families who were quartered in the courthouse and other public buildings, Delany put out a special edition of the paper. His story headed "PITTSBURGH IN RUINS!!" was reprinted in exchange papers across the country and was incorporated in later histories of the city.

Although he was not a graceful writer, he had developed a rough-and-ready style that was often effective. Some of his editorials were short and pointed. "We understand," he wrote in an early issue, "that a free colored boy by the name of Barclay belonging to Pittsburgh is now detained and imprisoned at Clarksville, Tennessee, and is to be sold for a slave! Will His Excellency the Executive of this Commonwealth demand the release of a free citizen of Pennsylvania? We think so!"

In others, he hammered away at injustice with a rat-tat-tat of adjectives: "What sensible and humane laws we have in this great free, despotic, tyrannical, aristocratic, poor, oppressing, prostitute forcing, woman defiling, cradle plundering, slave manufacturing America."

Writing on Mondays for a Tuesday deadline, he seldom

had time to polish his stories. Indeed, *The Anti-Slavery Bugle*, while praising *The Mystery*, suggested "another improvement, one which it needs very much—more care on the part of its proof readers." But an occasional misspelled word or misplaced comma didn't conceal the urgency of Editor Delany's message. He had much to tell his readers—and many pitfalls to warn them against.

Although the woman's rights movement was not yet under way, Delany was keenly aware of the position of black women. Alternating between scolding and pleading, he urged girls to set high goals for themselves instead of being satisfied with domestic work. At the same time he criticized the community for failing to provide "the true guardians of the rising generation" with adequate schooling. After reading his editorials on female education, the Reverend Charles Avery, a wealthy minister, started a high school for black youngsters which later became Avery College.

Minstrel shows were popular in the 1840s. White men with blacked-up faces sang, danced, and told jokes in what was supposed to be the style of black slaves, but which was actually an insulting caricature. Christy's Ethiopian Minstrels opened their performance with:

Now darkies, sing and play and make a little fun.
We'll dance upon the green and beat the Congo drum.
We're a happy set of darkies, and we're assembled here to
    play,
So strike the bones and tambourine, and drive dull care away.

Recalling the songs of the Mississippi boatmen, Martin took up his pen, "reproving in very severe style (too severely we think)," said the *Pennsylvania Freeman*, not only the minstrels, but also the newspapers that praised their performance.

Another popular form of entertainment was the traveling show of P. T. Barnum and others. They exhibited bearded ladies, midgets, giants, "mermaids," as well as misshapen individuals who were billed as "The Great Whatzit" or "The Nondescript—half-man, half-beast." Some of these freaks were blacks who permitted the showmen to make capital of their deformities in order to earn three meals a day. When "The Nondescript" was displayed in Pittsburgh, Delany angrily reported that rather than being "half-man, half-beast" the "Nondescript" was all hoax.

While fighting for dignity for his people, Delany continued to save his heaviest ammunition for organizations like the American Colonization Society. Charging that the society's primary motive was "the exile and expatriation of the entire free colored population and the decrepit helpless slaves," he wrote:

". . . Let the angry storms and beating winds refuse the unjust and cruel transportation; let the dark and crowning clouds of Heaven threaten the scheme with annihilation; let the thundering howls and terrific motion of this raging hurricane reject the wanton traffic, and the repulsing waves of the uncontrollable ocean dash back the putrid carcasses of their deluded victims to the American coast, to bleach and decay upon that soil, enriched by their sweat and blood! And may their restless shades arise, and cry aloud for justice!"

Slave catchers were another favorite target. Only a few hours' ride from the Virginia border, Pittsburgh was both a haven for fugitive slaves and a hunting ground for the men who pursued them. Sometimes Delany played more than an editorial role in this deadly game of hide-and-seek. On one occasion, a slaveowner and two police officers from Virginia put up at the Monongahela House. They were hunting for Daniel Lockhart, a slave who had escaped a month earlier. The policemen lured Lockhart to the hotel on a pretext. When he saw his former master, he realized that he had been tricked.

As his shouts echoed through the corridors, the hotel's black employees went into action. While some remained with the struggling fugitive to assure him that he had friends, others ran for Martin Delany and John Peck. Ten minutes later, Delany was leading a crowd of blacks to the Monongahela House. Taking the stairs on the double, they freed Lockhart from the policemen's grasp and hurried him away.

The Underground Railroad carried Lockhart to safety in Canada while his rescuers swore out a warrant for the arrest of the three Virginians. The charge—attempted kidnapping of a free black. There was little doubt that Lockhart had been a slave, but, explained one of the complainants, "I swore he was a free man because he was in the State of Pennsylvania where our laws recognize all men as free." Although the Virginians were discharged after a trial, the bold action of Pittsburgh's black community discouraged others from coming to the city on similar errands.

Not all of the slave-hunting stories had happy endings. Children were kidnapped, runaways captured, and sometimes colored men acted as informers. In the winter of 1847 *The Mystery* reported that Thomas Johnson, a black weaver, had helped a slaveowner locate a fugitive. Sparing no adjectives, Delany denounced him as a slave catcher and a traitor to his race. Smarting under the bludgeoning attack, Johnson sued *The Mystery*'s editor for libel.

Although Delany shrugged off the suit at first, his lawyer was worried. The old English rule of libel still prevailed in

Pennsylvania, he explained. He would not be permitted to prove that the *Mystery* story was accurate. Rather, the case hinged on a single point. Was it libelous to call a black a "slave catcher"?

Yes, a jury of twelve white Pennsylvanians decided. It was "slanderous and disgraceful" to call a colored man a "slave catcher." When Martin Delany returned to the court for sentencing a stern-faced judge, known for his dislike of abolitionists, ordered him "to pay a fine of $150 to the Commonwealth, to pay the costs of prosecution, and to stand committed until the sentence be complied with."

While Delany gave bail, promising to pay the fine within ten days, the courtroom buzzed with excitement. A hundred and fifty dollars, plus court costs! It was the heaviest penalty for libel ever imposed on an editor in Allegheny County. Where would he get the money? The fine could mean bankruptcy both for himself and *The Mystery*.

To his surprise, newspapers all over the state and as far west as Cincinnati condemned the fine as excessive. The press of Pittsburgh set up a collection box at the *Daily Dispatch* office and called on citizens to contribute. Meanwhile, lawyers and businessmen petitioned the governor. When the fine was due, the *Chronicle* reported: "We are pleased to learn that His Excellency, Gov. Schrunk, has remitted the fine imposed on Dr. Delany of *The Mystery* for a libel published in that paper . . . The Doctor must study the law of libel and not again permit his praiseworthy efforts in behalf of his race to bring him within its meshes."

The *Chronicle*'s use of "Doctor" was more than a courtesy title. Delany had resumed the study of medicine. Medical practice was changing and he could foresee the day when cupping and bleeding would be considered old-fashioned. In his spare time—between midnight and six A.M., his friends joked—he was reading medicine under the direction of Dr. Joseph Gazzam, the city's most prominent physician.

Riding a wave of optimism, he had begun to dream of going to medical school. It would be a long pull for a man of thirty-five with a wife and son, but not as impossible as it had seemed a decade earlier. Here and there colleges were accepting black students. John Peck's son, David, was completing his studies at Rush Medical College in Chicago— he would be the first black man to win a diploma from a United States medical school.

Delany was nodding over his anatomy book on a hot summer evening in 1847 when John B. Vashon dropped by with a notice for *The Mystery*. William Lloyd Garrison and Frederick Douglass were coming to Pittsburgh for two days of antislavery meetings. Delany had long wanted to meet Douglass, the fugitive slave who had become an abolitionist lecturer and writer. On the morning of their arrival, he left *The Mystery* office before dawn to join a welcoming committee on the Point. Garrison was expected later in the day, but Douglass was due in on the mail coach from Chambersburg.

The stagecoach pulled in a few minutes later. As a tall man, bronze of skin, with a shock of wavy black hair clambered down its steps, the Duquesne Brass Band struck up a tune. Introductions were performed by the light of the gas lamp on the corner. When it was Martin's turn, the newcomer pumped his hand enthusiastically.

"Martin Delany!" Frederick Douglass said. "You're the man I want to talk to."

> I had fear and anger and loneliness in my travels, but, the paradox that is America, there was much love too and goodwill. Perhaps the time will come when in parts of this nation I will not have to fear for my life.
> —JOHN A. WILLIAMS
> *in* This Is My Country Too, *1964*

10

VOICE IN THE WILDERNESS

During the Douglass-Garrison visit to Pittsburgh, Delany attended every meeting the two men addressed. But there was no opportunity for private conversation until he traveled with them on the Ohio to the next stop on their westward tour. John and George Vashon and young Dr. David Peck were also aboard. While they talked with Garrison, Delany and Douglass at last had a chance to exchange views.

Five years younger than Delany, Douglass had escaped from slavery in 1838. After hearing his first speech at an antislavery meeting in New England, Garrison invited him to become a lecturer for the Anti-Slavery Society. Completely self-taught, he quickly emerged as a powerful speaker and writer. "I got my education from Massachusetts Abolition University, Mr. Garrison, president," he liked to say. After his *Narrative of the Life of Frederick Douglass* became a bestseller, he went abroad to present the cause of the slave to the people of the British Isles.

There thousands flocked to hear his lectures. The trip became a personal triumph as well as a success for the abolition movement. Before his return to the United States, his English admirers raised a testimonial fund to enable him to support his family while devoting all his time to the cause. Douglass had suggested instead that the money be used to enable him to start a newspaper. Although his English friends were willing, Douglass was dismayed to find that Garrison and other abolitionist leaders disapproved of the project. A paper would ruin him financially—"the land is full of the wreck of such experiments," they said—and would interfere with his work as an antislavery speaker.

"It is quite impracticable to combine the editor with the lecturer," Garrison had written, "without either causing the paper to be neglected or the sphere of lecturing to be seriously circumscribed."

Douglass was well aware that Garrison had been lecturing as well as editing *The Liberator* for more than sixteen years. However, he was unwilling to offend the man who had "discovered" him. Therefore he shelved his newspaper plans and agreed to write a weekly column for *The Anti-Slavery Standard* while accompanying Garrison on this tour of the West. But their trip had scarcely begun when he realized that he had made a mistake. His experiences in Pennsylvania a few days earlier had confirmed this feeling.

At a meeting in Harrisburg, Pennsylvania's capital, Douglass' speech had been interrupted by a volley of rotten eggs— "slavery's choice incense"—and cries of "Throw out the nigger!" Pelted by stones and brickbats when he left the meeting hall, he had been saved from serious injury by a group of black men who acted as his bodyguard. On the mail coach from Chambersburg, he was refused the right to eat with the other passengers. For two interminable days and nights, as the coach traveled over the Alleghenies, he had scarcely tasted a mouthful of food.

It was then that he decided, as he wrote soon afterward, that a paper edited by blacks "would do a most indispensable work, which it would be wholly impossible for our white friends to do for us . . . The man who has *suffered the wrong* is the man to *demand redress*—the man STRUCK is the man to CRY OUT . . . We must be our own representatives and advocates."

Martin Delany, who had been editing such a paper for four years, was sympathetic to Douglass' plans. But Douglass wanted more than his approval. Would Delany work with him on the new project? Martin took only a split second to say "Yes."

As the steamboat puffed along the Ohio that August morning in 1847, the two men discussed the business and editorial problems of putting out a newspaper. Disagreeing like brothers, laughing like old friends, neither noticed that dinner time had come and gone until David Peck called it to their attention. Ordinarily, passengers were summoned to the saloon soon after leaving Pittsburgh, but today no dinner gong had sounded.

"For the very American reason that a goodly number of persons on board are colored," Douglass wrote in his account of the trip. "Some of us might have presumed to dine and thus have offended the white skinned aristocracy. So we preserve the peace by all going without our dinners."

But he and Delany were too buoyed up to care. Their discussion came to a halt only when the boat docked at Beaver, Pennsylvania. Disembarking, the abolitionist group traveled by omnibus to New Brighton, where they held afternoon and evening meetings in the upper room of a general store.

Garrison described the meetings in a letter to his wife:

"Over our heads were piled up across the beams many barrels of flour; and while we were speaking, the mice were busy nibbling at them, causing their contents to whiten some of our dresses, and thinking, perchance, that our speeches needed to be a little more *floury* . . . The meetings were addressed at considerable length by Douglass and myself, and also by Dr. Delany, who spoke on the subject of prejudice against color in a very witty and energetic manner . . . Black as jet [he is] a fine fellow of great energy and spirit."

Douglass' report on Delany was even more enthusiastic. In a dispatch to the *Pennsylvania Freeman* he wrote of his encounter with "that noble specimen of a man, Mr. Delany. He is one of the most open, free, generous and zealous laborers in the cause of our enslaved brethren, which I have met for a long time."

When Garrison and Douglass went on to Ohio the next day, Delany returned to Pittsburgh. Planning for the new paper was carried on by mail. Douglass decided to call it *The North Star,* after the pole star that guided runaway slaves to freedom. Where should it be located? Douglass, who lived in Massachusetts, wanted to leave New England to avoid a charge that he was competing with *The Liberator.* A first announcement in September said the paper would be published in Cleveland, Ohio. By November its locale had been switched to Rochester, New York.

With the money raised by his English friends, Douglass bought "an excellent and elegant press" and moved it and his family to Rochester. He was joined there by William C. Nell, a black Bostonian who had been active in the anti-slavery movement. When was Brother Delany coming?

Martin was not sure. Catherine had been listening to the plans for the paper with increasing uneasiness. The British fund guaranteed Martin's expenses for a few months. After that, what would happen? No one knew better than an editor's wife the financial uncertainties of a black weekly. In Pittsburgh where Martin had the respect of the community, he could always fall back on cupping and bleeding. But Rochester was unknown territory. Besides, another baby was expected soon and Catherine was reluctant to move far from friends and family.

In late November the Pittsburgh *Dispatch* carried a brief public notice: "M. R. Delany will be absent for several days. Mr. R. Vandevort, Dentist, Smithfield Street, will attend to his professional business. Due notice will be given of his return."

The "several days" became several weeks as Delany joined his colleagues in Rochester for their first editorial conference. Nell was to be publisher, with Douglass and Delany as co-editors. Douglass would remain in Rochester to put out the paper, while Delany traveled to line up agents, correspondents, and subscriptions. Since most of his work would be done in the West, his family would remain in Pittsburgh at least for the coming winter.

After the business matters had been settled, the three laid out the first issue of *The North Star*. Delany smiled as he looked at its masthead. A year earlier, *The Mystery* had dropped its biblical motto in favor of the more militant HEREDITARY BONDSMEN! KNOW YE NOT WHO WOULD BE FREE, THEMSELVES MUST STRIKE THE BLOW? The slogan that Douglass had chosen for *The North Star* read RIGHT IS OF NO SEX—TRUTH IS OF NO COLOR—GOD IS THE FATHER OF US ALL, AND WE ARE ALL BRETHREN.

The difference between the two slogans was typical of the difference between the two men. Although Douglass bore the scars of a slave driver's whip, he had spent most of his free years in the company of white abolitionists. His speeches and writings were influenced by these associations. Where Delany was likely to ask "Is it good for our black brothers?" Douglass would say, with Garrison, "My country is the world; my countrymen are mankind." Yet their difference had a meeting point. Each, in his own way, believed that America in a white skin could never be truly free as long as it continued to oppress America in a black skin.

Nell was a Garrisonian who believed that moral suasion would end slavery. In the first issue of *The North Star* he criticized "exclusive colored institutions" and urged black men to become "part and parcel of the general community."

Perhaps he was right, Delany thought. At any rate, they were both fine men and he was pleased with the association. After a whirlwind trip to Massachusetts where he and Douglass addressed several meetings "with excellent effect," he returned to Pittsburgh to wind up his affairs.

In a farewell editorial, he noted with some pride that eleven other black journals had sprung up since he had begun to publish *The Mystery.* The paper, he announced, was being turned over to a Publishing Committee. *"The Mystery* is still afloat," he assured his readers.

It remains afloat today. Purchased by the AME Church in 1848, it became *The Christian Herald,* the first religious black paper in the United States. Under the name *The Christian Recorder,* it is still published as a church weekly.

After arranging for a man to take over his cupping and bleeding practice, Delany was ready to depart for the West as soon as the new baby was born. The baby, a daughter, arrived with the new year, but she was frail and sickly. Then Catherine too fell ill. He spent anxious days and nights at her bedside.

Douglass wrote from Rochester: "Subscribers come in slowly

and I am doing all I can to keep our heads above water." Chafing at the delay, Martin started a series of editorial letters that would appear in *The North Star* for the next year and a half. Addressed to "Dear Douglass" and signed "Yours in behalf of our oppressed and downtrodden countrymen, M.R.D.," they contained his comments on national and local news, as well as reports of his activities on behalf of the paper.

At last, in mid-March, Catherine was well enough for him to leave. For five months he toured the West, crossing Ohio on horseback and in a rented buggy, then traveling by lake steamer to Michigan. Speaking in schools, churches, farmhouses, he stopped "wherever there are friends of humanity, both white and colored," often holding three meetings in a single day.

To black audiences he lectured on moral elevation. "We *must* become mechanics—we *must* become tradesmen—we *must* become farmers—we *must* become educated," he said over and over again.

To whites, he talked against slavery and prejudice. "The chief points on which he spoke," the *Anti-Slavery Bugle* reported from Salem, Ohio, "were the cruel and aggressive principle upon which slavery based its claim, the expedience of emancipation and the absurdity of prejudice against color. He speaks with vigor and his illustrations were clear and pointed." "From his earnest, grave and energetic manner," wrote the Cincinnati *Herald*, "it was evident that he felt the importance of the work he had to perform and that he had no time to lose in sentences made up of soft nothings."

His meetings over, he returned to his lodgings to dash off letters to Douglass. Writing by candlelight at the end of a strenuous day, he gave *North Star* readers their first close-up picture of the lives of free blacks in Ohio.

Few blacks lived in the eastern counties, but in Columbus,

Cincinnati, and Dayton he found "a large number of well-dressed and respectable colored," some of them quite wealthy despite the restrictions placed on them by the state's "infernal black laws." One "pro-slavery law" said that where less than twenty colored children lived in a school district, they could attend the "white" school, if no white objected. Where there were more than twenty children, a separate school was to be organized, financed not out of the general school fund but by the taxes paid by blacks. Thus, most of the schools for black children were supported by blacks who were also "shamefully and tyranically compelled to pay taxes for the education of the whites."

During a month's stay in Cincinnati, where he lectured day and night until he was "quite unwell," he visited the Colored Orphan Asylum, organized after the state institution refused to accept black orphans, and a cemetery operated by the United Colored American Association—"a most praiseworthy undertaking and how shameful the necessity of a separate burial place for the dead!"

One of the black elementary schools was "fine," but he was displeased with the high school located in "an out-of-the-way back-ground place as though to hide the pupils from public view." The curriculum, too, left much to be desired: "Knowledge of the elements of science, composition, or the correct construction of sentences appears to be foreign to the pupils . . . The greatest part of the time was spent in preparing for exhibitions which make great displays of seeming qualifications whether or not there be anything real."

He found news "the most cheering" in the large number of black-owned businesses in the city—a furniture factory, a blacksmithing establishment, a confectionery and public saloon, a daguerreotype gallery; and noted with approval that young black women worked at trades, leaving domestic work to "white girls of oriental extraction." The young men came in for criticism, however. Although some were carpenters, smiths, or shoemakers, many turned to steamboating as an occupation. Returning home with full pockets after a trip down the Mississippi, "the most they appear to think about is dress and pleasure . . . They do nothing but buggy-ride day after day until their capital is exhausted, and thus they get into debt for boarding and washing and out of credit with everybody."

Before he left Cincinnati, black citizens presented him with a tribute: "We feel proud that one like you, so well qualified both by nature and education shall report our cause; one who has not a drop of Anglo-Saxon blood," their spokesman said. "Not that we are prejudiced to color—for this idea we spurn, but for the simple reason that whenever a mind of higher order is exhibited among us some gossip or goose is ready to attribute it to a little speck of white blood coursing through our veins."

Delany liked the comment on his color, referring to it obliquely in a letter from Dayton soon afterward. Henry Bibb, a light-skinned former slave, had been lecturing in Dayton. "Our good co-laborer Henry Bibb," Delany wrote, was "much admired," but "they say that his talents emanate from the preponderance of *white* blood in him. This it will puzzle them to say of me!"

After Dayton he reported on his meetings with "the Randolph people." They were the 518 slaves of Senator John Randolph of Virginia. At his death in 1833, Randolph had set them free, leaving money to purchase farms for them in Ohio. His executors had bought land for them, but farmers armed with muskets soon drove the ex-slaves away. Drifting further west, they had found a refuge of sorts near the town of Milton where, after fifteen years, they were still waiting for their legacy.

Because of their ignorance of business, Delany found that they were continually being cheated by their white neighbors: "For instance in the purchase of a tub, which cost but one dollar, the storekeeper from whom the purchase was made, received a five-dollar note, which he kept. Another lost ten dollars in like manner. Old horses, old plows, and other farming utensils, worn out and good for nothing, are frequently sold to them at high prices, which, when the fraud is discovered, tends very much to their discouragement.

"I addressed them in a kind of bush meeting in the woods. . . . Mr. C. H. Langston, a talented young colored gentleman, who volunteered his services to travel with and assist me for a while, also spoke to them."

Charles Langston was a Virginian whose white father had left money to send him and his younger brother, John, to Ohio. A graduate of Oberlin and a gentleman farmer, Charles Langston devoted most of his time to the cause of black liberation. He traveled with Delany in Ohio and Michigan, helping to collect subscriptions for *The North Star*.

Delany also received assistance from white Ohioans. In some places, churches and courthouses were opened to him. In others he held meetings in abolitionists' cramped parlors. Once when heavy rains made the roads impassable for a man on horseback, a wagonload of antislavery people drove him to the country so that he could meet with farmers. They were drenched with rain on the way home, but "What is that to the sufferings of the downtrodden bondsmen?" a woman asked.

"I have been treated like a man, without exception, at every hotel at which I stopped," he exulted in an early letter to *The North Star*. "At New Garden the proprietor kept my horse and otherwise treated me with kind favors and refused to take pay."

A month later when he traveled along the National Road, the great highway to the West that ran from Maryland to Missouri, he had a different story to tell:

"I cannot permit myself to believe that there is in either Asia or Africa a tribe or clan of heathen among whom a stranger would not meet with more civility than I received from Lloydsville to Zanesville . . . Aged men and women, young men and maidens, the mechanics in their shops, the farmers in the field, all, all, hallowing, disparaging, pointing the finger full in one's face and even throwing stones and blocks. Respectable-looking women, standing in the doors of fine-looking houses call out, full in one's hearing, 'Come, here goes a nigger!'

"Where the adults fail, the children, true to their education, fully make up the deficiency. Engaged intensely as they may be at their innocent sports and playful gambols, they are never too busy to notice and hurl forth their wonted abuse at a 'nigger,' frequently accompanied by a missile."

. . . Children . . .

In his wallet there was the telegram he had received a week earlier from Catherine. Their little daughter was dead. His first impulse was to return home. Calling off a scheduled lecture, he had walked the streets of an Ohio town, a stranger and alone. But there was work to be done. The next day he was on his way again.

Touring western Ohio with Langston in late June, Martin was again in an exuberant mood. Meetings were going well and he had a fat batch of subscriptions to send to Douglass. After a long day's drive they stopped for the night in the village of Marseilles. It seemed a peaceful little town. The sun had set and a group of men were using the last minutes of daylight to pitch quoits along the main street. Although they halted their game to stare as the two blacks entered the hotel, Martin ascribed this to normal curiosity. Perhaps they had never seen a black man before. He was further reassured when the hotel proprietor welcomed them and offered to arrange for a meeting in the local schoolhouse.

As they walked along dark streets to their engagement, Martin's skin began to prickle. A crowd of men and boys had fallen in step behind them. Forty or fifty of them entered the school room. Their leader adjourned the meeting before it began, calling it a "darkey burlesque!"

By the time Martin and his companions returned to the hotel the crowd had doubled in size and was still growing. Watching from an upstairs window, he thought that all the men and boys in the neighborhood who could throw a brickbat were now assembled.

Shouting for tar and feathers, they rolled a tar barrel into the street and smashed it open. But the barrel was almost empty and they used it instead to start a bonfire. The flames mounted until the fire could be seen for miles around. The cries of the crowd grew louder, more menacing.

"Burn them alive! Kill the niggers!"

"Niggers, come out, or we'll burn down the hotel over your heads!"

While the handful of men inside the hotel listened, the leaders of the mob decided to drag the blacks out and sell them in the South.

"The black one'll bring fifteen hundred dollars easy."

But "the black one" had no intention of being captured. Although he had accepted the doctrine of non-violence since his teenage years in Pittsburgh, he then and there renounced it. "My friends may censure me for this," he wrote to *The*

North Star afterward, "but we are not slaves, nor will we tamely suffer the treatment of slaves."

He urged Langston, who was light-skinned enough to pass for white, to leave the hotel by a rear door. When Langston refused to abandon him, they blockaded the stairs with chairs. Martin returned to his post at the upstairs window, armed for all to see with a hatchet and butcher's knife.

"Then came the most horrible howling and yelling, cursing, and blasphemy. There is no tongue can express nor mind conceive the terrible uproar of this night's proceedings," he wrote. "The roaring of drums, beating of tambourines, blowing of horns, smashing of store boxes and boards for the fire, all going at once, incessantly for the space of four hours.

"The wretches, not possessing courage sufficient to drag us by force into the street, conceived of the plot of disabling our horse and breaking our buggy to pieces. Two or three gentlemen, overhearing the plot, secreted the horse and buggy in the barn of a neighbor.

"After rioting around the hotel until past one o'clock, having burnt all the spare store boxes, the mob concluded to retire until morning, not without giving strict instructions to the ostler boy who slept in the bar-room of the hotel, that should we attempt to flee, to give speedy notice."

Delany and Langston managed a few hours sleep before their buggy was brought to the door at dawn. A half-dozen men standing watch in the street showered them with stones as they drove away.

It had been a long night, and a decisive one for Martin Delany. He had looked into the faces of men who hated him enough to kill him, not for anything he had done, but simply for what he was—a black American. The crackling flames and the roar of "Kill the nigger!" would remain with him always.

"We left that place untarred, and even unfrightened, as we were reconciled as to the course we should pursue," he concluded his report to *The North Star*. "We arrived in Sandusky City on Friday evening, the 30th inst., and shall proceed from there to Detroit where there is a very interesting slave case pending before the U. S. Court, Judges McLean and Wilkins. I shall report you concerning this case from Detroit. Yours for God and Humanity, M.R.D."

11

YEARS OF REVOLUTION

From Michigan, Martin traveled east again to participate in
the First of August celebration in Rochester. Alongside
Douglass, Delany marched in a parade from the Colored
Baptist Church on Ford Street to the public square. After
the uncertainties and dangers of his western tour, it gave him
deep comfort to see black people's banners carried by black
hands through the streets of a city. One, emblazoned with
a cross, said, WITH THIS WE OVERCOME. Another,
ETHIOPIA STRETCHES FORTH HER HANDS TO GOD.
A third, carried by school children, proclaimed KNOWL-
EDGE IS POWER.

More than two thousand people, white as well as black,
were waiting in the square when Douglass climbed up to the
speakers' platform. "We live in times which have no parallel
in the history of the world," he told his listeners. In the past

months revolutions had shaken Europe. The French people had overthrown King Louis Philippe and had proclaimed freedom for the slaves in their West Indian colonies. Only in "our own great country—great in numbers—great in wealth—great in hypocrisy—and great in atrocious wickedness" did "three million slaves drag their heavy chains."

Martin applauded vigorously. The more he saw of this man the better he liked him. His eight months as an editor had changed Douglass, bringing him closer to black people and their problems.

The next day Delany and Douglass went over their accounts. The big ledger book in which Nell recorded *The North Star*'s income told a familiar story—"a very long list of non-paying and a very short list of paying subscribers."

All the money from England was gone and Douglass had mortgaged his home in order to pay the printer. Nevertheless, neither man was pessimistic. The paper had been enthusiastically received both at home and in England. They felt sure that if they could keep it going for a year, their books would balance. After deciding that Martin should head east in the fall, the two went to Buffalo where the Free-Soil Party was holding a convention.

The year 1848, a year of revolution in Europe, was a presidential election year in the United States. The chief campaign issue was the extension of slavery. A peace treaty with Mexico, signed in February, had added vast new lands in the West. Should this territory (which would become California, Utah, Arizona, Colorado, and New Mexico) be slave or free? The question became more compelling after the discovery of gold in California started a stampede to the West.

Freedom-loving Whigs and Democrats who were dissatisfied with their parties' choice of candidates had formed the Free-Soil Party. Although they were not out-and-out abolitionists, they opposed slavery in the territory taken from Mexico and had chosen as their slogan "Free Soil, Free Speech, Free Labor, and Free Men."

In Buffalo, thousands of delegates and visitors crowded into a huge canvas tent set up in the center of the city. Thousands more milled around outside, trying to get within earshot of the speakers. Martin enjoyed the excitement of his first political convention. He was a center of attraction on the opening day when delegates were deciding on their candidate for President.

The front runner was Supreme Court Justice John McLean —the same Judge McLean who had presided over "the very interesting slave case" Martin had covered in Detroit. The case involved a slaveowner who sued six Michigan men for damages because they had helped the Crosswaits, a family of runaways, escape to Canada. His suit was based on the Fugitive Slave Law of 1793, which said that anyone assisting slaves to escape "knowing them to be slaves . . . shall pay for each slave, the sum of five hundred dollars."

The defendants replied that they had not known that the Crosswaits were slaves. In his charge to the jury, Judge McLean explained that it was not necessary to *know* that the Crosswaits were slaves. As long as the slaveowner *claimed* that they were, the defendants were liable to punishment.

Martin had written a three-column account of the trial for *The North Star* in which he expressed his disappointment in McLean.

"I did not find him that independent and liberal-minded jurist that, from all I had heard of him, I had reason to expect. He did not once express his abhorrence of slavery, but avoided commitment by simply saying: 'whatever may be our feelings' and so forth, 'the law' is thus and so.

"Previous to this decision colored persons had some slight

semblance of liberty but now every vestige has been wrested from us—each and all of us may at any moment be arrested as the property of another. Kidnapping by the act of Congress and the decision of American Judges, has been legalized."

With copies of *The North Star* in their hands, delegate after delegate came up to question Martin. Was he the author of the article on McLean? Had he actually heard the judge deliver the charge or was his account secondhand?

At the end of the day, Salmon P. Chase, who later became Chief Justice of the Supreme Court, mounted the rostrum. The name of John McLean had been dropped as candidate for the presidency—"for reasons sufficiently satisfactory to the executive council." Instead the Free-Soil Party was nominating Martin Van Buren. Van Buren was not noted for antislavery sentiments either, but for a fleeting moment Martin Delany could feel like a kingmaker.

The Free-Soil Convention was followed by a National Convention of Colored Freemen, held in Cleveland. Douglass and Delany boarded in the home of John Malvin, the black captain of a canalboat. The two *North Star* editors were convention leaders, Douglass as president and Delany as chairman of its Business Committee.

While the delegates, meeting in Cleveland's courthouse, sang "Come Join the Abolitionists" and other liberty songs, the Business Committee drafted a series of resolutions. Most of them were passed without debate. No one was surprised when the convention condemned slavery and prejudice, endorsed education, and urged black people to support the Free-Soil Party and *The North Star*. Some men were disturbed, however, when Martin read Resolution 4:

"That the occupation of domestics and servants among our people is degrading to us as a class, and we deem it our bounden duty to discountenance such pursuits, except where necessity compels the person to resort thereto as a means of livelihood."

Eager to drive home his point, which he considered basic to the elevation of black people, Chairman Delany said: "I would rather receive a telegraphic dispatch that my wife and children had fallen victims to a loathsome disease than to hear that they had become the servants of any man."

Shouts of disapproval greeted this extravagant statement.

"No useful labor is degrading," a barber scolded.

"Those in the editorial chair and others who are not servants must not cast slurs on those who are from necessity," said a minister.

After Delany explained that he had not meant to insult anyone, Douglass suggested a compromise: "Let us say, what is necessary to be done is honorable to do—and leave situations in which we are considered degraded as soon as necessity ceases."

A white newspaperman found this earnest discussion comical. "The colored race at the North are determined hereafter to abandon shaving beards, blacking boots and carrying trunks," he reported to the New York *Herald*. "A revolution is threatened by the new movement, from the crown of the head to the sole of the foot, including boots, breeches and beards."

His feelings of superiority led him to ignore two other resolutions that were revolutionary for their day. Recalling his night in Marseilles, Delany proposed: "Whereas we find ourselves far behind the military tactics of the civilized world, Resolved that this Convention recommend to the colored Freemen of North America to use every means in their power to obtain that science, so as to enable them to measure arms with assailants without and invaders within."

His listeners, who had grown up believing in non-violence, rejected the idea of colored men arming themselves, even for self-defense. They also found his resolution about women too radical:

"Whereas we fully believe in the equality of the sexes, therefore, Resolved that we hereby invite females hereafter to take part in our deliberations."

The first Woman's Rights Convention in the United States had been held two months earlier, but even black men fighting for equality were not ready to accord it to women. The debate ended with another compromise suggested by Frederick Douglass. The convention had ruled that "all colored persons" could be delegates. Therefore, he moved that the word "persons" be understood to include women.

After giving three hearty cheers for "Elevation—Liberty—Equality—Fraternity," the convention adjourned. Although the delegates planned to meet the following year, the next Colored National Convention was not held until 1853. By then Martin Delany was moving in another direction.

On his way east, Martin stopped in Pittsburgh to see his family. He hadn't realized how much he had missed them until he sank back in his favorite chair with Toussaint on his lap and Catherine alongside him. In the six months that he had been away, Toussaint—called "Saint" by everyone—had changed from a plump toddler to a sturdy boy with a mind and will of his own. For a week, while Pati cooked his favorite dishes and Catherine caught up with his mending, father and son became reacquainted. Then he was on his way again.

Philadelphia . . . Columbia . . . Lancaster . . . Reading . . . Hollidaysburg . . . Carlisle . . . York . . . Harrisburg . . . Wilmington . . . Meetings, conventions, lectures. He talked, afternoon and evening, until his voice was too hoarse to be heard. Then he poured out his enthusiasm in letters to *The North Star*.

In Philadelphia he had "a glorious meeting" with black abolitionist Charles Lenox Remond. When Douglass and Henry Highland Garnet, a militant minister from New York, joined them, "Garnet, Douglass, Remond and myself, all had the pleasure for the first in time in our lives of meeting and shaking glad hands together! Truly the God of Liberty was lavish with favors."

In Carlisle he went to an "excellent colored school" where a boy "wrote sums on the blackboard and worked them out with the facility of a counting house clerk." In Columbia he toured the coal and lumber yards owned by Smith and Whipper—"the most extensive colored business north of the Mason-Dixon line"—and was "pleased to see colored men laboring side by side with white" in the pits and furnaces of the area.

Visting Harrisburg for the first time since he was a boy, he attended a state convention of colored citizens. With Remond and a committee of black Pennsylvanians he called on the governor to ask once again that colored men be allowed to vote. Although the governor greeted them as "gentlemen and fellow human beings" and listened courteously, he made no promises.

Not all of Martin's impressions were favorable. In Lancaster ministers preached that "colored should be humble and low-spirited, suffering a life of sorrow in order to get to heaven." Wilmington had "quite too many churches for the population." And when he called at a colored school, a white teacher rudely turned him away. "It was evident that she considered it impudent for a colored person to visit the schools as an inquirer."

Although Wilmington's free blacks readily subscribed to

The North Star, the post office people blocked the delivery of their papers. "They say we are imposters—that there is no *North Star* in existence save in heaven—that the paper was sent by mistake to Baltimore . . . What can you expect in a slave state?"

For two months Martin remained in Philadelphia, which had a black population of 25,000—more than in the whole state of Ohio. Speaking in the city and in towns near by, he foresaw the day when "we shall stand up in the might and majesty of our manhood and declare that slavery shall cease . . . Let us have but one mind, one purpose, one cause and one determination—yea, and but one watchword—Let my people go!"

Fired by his enthusiasm, Philadelphia's black women formed a North Star Association to solicit subscriptions and to organize a Christmas Fair for the benefit of the paper. The Fair was a huge success, netting $100 for *The North Star* and $100 for the relief of runaway slaves. Its high point came when Delany introduced two young fugitives who had arrived in Philadelphia that morning.

Four days earlier William and Ellen Craft had been slaves in Georgia. Desperate for freedom, they had worked out a bold plan of escape. Twenty-two-year-old Ellen, who was light-skinned, had posed as a planter's son, William as her servant. Using money that William had earned at night work, they traveled north by steamboat and train, putting up at the best hotels along the way. Although no one penetrated their disguise, they had several close calls. Ellen was near collapse by the time they reached Philadelphia. After their dramatic appearance at the Fair, Underground Railroad workers hid them outside of the city and later sent them on to Boston.

After the Fair the women organized a permanent Woman's Association to support the Negro press and to hire lecturers for their own education. Delany was the only man present at their first meeting. Addressing them "on the importance of elevation," he then read them a constitution that he had drawn up for their benefit. The constitution "was taken up by sections and after mature deliberations, adopted."

Despite all of Martin's efforts in Philadelphia, *The North Star*'s finances were growing shakier with each succeeding issue. Catherine, too, was feeling the pinch. Their savings were gone and she had used up the small legacy left by her father. While "several excellent colored ladies" in Philadelphia helped out with gifts of clothing, Martin was forced to borrow $50 from the sum raised at the Fair for her food and rent.

After a quick visit to Pittsburgh he went to Rochester to confer with Douglass. Their ledger recorded what they both knew—that they were spending $60 a week and taking in a little more than $25.

Was it true, as Douglass wrote in a burst of indignation, that Negroes thought that a colored man's paper should be supported by white people, while Negroes received free copies? Delany disagreed. Although there were more than 80,000 free black families in the United States, a third of them lived in the South and could not subscribe to the paper. That left upward of 60,000—

"And of this number two-thirds can't read," he pointed out in an article in *The North Star*. "So there are only 20,000 who can understand the paper and of these half can't afford it. Two things are necessary before our people will become interested in newspapers—common education and *means*."

Blacks were not uninterested in *The North Star*, he concluded, but for most black Americans the printed word was a luxury. If the paper was to continue, it would need other sources of income.

Volunteering to make one last try, Martin spent the spring months touring Ohio, seeking donations as well as subscriptions. But the paper was still in the red when Frederick Douglass wrote a notice for its June 29, 1849, issue:

"After the present number, by a mutual understanding with our esteemed friend and coadjutor, M. R. Delany, the whole responsibility of editing and publishing *The North Star* will devolve upon myself. I am happy to state that while the copartnership which has subsisted between myself and M. R. Delany is now terminated, his interest in the success of the enterprise remains unabated; and he will continue to contribute by his pen, as formerly, to the columns of *The North Star;* and do all, consistently with his other duties, toward making the paper prosperous to its editor and valuable to its readers. It is proper for me to state that thus far, Mr. Delany has been a loser (as well as myself) by the enterprise; and that he is still willing to make sacrifices that our favorite sheet may be sustained."

Back in Pittsburgh, Martin turned to familiar routines. He resumed his practice as a cupper and bleeder, wrote an occasional letter for *The North Star,* attended lectures, and spoke at local antislavery meetings. With Saint riding on his shoulders, he and Catherine walked across the bridge to Allegheny for Sunday dinners with his parents. After a second son, named for his co-worker Charles Lenox Remond, was born, he moved his family to a larger house on Smithfield Street.

But Pittsburgh had begun to seem small and circumscribed, his friends provincial, his work dull. When a group of Ohioans asked him to start a paper for the colored people of the West he was tempted to accept. Cold logic told him, however, that the paper would fail.

"During seven years as editor of different papers, I have

labored for naught and received nothing," he replied. "To embark in a new enterprise of this kind would be certain starvation of my family. My ardent desire for the elevation of our race has caused me to sacrifice more than my share."

After urging the Ohioans to "rally around the *North Star*," he added: "I have no ambition whatever for popular fame . . . I have determined to remain in obscurity, wishing Godspeed to our public great men."

Catherine must have smiled to herself at this disclaimer. Martin was anything but satisfied with obscurity. For more than a decade he had preached the gospel of elevation. Set your sights high . . . Excel . . . Strive for equal attainments with the whites.

Now in moments of gloomy self-appraisal, he saw himself as a failure. Men who were less ambitious—the barbers, the boatmen, even the waiters at the hotels on the Point—owned their own homes and other real estate in the city. Many of the new generation of blacks—youngsters like George Vashon, David Peck, Charles Langston—were college-trained. But here he was, at thirty-seven, with a second-rate education, a second-rate profession, and not a penny to his name.

When he read in *The North Star* that two black men had graduated from the medical school at Bowdoin in Maine, he came to a decision. Dusting off his medical books, he asked Dr. Francis LeMoyne, his friend from the Liberty Party, if he could read medicine under his direction. This time he was going to finish his studies and go to medical school.

Once the decision was made he buckled down to a year of hard work. By the fall of 1850 he had saved enough money for Catherine and the boys to live on while he was away. The winter course of lectures in most medical schools started in November and lasted four months. Since two terms were all that were required, he planned to be back home the following July with his diploma.

Pittsburgh's doctors were all graduates of the University of Pennsylvania or of Jefferson Medical College, both in Philadelphia. It was not difficult to enroll in these schools. An applicant had to have a letter showing that he had studied medicine for three years with a reputable physician. Then, if he was of good moral character and could pay the tuition, he was accepted. It was not difficult to enroll—if he were white.

Martin applied to both schools. Answers came back promptly. The University of Pennsylvania Medical School does not accept colored students . . . Jefferson Medical College does not accept colored students.

He next wrote to schools in New York. Albany Medical College did not accept colored. Geneva Medical College— he was banking on Geneva, which had given a medical degree to Elizabeth Blackwell the year before. A college that would admit a woman would surely take a man even if his skin was the wrong color. But Geneva Medical College also said no to Martin Delany.

A Pittsburgh merchant suggested Pittsfield Medical College, a well-established school in western Massachusetts. He offered to write a letter of introduction to the dean, an old friend of his. Martin was preparing an application to send there when he was interrupted.

On September 18, 1850, Congress passed a Fugitive Slave Law far more drastic than the law of 1793. If a white man took an oath that a black was his slave, federal marshals and commissioners were obliged to return him to slavery and "all good citizens" were "commanded to aid and assist." Any black was liable to arrest and sale as a slave on the claim of any white. The law, which denied blacks the right to testify in their own behalf or to have a jury trial, was an open invitation to slave catchers.

Panic swept black communities. Six days after President Millard Fillmore signed the law, thirty-five blacks left Pittsburgh for Canada. Three days later more than a hundred and fifty followed them. Before the month was out there was a shortage of waiters at the hotels and of hands on the waterfront.

"The scene preceding the flight would have excited the sympathy of the most cold-hearted," Pittsburgh's *Commercial Journal* reported. "Mothers and daughters, fathers and sons, brothers and sisters, were clinging to one another in despair at the thought of a separation which they seemed to feel would be for life."

Similar scenes were enacted all over the North. In Rochester all but two members of the Colored Baptist Church on Ford Street crossed the border to Canada. A hundred men, women, and children left Buffalo. Thousands more, including spokesmen like Henry Bibb, abandoned homes and jobs in Philadelphia, Cincinnati, Boston, New York to find a haven outside the United States.

Martin could not keep silent. Shelving his medical school application, he joined with other abolitionists to plan resistance to the law. He felt not fear but cold rage when he rose to address a mass meeting in the market house in Allegheny on September 30. The speakers who preceded him—Allegheny's mayor, the congressman from the district, prominent local citizens—had urged people to petition for the law's repeal.

Martin thought this a futile action. "To suppose its repeal is to anticipate the overthrow of the Union. Leaving morality and right out of the question, the Fugitive Slave Law is *necessary* to the National Compact. We must look at *facts* as they really are," he said.

"What can we do? Shall we submit to be sent into bondage? Shall we fly, or shall we resist?

"Honorable mayor, whatever ideas of liberty I may have have been received from reading the lives of your revolutionary fathers. I have therein learned that a man has a right to defend his castle with his life, even unto the taking of life.

"Sir, my house is my castle. In that castle are my wife and children. If any man approaches that house in search of a slave, let it be [the President] surrounded by his Cabinet as his body-guard, with the Declaration of Independence waving above his head as his banner, and the Constitution upon his breast as his shield—if he crosses the threshold of my door, and I do not lay him a lifeless corpse at my feet, I hope the grave may refuse my body a resting-place and righteous Heaven my spirit a home. No! he cannot enter that house and we both live."

Black leaders shared his mood of defiance. Speaking in Faneuil Hall in Boston, Frederick Douglass said: "We must be prepared, should this law be put in operation, to see the streets of Boston running with blood."

"Should any wretch enter my dwelling to execute this law, I'll seek his life, I'll shed his blood," Robert Purvis warned at a meeting near Philadelphia.

"I don't respect the law—I don't fear it—I won't obey!" said Reverend Jermain W. Loguen in Syracuse.

The non-violent movement died in that fall of 1850. One by one, white abolitionists joined blacks in vowing to resist "this filthy enactment." "If a man attacks you to return you to slavery, you have the right to resist the man unto death," Reverend Theodore Parker told William Craft as he hid him from slave catchers. "Every fugitive slave is justified in arming himself for protection and defense," William Lloyd Garrison wrote.

The non-violent movement died and Martin Delany looked at *facts* as they really were. He had always believed that slavery would some day come to an end in the United States. Much of his optimism drained away when the 1850 Fugitive Slave Law was passed.

Still, law or no law, life must go on. If he was to enter the winter course at Pittsfield, he must hurry. It was too late to mail an application. He would apply in person. After collecting letters of recommendation, he said good-by to Catherine and the boys and set out for Massachusetts.

Response to a petition to the Faculty
of Medicine from Harvard medical
and dental students has resulted in the
offering of 23 places to minority group
applicants to the Harvard Medical
School and the Harvard School of
Dental Medicine. Places have been
offered to 20 black students of the
135 who applied to the medical school
and three of the 27 black students who
applied to the school of dental
medicine.
—*Director of Medical Information*
Harvard University, March 24, 1969

12

LET BLACKS BE
EDUCATED, BUT—

Dr. Oliver Wendell Holmes had a difficult decision to make.
As dean of the faculty of Harvard's Medical School, it was his
job to check the credentials of all who applied for admission.
The winter term had already started, but here was another
applicant presenting letters of recommendation—and problems galore.

Holmes shuffled through the letters, then picked one at
random. It was signed "F. Julius LeMoyne, M.D."

"Permit me to introduce to your favorable notice the
bearer Mr. M. R. Delany . . . He has been reading under my
direction for the past twelve months . . . I can cheerfully

vouch his good morals & gentlemanly conduct. You will sub-
serve the cause of science, justice & humanity if you will accord him the full benefits of Your institution."

Uncomfortably aware of the man sitting on the other side
of the desk, Holmes reached for a second letter.

Joseph I. Gazzam, M.D., wished "to assure all whom it may
concern" that "M. R. Delany commenced the study of medicine under my direction in October 1846 and continued until
March 1848 . . . industrious and made satisfactory progress
. . . has always deported himself as an excellent member of
society . . . know him to be an excellent and trustworthy
man."

Holmes stole a glance at Delany. For a moment, their eyes
met. Then the dean resumed his reading.

"We the undersigned, Physicians of the city of Pittsburgh,
having known Mr. Martin R. Delany for a number of years,
take great pleasure in certifying to his upright and honorable
conduct . . . recommend him to the Medical Faculty . . . as
worthy of their favorable consideration."

Martin's face was impassive. He felt sure that Dr. Holmes
was stalling for time, examining each dotted "i" and crossed
"t," while he phrased a refusal.

The day before, Dr. Henry Childs, dean of Pittsfield Medical
College, had gone over these same letters word by word, line
by line, as if he were studying the writings of Hippocrates.
Then, peering at him over steel-rimmed spectacles, he had
asked, "Do you intend to go to Africa?"

When Martin shook his head, Dr. Childs murmured re-
grets. Pittsfield had accepted three colored students in recent
years, but they were all men sent by the Colonization Society,
to be trained for medical practice in Liberia.

"We have had applications to educate colored students to

practice medicine in this country which have been uniformly refused," he said. "I trust you understand."

Martin understood all too well. One of his many grievances against the leaders of the Colonization Society was their willingness to prepare blacks for useful work—outside of the United States. Swallowing his anger he picked up his letters and turned to leave. As he opened the door, Dr. Childs broke the silence.

"Why don't you try Dr. Holmes at Harvard?"

Why not? On an impulse Martin had climbed aboard the stagecoach for Boston. After all, Boston was noted as an antislavery stronghold. It was the "Cradle of Liberty" and the home of *The Liberator*. And Harvard was the alma mater of such distinguished abolitionists as John Quincy Adams and Wendell Phillips. He tried to remember what he knew about Holmes. Author of an important paper on childbed fever. Hadn't he also written *Old Ironsides,* the poem that every American schoolboy memorized? As the stagecoach jounced over the icy rutted road Martin recalled a stanza:

> Ay, tear her tattered ensign down!
>   Long has it waved on high,
> And many an eye has danced to see
>   That banner in the sky.

Martin had walked slowly up the steps of the Medical School on North Grove Street. Harvard was his last hope. If Holmes turned him down—what would he do if Holmes turned him down?

He gripped the arms of his chair anxiously as the dean scanned the last of the letters. The doctors of Allegheny reported Martin Delany to be "an upright and intelligent man." Three Pittsburgh ministers described his "unexceptionable

moral and religious character . . . He is a man of considerable intellectual power and of great and persevering energy.
He is entitled to the favorable consideration of good men."

Good men! Holmes sighed. Who were the good men? The
gentlemen of Beacon Hill who would be affronted if he admitted Delany to the Medical School or abolitionists like
Cousin Wendell Phillips who would be affronted if he didn't?

Boston was split wide open over the Fugitive Slave Law.
A month earlier, when the owners of William and Ellen
Craft sent agents to the city to capture the runaway couple,
not only radicals like Cousin Wendell, but also lawyers, doctors, ministers had defied the law and helped the Crafts
escape to England. Even aging Cousin Josiah Quincy, a
former president of Harvard College, had sided with them.

Holmes had no taste for causes. Although he thought
slavery "a dreadful business," he had refused to join the
abolitionists. Yet it was difficult to remain neutral in these
trying times.

Only a fortnight ago the managers of the Massachusetts
Colonization Society had written to ask him to admit Daniel
Laing and Isaac Snowden, "two young men of color" to the
winter course of lectures. They were "pursuing medical studies
for the purpose of practicing in Liberia where their services
are greatly needed."

After earnest discussion the Medical Faculty had voted
to accept the two men. They had been attending lectures for
more than a week. So far he had heard no rumbles of
discontent. But what would happen if a third black joined
them, a black who intended to practice in the United States?

Swiveling around in his chair, Holmes found Martin's un-
blinking gaze disturbing. Blast the fellow! What should he
tell him? Holmes cleared his throat, and the words that
came out were a surprise to them both. "The fee for the course

of lectures is $80. Tickets for the Dissecting Room are $5 and there's a $3 fee for matriculation, payable to me."

Fumbling with his wallet, Martin counted out three dollars. He signed the student register in bold black script— Martin Robison Delany—thereby obligating himself to submit to the laws of Harvard University and the direction of the Faculty of Medicine.

The two men rose, taking each other's measure. They were the same height, almost the same age. They shared a common interest in curing the sick. But one was a Boston aristocrat and the other the son of a slave. The gulf between them was almost unbridgeable.

Martin murmured a "thank you" and left to pay his fees to the bursar. It was dusk when he walked across Boston Common, taking great gulps of the frosty air to keep from shouting. First, a stop at the telegraph office to send a jubilant message to Catherine. Then he must call on William Nell who had left *The North Star* and lived in Boston again.

Nell helped him to find a boardinghouse and introduced him to Snowden and Laing, his fellow students. They were upstanding, ambitious young men. Snowden was the son of a minister whose church had been a center for antislavery and Underground Railroad activity. Although both Snowden and Laing were printers who owned their own presses, they had become discouraged about their prospects in the United States. When Liberia became an independent republic in 1847, they had decided to emigrate. Applying to the Colonization Society for passage, they had been told that there was an oversupply of printers in the new republic and a shortage of doctors. The society had enabled them to read medicine with a Boston doctor and enter medical school.

Flanked by his two companions, Martin entered the lecture hall at the Medical School the next morning. The noisy room fell silent. Elbows nudged elbows, necks craned as 113 white students strained to see their new black classmate.

Was there a sigh, a groan? Martin wasn't sure. At any rate, no one said a word.

No one spoke to them when the lecture was over and the trio walked down the corridor to the next class. No one talked to them in the Dissecting Room or the library. Or in the student room where in an atmosphere of easy camaraderie the class memorized the names of bones from a skeleton suspended over the table.

In each room a no man's land of empty benches separated the three blacks from their classmates. They walked alone to the lectures at the Massachusetts General Hospital around the corner and they sat apart in the operating theater there.

No matter, Martin thought. He hadn't come to Harvard to make friends with these youngsters who were half his age. He had come to study medicine. And he was getting his fill of that.

9 A.M. Dr. Jacob Bigelow: the history of drugs and their medical uses.

10 A.M. Dr. Josiah Cooke: chemistry.

11 A.M. Dr. John Ware: the history and treatment of diseases.

12 A.M. Dr. Walter Channing: obstetrics.

1 P.M. Dr. Oliver Wendell Holmes: anatomy and physiology.

Holmes, called "Uncle Oliver" by the students, was the most popular lecturer in the school. Martin's head ached from four hours of note-taking when he climbed the steep flight of steps to the amphitheater at one. The wooden benches were hard, the air thick with tobacco smoke. But all discomfort was forgotten when Holmes began to talk. Standing behind a cadaver that his assistants had prepared for the day's lesson, he used humor and poetic imagery to make his students see the human body as a delicate beautiful piece of machinery.

"These, gentlemen," he would say as he pointed to the lower portion of the pelvic bones "are the tuberosities of the ischia, on which man was designed to sit and survey the works of Creation."

It was scarcely necessary to write "tuberosities of the ischia" in one's notebook. They were fixed in the mind forever by Holmes' phrase.

The microscope was not yet a physician's tool, but he encouraged his students to look through its magnifying tubes to see the cells that a German physiologist had recently described as the basic building blocks of all plant and animal life. What was their origin? How did they grow? No one yet knew.

Peering through the microscope or working in the Dissecting Room after the day's lectures were over, Martin shared Dr. Holmes' appreciation of the marvelous way that heart, lungs, blood vessels fitted into the chest cavity. For the first time he was really *seeing* organs, tissues, bones instead of reading about them.

Three afternoons a week the class toured the wards of Massachusetts General Hospital. At the bedsides of patients, Dr. Jacob Bigelow pointed out the symptoms of typhoid, scarlet fever, tuberculosis, while students made notes on the course and treatment of each disease. Bleeding and strong purges were going out of fashion. In their place, physicians recommended improved hygiene, fresh air, exercise, and nutritious food. "To *cure* a patient is simply to *care* for him" had become a popular saying.

If an operation was scheduled, they filed into the operating theater to watch Dr. Henry Bigelow at work. Four years earlier in this same room Dr. William Morton had demonstrated that ether deadened pain during surgery. Dr. Bigelow had written up the demonstration for the medical journals but it was Dr. Holmes who proposed that the effect of this great discovery be named anaesthesia.

Martin was familiar with many of the techniques that the other students were seeing for the first time during their sessions in the hospital. He had been taking pulses and using stethoscope and scalpel for fifteen years. But he had a hard time with the Latin phrases with which the professors peppered their lectures. His classmates, recent graduates of Harvard or Yale, nodded wisely when they heard *similia similibus curantur* or *dolor, rubor, tumor, calor.* Martin jogged his memory for the Latin that Molliston Clark had taught him and boned up at night.

Early in December the three outcasts learned that they were to be joined by a fourth. Harriot Kezia Hunt, a Boston lady of good family, had applied for admission to the lectures. The faculty voted to admit her "provided her admission be not deemed inconsistent with the Statutes" of the university. When Holmes so informed Harvard's president and Board of Overseers they replied that they had no objection to admitting female students to the lectures "if the Medical Faculty deem it expedient." However, they cautiously expressed "no opinion as to the claims of such Students to a Medical degree."

Personally, Holmes was of two minds. "His kindly nature inclined him to the claims of the other sex," a colleague later wrote, but it was "interesting as an index of his delicacy and purity, that he affirmed that he was willing to teach anatomy, but not with men in the same classes; and, above all, that he should insist on two dissecting rooms, which should strictly separate the sexes."

Holmes never had to face a coeducational anatomy class. On the afternoon of December 10 the medical students had a meeting to which Delany, Laing, and Snowden were not invited. With scarcely a dissenting vote the students passed a resolution to protest the admission of a woman to the medical school lectures. At the same time they declared their objections to black fellow students, in a resolution "passed by a very large majority":

> Whereas blacks have been admitted to the lectures of the medical department of Harvard University
> Therefore
>
> *Resolved* That we deem the admission of blacks to the medical Lectures highly detrimental to the interests, and welfare, of the Institution of which we are members, calculated alike to lower its reputation in this and other parts of the country, to lessen the value of a diploma from it, and to diminish the number of its students.
>
> *Resolved* That we cannot consent to be identified as fellow students with blacks; whose company we would not keep in the streets, and whose Society as associates we would not tolerate in our houses.
>
> *Resolved* That we feel our grievances to be but the beginning of an evil, which, if not checked will increase, and that the number of respectable *white* students will, in future, be in an inverse ratio to that of *blacks*.
>
> *Resolved* That we earnestly request the Medical Faculty of the University to listen to this our remonstrance against the presence of such persons, and spare us the necessity of being in such company, or of compelling us to complete our medical studies elsewhere.
>
> *Resolved* That a copy of these resolutions be presented to the Medical Faculty.

Resolved That we have no objection to the education and elevation of blacks but do decidedly remonstrate against their presence in College with us.

Two years earlier, Martin had listened to a lynch mob shouting "Kill the nigger!" These well-bred young gentlemen from New England would never be so crude. But there were many ways to destroy a man. Wielding polite phrases the way a surgeon used a scalpel, they had cut to the bone.

Nor were his feelings assuaged a day later when counter-protests reached the desk of Dr. Holmes. One, signed by twenty-six of his classmates, expressed "their dissent from the resolutions adopted by the class in regard to the colored students . . . Their prejudices would perhaps lead them to wish that no occasion had occurred for the agitation of this question; but, as students of science, above all, as candidates for the profession of medicine, they would feel it a far greater evil if, in the present state of public feeling, a medical college in Boston could refuse to this unfortunate class any privileges of education, which it is in the power of the profession to bestow."

A second, with twenty-two names signed to it, said: "The undersigned not fully agreeing in the foregoing do from motives of their own protest against the proceedings of yesterday."

For two nights the faculty met at Dr. Holmes' house on Montgomery Place to decide how to respond to the students' petitions. At last it was agreed that Dean Holmes would call on Miss Hunt to persuade her to withdraw her application. Since the colored students had paid for the winter lectures and had "thereby acquired rights, of which they cannot properly be divested," they would be permitted to complete the winter term. But they would be barred from any other course of lectures at Harvard Medical School.

The public had already learned of the controversy from a letter in the Boston *Journal* in which a medical student protested being "classed with blacks, whom they themselves, their professors, and the community generally, consider to be of inferior mental ability . . . Let blacks be educated," the letter concluded, "but do not *compel* white men to become martyrs and to fraternize with them." .

To Dr. Holmes fell the ticklish assignment of notifying the black students and the Massachusetts Colonization Society of the decision. The students were easily disposed of. Dean Holmes called them to his office and bluntly informed them that they must leave the medical school after the winter lectures were over.

Now came the harder task of notifying the influential spokesmen of the Massachusetts Colonization Society. As though hoping for a sympathetic judgment from yet-to-be written history books, Dean Holmes drafted and redrafted a letter.

"In conformity to your request . . . the Medical Faculty of Harvard University voted to furnish tickets of admission to certain colored students, introduced by you, as destined for the settlement at Liberia.

"The result of this experiment has satisfied them that the intermixing of different races on a footing of equality and personal proximity during the course of lectures—"

Holmes broke off and tried again.

"The result of this experiment has satisfied them that the intermixing of the white and black races in their lecture rooms is distasteful to a large portion of the class and injurious to the interests of the school—therefore

"At a meeting of the Faculty it was voted that the Dean be instructed respectfully to inform the gentlemen acting as agents for the Colonization Society, that this Faculty deem it inexpedient, after the present course, to admit colored students to attendance on the medical lectures."

If Dean Holmes was concerned that his letter might cause an outcry in the abolitionist press, he needn't have been. *The Liberator* never told the story of the black men who were dismissed from Harvard Medical School. The abolitionists did not protest—nor did the anti-abolitionists. As for the history books—silence. The drafts of Dr. Holmes' letter, the minutes of the faculty meetings, and the student petitions reposed unread in the archives of the medical school, for more than a century. Holmes' biographers and the biographers of his illustrious son, Supreme Court Justice Oliver Wendell Holmes, failed to mention the incident. Perhaps it did not seem significant to them.

After leaving Harvard, Isaac Snowden and Daniel Laing were able, with the help of the Colonization Society, to finish their medical studies at Dartmouth and to do postgraduate work in Boston and London. When they embarked for Liberia in 1854, "They took with them good medical libraries and a good supply of surgical instruments," the Society's annual report said.

That left Martin Delany, black man, who wanted to become a doctor in the land of his birth. All during December, January, February he had expected Boston's liberals to rally round. Week after week he scanned *The Liberator* for news of an outcry. In January the paper carried articles about the Crafts, who had reached England. In February it headlined the arrest of Shadrach, a fugitive slave, and his rescue from jail by a crowd of black men. In March, when the winter term at the medical school came to an end, he found an article on page three. Headed PETITION—CIRCULATE IT, it read:

> The following petition needs no explanation; and the readers of *The Liberator* will need no arguments to induce them to sign it. If those who feel an interest in the subject will circulate this within a few days, and forward it to the Anti-Slavery Office we will endeavor to make good use of their names.
>
> "To the Board of Overseers of Harvard College:
>
> The undersigned respectfully ask your Honorable Body to take such measures as shall open the classes of the Undergraduates and those of the Schools of Theology, Law, Medicine and Science, to all persons, without distinction of color."

That was the extent of the abolitionists' reaction to the barring of blacks from Harvard—thirteen half-hearted lines at the bottom of a column on page three.

Martin was bewildered. When black students were turned away from other schools and colleges, there had been loud outcries. Where were the protests now? Even black people were silent. William Nell had been ill all winter. Recuperating from an attack of pneumonia, he was writing a book about black men who had served in the wars of the United States. Martin contributed a section on John B. Vashon's experiences in the War of 1812—but Nell did not speak in his behalf. Other black Bostonians were preoccupied with a more pressing problem—the defense and rescue of fugitive slaves—and had no time to tackle Harvard.

The abolitionists' failure to protest may have stemmed from the factional differences that plagued their movement.

Garrison and the Garrisonians despised the Colonization Society and were warring with Frederick Douglass, who differed with them on a number of issues. This could have seemed sufficient reason for ignoring the problems of the medical students, two of whom were Colonizationists and the third closely linked with Douglass.

To Martin Delany their silence underlined charges sometimes made against the white emancipationists—that they were interested in the slaves of the South but not in the free blacks of the North. That despite their fine words they did not want blacks to rise to positions of equality, did not want to rub elbows with them on the campus of Harvard College.

A year later he would write of his "sad, sad disappointment" with the abolitionists: "We find ourselves occupying the very same position in relation to our anti-slavery friends as we do in relation to the pro-slavery part of the community—a mere secondary, underling position."

Slumped in a chair in his cheerless rented room in Boston Delany pondered his future. Even without his M.D. degree, no law or regulation would prevent him from practicing medicine. Yet he was reluctant to return to Pittsburgh, ashamed to tell the friends who had given him a fine send-off that he was only half a doctor, as in the eyes of his white countrymen, he was only half a man.

Above all what would he say to Saint and little Charlie when they grew older? Could he still tell them what he had believed for so long, that perseverance and hard work would bring success and win respect from the white community?

> Our nation is moving toward two
> societies, one black, one white—
> separate and unequal.
> —*Report of the National Advisory
> Commission on Civil Disorders, 1968*

13

WHAT THEN SHALL WE DO?

Without returning home, Delany went from Boston to western New York and Ohio to give lectures on anatomy and physiology. In the decades before the Civil War, lectures were a popular pastime as well as an educational force. With few magazines, and no radio or television, people crowded into auditoriums to hear the latest reports on science, literature, public affairs.

During his hours in the Dissecting Room, Martin had seen that there were no anatomical differences between white men and black. The sizes and shapes of their brains, the configurations of their bones, even the structure of their skins were identical. With the help of Dr. Holmes' microscope he had solved, for himself, the puzzle of varying skin colors. Examining human skin under the microscope, he had seen the same kind of coloring matter, which he called "rouge,"* in both black and white samples.

---

* Later scientists with better microscopes were able to see the granular structure of Delany's "rouge." They named the pigment "melanin."

"The pigment that makes a Negro's complexion black is the same in properties as that which makes the ruddy complexion of the white man. In a Negro's skin the rouge is more concentrated, hence it looks black," he explained in his lectures.

To his listeners, most of whom believed in the curse of Ham as the cause of blackness, this was significant news. And it had a double impact on black audiences, who were delighted to hear one of their own people speak with so much knowledge and authority.

Their applause helped to restore Martin's self-esteem. He returned to Pittsburgh, if not a conquering hero, at least outwardly reconciled to practice medicine for the rest of his days, without a Harvard degree. He moved his family again, this time away from the integrated neighborhood on the Point to a house on Arthur Street, in a growing all-black section that Pittsburghers called "Hayti."

When he had been a cupper and bleeder, doctors had asked him to tend white patients. As a doctor, his practice was limited to blacks, except during a cholera epidemic when every trained hand was needed. Three hundred people, including Samuel Delany, Sr., died during the epidemic. After it was over, Pittsburgh's Board of Health and City Council presented Dr. Delany with a parchment scroll testifying to his skill as a physician. He hung it, suitably framed, on his office wall and went back to being "the colored doctor." Most of his patients were poor. Scratching to make ends meet, he often earned less as a physician than he had as a cupper and bleeder.

For a time, he supplemented his income by serving as principal of the Colored School. Black parents had been protesting the inadequate schools for their children ever since the passage of the free-school law in the 1830s. Denied seats in classrooms with whites, black youngsters were not given a share of the school taxes until their parents threatened the school board with a law suit. When at last a public Colored School was organized, its teacher, John Templeton, died unexpectedly. Delany agreed to run the school for a month, until a substitute could be found. He stayed for a year, shattering precedent and winning instant popularity with his pupils by abolishing the practice of flogging.

Until 1856 Martin Delany remained in Pittsburgh as doctor, teacher, community leader. When John B. Vashon died, Delany chaired the public meeting held in his old friend's honor and wrote his obituary for *Frederick Douglass' Paper* (as *The North Star* was now called). He became Worshipful Master of the St. Cyprian Lodge of the Masons and published a short history of black Freemasonry. He presided at First of August celebrations, attended state conventions of colored men, drew up petitions asking for the right to vote. He sheltered fugitive slaves and sent them on to Canada on the Underground Railroad.

When a telegram from Philadelphia warned that a slave-owner was heading for Pittsburgh with a boy who had been kidnapped, Delany met the pair at the depot and freed the boy as he left the train. The youngster had been lured from Jamaica, in the British West Indies, by the promise of a good job in the United States. Delany questioned him after arranging for the British consul to return him to his home. He discovered that a ring of slave catchers regularly visited the West Indies to kidnap and enslave black children. In an angry letter to the Jamaica *Morning Journal* he warned West Indians against these "unprincipled Americans":

"It is better to live on one banana or yam, and a cup of water a day and be free, than to be a slave, especially in this country which is the worst and meanest upon which

Heaven's sun ever shone. No colored person in the United States is really free. Bury your bones in the sunny clime of your own beautiful isle, rather than come to this slave-holding, oppressing country."

Martin's days were full—and empty. He could see few signs of progress for his people. Every month men and women were arrested and returned to slavery because of the Fugitive Slave Law. And every month saw the passage of more laws restricting blacks. The new state of California refused to admit blacks' testimony in the courts. The Territory of Oregon refused to admit blacks, period. Indiana banished them and even Pennsylvania's legislature was considering an "Act to Prohibit the Emigration of Negroes and Mulattoes into this Commonwealth."

In the spring of 1852 Martin's dissatisfactions drove him to New York. Ostensibly he went to sell the rights to an invention. The Pennsylvania Railroad was extending its tracks to Pittsburgh, but its cars still crossed the Alleghenies on the Portage Road, using cumbersome stationary engines to haul the cars up and down a series of inclined planes. After many trips on the old Portage Road, Martin had devised a scheme that would do away with the stationary engines and permit locomotives to cross the mountains under their own steam.

Impressed with his working drawings, Dr. James McCune Smith introduced him to a lawyer so that he could patent the invention before attempting to market it. After weeks of correspondence with the Patent Office in Washington, the lawyer returned the drawings. Only U.S. citizens could obtain patents, he had been informed. And black Martin Delany was not considered a citizen of the United States.

Martin accepted the news as one more bit of evidence that colored people could never expect justice from whites.

A day later he was asked to speak to the pupils of a colored Sabbath School. What should he tell them? That their country despised them? That they could never improve their situation?

Looking into their well-scrubbed expectant faces, he could not bring himself to say this. Instead he made the conventional remarks, praising their achievements and urging them to keep up their good work. Afterward he turned to their teacher to ask, "But to what end are all these attainments? Where is the field for their future usefulness?"

A correspondent for *Frederick Douglass' Paper* who overheard the interchange wrote "This certainly is indicative of despair."

Despair? Yes. But Martin had worked through from anger to despair to a new determination. While waiting for word from the Patent Office, he had started to write a pamphlet to acquaint "one part of the American people with the other."

"The colored people are not yet known, even to their most professed friends among the white Americans; for the reason, that politicians, religionists, colonizationists, and abolitionists, have each and all presumed to *think* for, dictate to and *know* better what suited colored people, than they knew for themselves . . . Their history—past, present, and future has been written by them who . . . are not their representatives, and therefore, do not properly nor fairly present their wants and claims among their fellows . . . We design disabusing the public mind, and correcting the false impressions of all classes upon this great subject."

Holed up in his New York boardinghouse he worked night and day for a month. The ideas came tumbling out faster than his pen could keep up with them. His pamphlet became a book: *The Condition, Elevation, Emigration, and*

*Destiny of the Colored People of the United States Polit-
ically Considered.*

The first full-length piece of political analysis by a black
American, *Condition, Elevation, Emigration* was a combina-
tion of hardheaded critical thinking and indignant outcry.
Martin had ransacked his own knowledge of many subjects to make his points—history, geography, ethnology, theology, biography. His book boiled down to several simple
propositions and some not so simple conclusions:

We are Americans. . . . For more than 200 years, we have
cleared the forests, planted the crops, built the cities. We
are "the bone and sinews of the country."

We have been good citizens. Despite the stumbling blocks
placed in our way, black Americans have been poets and
warriors, musicians and doctors, artists, lawyers, ministers,
businessmen.

But our country has failed us. "We are slaves in the midst
of freedom . . . aliens to the laws and political privileges
of the country."

Even our antislavery friends have broken their promises.
Twenty years ago, they urged us to give up our separate
struggle for equality. "They earnestly contended' that they
(the whites) had obstructed our progress and now it was
their bounden duty to make full amends . . . In a word,
as they had oppressed and trampled down the colored people,
they would now elevate them . . . It was expected that
colored boys would get situations in their shops and stores,
that in Anti-Slavery establishments, colored men would have
the preference . . . But it has not been done . . . We are
still occupying a miserable position in the community, wherever we live."

For too long, we have let whites think for us. After the
Anti-Slavery Society was formed, "colored men stopped sud-

denly, and with their hands thrust deep in their breeches-pockets, and their mouths gaping open, stood gazing with astonishment, at the stupendous moral colossal statues of our Anti-Slavery friends."

We must act for ourselves. "We are a nation within a nation; —as the Poles in Russia, the Hungarians in Austria, the Welsh, Irish and Scotch in the British dominions. But we have been, by our oppressors, despoiled of our purity, and corrupted in our native characteristics, so that we have inherited their vices, and but few of their virtues, leaving us really a *broken people."*

What then shall we do? "We must go from our oppressors . . . We love our country, dearly love her, but she don't love us—she despises us, and bids us begone."

Where shall we go?

Not to Liberia. Although "we desire the civilization and enlightenment of Africa, Liberia is not an Independent Republic but a pitiful dependency of the American Colonization Society."

Not to Canada. Although it offers a temporary haven for the fugitive slave, "the Canadians are descended from the same common parentage as the Americans" and Canada will inevitably be annexed to the United States.

Central and South America must be our future home. Twenty-one million colored people—"our brethren—because they are precisely the same people as ourselves . . . stand with open arms ready to receive us. The climate, soil, and productions—the vast rivers and beautiful sea-coast . . . the song of the birds . . . bids us go. We shall make common cause with the people and shall hope to assemble one day . . . and form a glorious union of South American States."

Delany was not as sure of himself as he sounded. Pacing the room as he worked on the final section, he thought of objections that people would raise and, one by one, batted them down.

Leaving the United States would not mean deserting the cause of the slave. Instead the example of a free black nation in the Americas would hasten the day of emancipation. And as for the fugitives, "he who can make his way from Arkansas to Canada can find his way from Kentucky to Mexico."

Nor would black Americans find it difficult to adjust to the language and customs of the people south of the Rio Grande: "Spanish is the easiest of all foreign languages to learn . . . many who might think that they could not become reconciled to the new order of things should recollect that they were once in a situation in the United States (in *slavery*) where they were compelled to be content with customs infinitely more averse to their feelings and desires . . . Talk not about religious biases—we have but one reply to make. We had rather be a Heathen *freeman,* than a Christian *slave.*"

He was still revising the book when a chance encounter gave him the opportunity to try out some of his arguments. The educated young men who, he once had hoped, would knock down the barriers of prejudice, were not faring well. George Vashon had completed his law studies, but had been refused admission to the Pennsylvania bar because of his color. Robert Douglass, a talented portrait painter and daguerreotypist, had gone to the West Indies because he was unable to earn a living in his home town of Philadelphia. Now David Peck, who had been practicing medicine for two years, had given up in disgust. He was in New York waiting for passage on a boat to California.

"Why California?" Martin challenged him. "Go to Central America instead—where your color will be in your favor."

"Central America?" Peck was dubious. "Where?"

"San Juan del Norte!"

San Juan del Norte was a port city in Mosquitia, a kingdom bordering on the Caribbean, whose people were Indians who had intermarried with runaway slaves. Now a part of Nicaragua and Honduras, it was then under British influence. It had become important to the United States since the discovery of gold in California. Instead of making the long voyage around Cape Horn, gold hunters from the East were disembarking at San Juan del Norte to travel by river boat and overland to the Pacific.

Cornelius Vanderbilt, the American shipping magnate, had acquired exclusive rights to passage up the San Juan River and across the Isthmus of Nicaragua. Stock in his Accessory Transit Company had quadrupled in value since the American chargé d'affaires to Central America had described San Juan as "the only possible Atlantic terminus for the only possible ship-canal route across the continent."

Acting on Martin's suggestion, David Peck went to Mosquitia. Weeks later he sent Martin an enthusiastic letter, telling him that if he wanted to be mayor of San Juan, he should come on down! And bring your own council of state, he added. "We need administrators, lawyers, teachers."

Peck had arrived in San Juan during a struggle between British and American interests for control. Agents of Vanderbilt's Transit Company and a group of New Orleans businessmen had formed an American party, aimed at taking over from the British officials, most of them black men from Jamaica, and their local supporters. Once in power, they planned to limit the voting right to whites.

When the natives of San Juan, the black Britishers, and a handful of colored men from New York called a meeting to oppose the "cotton Americans," Dr. Peck was asked to be chairman. Using the political know-how acquired at colored conventions in Pennsylvania, he helped them to organize their own party. On election day the "cotton Americans" were defeated by a large majority. Now black men from the West Indies and New York were sitting on the town council, and David Peck of Pittsburgh was physician of the port of San Juan del Norte.

Here was proof that Martin was on the right track. But first he must bring out his book. After making arrangements to have it published in Philadelphia, he spent his last days in New York lecturing on physiology to raise money to pay the printer's bill.

On the train to Philadelphia, he worried over the manuscript again. Was he sure that he was right? The facts he had marshaled led to only one conclusion. If they were to live like men, colored people must find a home outside of the United States. And David Peck's letter, carefully tucked in his wallet, confirmed his choice of Central America. Yet as he stared out of the coach window, his mind went back to a shabby room in Pittsburgh and two young men who agreed that they must see Africa one day.

While the train rolled on, he wrote an appendix "giving the plan of the author, laid out at twenty-four years of age, but subsequently improved." Titled "A Project for an Expedition of Adventure to the East Coast of Africa," it envisioned black Americans building a railroad across Africa from the Red Sea to the shores of the Atlantic Ocean. Although he had put aside this plan in favor of a black republic in the Western Hemisphere, "we still lay claim to the project, which one day must be added to our dashing strides in national advancement, successful adventure and unsurpassed enterprise."

Still he was troubled. The book meant a break with everything black men had been working for. Was he really prepared to take a public stand against friends, mentors—and his native land?

"That all?" the printer grunted as he took the closely written sheets of paper from Martin.

"Wait!" Scribbling on the back of an envelope, Martin added a dedication page to his book:

SINCERELY DEDICATED

TO THE AMERICAN PEOPLE

NORTH AND SOUTH

BY THEIR MOST DEVOUT

AND PATRIOTIC FELLOW-CITIZEN

THE AUTHOR

It was as if he were making one last plea to the United States. Would anybody hear him?

> The problem of the twentieth century
> is the problem of the color line.
> —W. E. B. Du Bois, *1900*

14

BLACK AND PROUD

An author is never so vulnerable as when the first copies of his book come off the press. Seen in type, once-pleasant conceits look bumbling, elegant phrases seem pretentious, and the book abounds in mistakes that he hopes that readers will blame on the printer. He is doubly vulnerable if the book happens to appear on his fortieth birthday—a day which finds every man asking, "What have I accomplished? Where am I going?"

Martin Delany was no exception. When *Condition, Elevation, Emigration* was published in early May 1852 his joy at seeing his first sustained piece of writing between covers was mixed with regret. Misspelled names, wrong dates, awkward passages leaped out at him as he turned the pages. The printer had neglected to show him proof sheets so that he had been unable to correct obvious errors. Perhaps his prefatory note in which he apologized for "the hurried manner in which it has been composed" and warned the reader not to expect "elegance of language and terseness of style" would disarm his critics.

At any rate, it was too late for changes now. Feeling a

little like a mother who abandons her baby to the cold cruel world, he mailed copies of the book to the antislavery and black newspapers. How would they respond to his message?

He was still in Philadelphia, staying with James J. G. Bias, another black doctor, when the *Pennsylvania Freeman* carried a short notice of *Condition, Elevation, Emigration*. Oliver Johnson, editor of the *Freeman* and a stalwart of the American Anti-Slavery Society, dismissed the book with a few cutting phrases. Delany's facts were "bunglingly and egotistically presented . . . mixed up with much that is of questionable propriety and utility . . . The manner in which the author has used his materials deprives his work of all value. We could wish that, for his own credit, and that of the colored people it had never been published."

Delany had expected criticism from the abolitionists. *Condition, Elevation, Emigration* made points that no black man of stature had made before. But he had looked forward to a reasoned discussion rather than a curt put-down. Johnson's review was a slap in the face.

Still smarting, Delany struck back. The next issue of the *Freeman* printed his letter to the editor: ". . . The object of your remarks evidently has been to disparage me and to injure the sale of the book, especially among the colored people . . . which but furnishes a striking proof of *your* Negro-hate, in common with many of your less pretending fellows. You also charge me with egotism, which is but a prejudicial sneer at a black man, for daring to do anything upon his own responsibility . . . There is not one word, which to an unprejudiced mind, will be tortured into egotism . . . Under the circumstances, the attack was cowardly. I despise your sneers and defy your influence."

He was somewhat mollified when *The Liberator* carried a long friendly report on *Condition, Elevation, Emigration* a week later. William Lloyd Garrison hoped that it would be read by all Americans: "It contains so many valuable facts and cogent appeals that its dissemination cannot fail to remove many groundless prejudices. Dr. Delany is both 'black and comely'—so black as to make his identity with the African race perfect . . . He is a vigorous writer, an eloquent speaker, and full of energy and enterprise. The sketches he has made of several literary and professional colored men and women are not only authentic and highly interesting, but will greatly surprise those, who, having been taught to consider the colored population as a very inferior race, are profoundly ignorant as to all such instances of intellectual power, moral worth and scientific attainment."

After pointing out some factual errors, Garrison tackled Delany's conclusions. "We are sorry to see a tone of despondency . . . in the concluding portion of this otherwise instructive and encouraging work . . . The idea of separation is not only admitted, but strongly urged, and in a very plausible manner. Accordingly, Dr. Delany advices the free colored populations to 'emigrate to Central or South America, and even to Mexico and the West Indies' . . . We are desirous of seeing neither white nor black republics, as such . . . It never can be true that the proud and baneful prejudices, which now so cruelly alienate [Americans] from their colored brethren, may not, will not, must not yield to the sword of the Spirit, to the word of God, to the blessed weapons of Truth and Love."

Fair enough. Although Delany no longer had faith in the "weapons of Truth and Love," he thanked Garrison for "the very favorable and generous notice" and promised to correct the factual errors in the next edition.

"I would as willingly live among white men as black, if I had an *equal possession and enjoyment* of privileges," he explained in a letter to *The Liberator*. "But I must admit that I have no hopes in this country—no confidence in the American people—with a *few* excellent exceptions."

Garrison had opened the debate. Now others would join in. Delany was eager for black reactions. Several white abolitionists had sent him complimentary letters, but he was waiting to hear from Dr. James McCune Smith and Frederick Douglass.

He waited in vain. Few comments from blacks appeared in the antislavery or black papers. The book was mentioned in *The Voice of the Fugitive* which Henry Bibb was editing from Canada, but *Frederick Douglass' Paper* did not review *Condition, Elevation, Emigration* although it printed book reviews in almost every issue. Hurt, bewildered, angry, Martin kept silent for two months before writing to upbraid Douglass:

"The *Condition, Elevation, Emigration and Destiny of the Colored People*, a copy of which I sent you in May on its issue has never been noticed in the columns of your paper. It was not necessary that you should implicate yourself with the sentiments therein contained. You could have given it a supplementing notice, by saying that such a work had been written by me (saying anything else about or against it that you pleased) and let those who read it pass their own opinions. But you heaped upon it a cold and deathly silence.

"This is not the course you pursue to any issue, good or bad, sent you by white persons; you have always given them some notice. I desire . . . simply to be treated as justly as you treat them. I care but little what white men think of what I say, write, or do; my sole desire is to benefit the colored people . . .

"I desire that our people have light and information upon the available means of bettering their condition . . . We never have had any settled and established policy of our own—we

have always adopted the policies that white men established
. . . No people can go on this way.

"We must have a position, independently of anything pertaining to white men . . . I weary of our miserable condition, and [am] heartily sick of whimpering, whining and sniv-
eling at the feet of white men . . ."

Douglass printed Delany's letter without comment—and
continued to ignore his book.

Still Martin did not give up. Shuttling back and forth between Pennsylvania and New York with a satchel of books in
one hand and David Peck's letters in the other, he buttonholed
friends and lectured to strangers in an effort to round up a
corps of settlers for Central America. Few bought either his
book or his program.

Even Catherine, loyal and long-suffering, fell silent when
he spoke of exchanging their home in Pittsburgh for the
doubtful comforts of a thatched hut in a dusty tropical town.

Victor Hugo once said: "No army can withstand the
strength of an idea whose time has come." The year 1852
was clearly not the time to preach the idea of emigration
to colored Americans. The publication of Harriet Beecher
Stowe's *Uncle Tom's Cabin* was the major antislavery event
that year. As millions wept for Uncle Tom, free blacks felt
sure that some of the sympathy evoked by the book would
rub off on them. Frederick Douglass' election as secretary of
the Free-Soil Party's national convention was another hopeful sign. Although the party favored the containment of slavery rather than its extermination, most blacks supported
John P. Hale and George Julian, the Free-Soil candidates
for President and Vice-President. In the weeks before election
day *Frederick Douglass' Paper* carried their names on the
masthead, imprinted on an American flag.

Uncle Tom's Cabin sold 300,000 copies in 1852, *Condi-*

tion, Elevation, Emigration less than a thousand. Delany had promised to correct his errors when he brought out a second edition, but the second edition was never printed. Instead, he returned to Pittsburgh, feeling that he had lived through the darkest period of his life.

The news from Central America rubbed salt into his wounds. Cornelius Vanderbilt's Transit Company had defied the orders of San Juan's town council. When the City Marshal, a black man from New York, attempted to enforce them, the United States sloop-of-war *Cyane* steamed into the harbor and landed a company of Marines. With the Marines standing guard at the Transit Company offices, the town council resigned in a body. New York newspapers printed their protest to "the civilized world against this unlawful occupancy of their territory and subversion of their laws." A year later the long arm of the United States reached out once more: a U.S. warship bombarded San Juan del Norte and burned the port city to the ground.

Penniless and dispirited, Martin resumed the practice of medicine. Slowly he regained his buoyancy. His book had failed, but here and there others were taking up his theme. At a convention in Ohio, Charles and John Mercer Langston proposed a mass emigration of colored people from the United States. Writing from Jamaica where he was pastor of a church, Henry Highland Garnet urged free blacks to move to the West Indies. In New England, James Theodore Holly, a shoemaker turned minister, spoke in favor of Canada as a homeland for black people.

In the summer of 1853 black men met in Rochester for their first national convention in five years. Under Frederick Douglass' leadership, they made plans for a manual labor college for black youth, an employment agency for black workers, and a national black museum and library. "We intend to plant our trees on American soil and repose in the shade thereof," one of the delegates declared.

Martin Delany did not attend. Instead, he challenged their program by calling all men in favor of emigration to meet in Cleveland the following year. "We must make an issue, create an event, and establish a position *for ourselves*. It is glorious to think of, but far more glorious to carry out," he wrote.

With the first announcement of the National Emigration Convention, the "cold and deathly silence" that had greeted *Condition, Elevation, Emigration* was broken. Column after column in black weeklies was given over to a battle between the emigrationists and those who wished to remain on American soil. Frederick Douglass called the forthcoming convention "unwise, unfortunate and premature." John Jones, a well-to-do tailor from Chicago, accused Delany of creating disunion. Philip Bell, a co-editor of the old *Colored American,* charged him with "being false to his brethren, recreant to the principles he has heretofore espoused." Terming the emigration scheme "infamous," Bell said: "It is the work of an evil spirit who would rather 'rule in hell, than reign in heaven.' "

Quick to defend "this great movement of establishing our nationality," Delany ridiculed "those who love to live among whites better than blacks." James M. Whitfield, a twenty-three-year-old poet-barber, also took up the struggle. Emigration was preferable to "crawling in the dust to the feet of our oppressors," he wrote. "I believe it to be the destiny of the Negro to develop a higher order of civilization and Christianity than the world has yet seen." After Douglass called Delany "querulous" and "dictatorial," young Whitfield dedicated his first book of poetry, *America and Other Poems,* to "Martin R. Delany . . . as a small tribute of respect for his character, admiration of his talents and love of his principles by the Author."

Although the debate often generated more heat than light, it publicized the question that *Condition, Elevation, Emigration* had raised. Should blacks remain in the United States where under the best of circumstances they would always be a minority, or should they establish a homeland of their own? On a sultry August day in 1854 more than a hundred black men and women from ten states and Canada met in a Cleveland church to try to arrive at an answer.

The Emigration Convention was Martin Delany's show from beginning to end. Two decades of attending meetings where fine-sounding resolutions were passed but rarely implemented afterward had left him with decided opinions about how conventions should be run. As President pro tem, chairman of the Business Committee, and keynote speaker, he saw to it that his was "not merely a talking and theoretical, but an *acting* and practically *doing* Convention."

Sessions began on time and ran with clockwork efficiency. "Few conventions of whites behave themselves more orderly or observe parliamentary rule more exactly, or discuss important topics with more ability and self-possession," the Cleveland *Morning Leader* reported.

Not the least of Martin's innovations was the presence of women delegates with full power to speak and vote. Mary Bibb, widow of Henry Bibb who had died three weeks earlier, was elected second vice-president, Catherine Delany was one of Pittsburgh's representatives, and four other women sat on the Finance Committee. When a "Declaration of Sentiments" was drawn up, one resolution said: "The potency and respectability of a nation or people, depends entirely upon the position of their women; therefore, it is essential to our elevation that the female portion of our children be instructed in all the arts and sciences pertaining to the highest civilization."

Equally unusual were two resolutions that followed:

"—That we shall ever cherish our identity of origin and race, as preferable, in our estimation, to any other people.

"—That the relative terms Negro, African, Black, Colored and Mulatto, when applied to us, shall ever be held with the same respect and pride; and synonymous with the terms Caucasian, White, Anglo-Saxon and European, when applied to that class of people."

For the first time in American history black people were asserting a positive pride in their race. Chairman Delany elaborated on this the second day of the convention when sixteen hundred blacks and whites crowded into the church to hear his "Report on the Political Destiny of the Colored People." In a sharper, more confident summary of *Condition, Elevation, Emigration* he urged blacks to leave the United States. The dream of integration that had sustained a generation of free blacks was wrong.

"Our friends have for years been erroneously urging us to lose our identity as a race, declaring that we were the same as other people . . . The truth is, we are not identical with the Anglo-Saxon or any other race . . . We have inherent traits, and native characteristics, peculiar to our race and all that is required of us is to cultivate these to make them desirable and emulated by the rest of the world."

Blacks are different but not inferior, he continued. "The white race may probably excel in mathematics, sculpture and architecture, commerce and internal improvements. But in language, oratory, poetry, music and painting, and in ethics, metaphysics, theology and legal jurisprudence; in plain language—in the true principles of morals, correctness of thought, religion and law or civil government, there is no doubt that the black race will yet instruct the world."

In words not greatly different from those written half a century later by Dr. W. E. B. Du Bois, Delany predicted that "the great issue" facing the world "will be a question of black and white—and every individual will be called upon for his identity with one or the other."

"The blacks and colored races are four-sixths of all the population of the world . . . The white races are but one-third of the population of the globe—or one of them to two of us—and it cannot much longer continue that two-thirds will passively submit to the domination of this one-third.

"For more than two thousand years, the determined aim of the whites has been to crush the colored races. The Anglo-Saxon has taken the lead in this work of universal subjugation. But the Anglo-American stands pre-eminent for deeds of injustice and acts of oppression.

"We admit the existence of great and good people in America, England, France, who desire a unity of interests among the whole human family, of whatever origin or race.

"But it is neither the moralist, Christian, nor philanthropist whom we now have to combat, but the politician—the civil engineer and skillfull economist, who direct and control the machinery which moves the nations and powers of the earth."

As for the philosophy of non-resistance, Delany said: "Should we encounter an enemy with artillery, a prayer will not stay the cannon shot; neither will the kind words nor smiles of philanthropy shield his spear from piercing us through the heart. We must meet mankind, then, as they meet us—prepared for the worst, though we may hope for the best. Our submission does not gain for us an increase of friends or respectability—as the white race will only acknowledge as equals those who will not submit to their rule."

To win respect, a black republic in the American tropics was a necessary first step: "Shall the last vestige of an opportunity, outside of the continent of Africa, for the national development of our race, be permitted to elude our grasp and fall into the possession of the whites? This, may Heaven forbid. May the sturdy, intelligent Africo-American sons of the Western Continent forbid."

After a discussion of the report, which was unanimously adopted, H. Ford Douglass, a free colored man from New Orleans, stole the spotlight for an hour. Answering an opponent of emigration who had appealed to the delegates' patriotism, young Douglass warned his listeners against "a sickly sentimentality."

"I can hate this Government without being disloyal, because it has stricken down my manhood, and treated me as a saleable commodity," he said. "I can join a foreign enemy and fight against it, without being a traitor, because it treats me as an ALIEN and a STRANGER.

"When I remember that from Maine to Georgia, from the Atlantic waves to the Pacific shore, I am an alien and an outcast, unprotected by law, proscribed and persecuted by cruel prejudice, I am willing to forget the endearing name of home and country, and as an unwilling exile seek on other shores the freedom which has been denied me in the land of my birth."

There was a sharp intake of breaths when Douglass offered to take up arms against the United States. No gathering of American blacks had heard such sentiments expressed before. "He kept the house in a ferment of emotion," the secretary dryly reported in the minutes.

By the third day the speeches were over and it was time to plan for action. Delany had come to Cleveland with a blueprint for a permanent organization—a National Board of

Commissioners that included, in addition to the usual officers, a Foreign Secretary and a Committee on Foreign Relations. It would be their job to collect information on the geography, politics, and economy of countries that might welcome Africo-American settlers. After conducting inquiries by mail, the commissioners were to travel to these countries for a first-hand study of conditions. Envisioning a long period of research and investigation before a mass emigration could be organized, the constitution of the National Board called for monthly meetings, annual reports, and conventions every two years.

With Martin Delany as President, the Board of Commissioners began to take care of business. He and his Foreign Secretary instituted a lively correspondence with officials in Central and South America, Jamaica, and Cuba. His first annual report described the political situations in these countries and in the Sandwich Islands (now Hawaii), which was also under consideration as a homeland. In the summer of 1855 James Theodore Holly was sent to Haiti as the Board's representative at the court of Emperor Faustin Soulouque. Returning full of enthusiasm after a month's visit, Holly reported on his mission when the Emigration Convention again met in Cleveland in 1856.

By that time, Martin Delany had left the United States.

I have just returned from Canada.
I have gazed for the first time upon
Free Land, and, would you believe it,
tears sprang to my eyes and I wept.
Oh, it was a glorious sight to gaze on
a land where a poor slave, flying
from our glorious land of liberty,
would in a moment find his fetters
broken, his shackles loosed, and
whatever he was in the land of
Washington, beneath the shadow of
Bunker Hill Monument or even
Plymouth Rock, here he becomes a
man and a brother.
—FRANCES E. W. HARPER, *1856*

15

NORTH OF THE BORDER

"We are pleased to state to our readers" the *Provincial Free-man* of Chatham, Canada said in its February 22, 1856, issue "the arrival of our esteemed and talented friend, Dr. M. R. Delany, of Pittsburgh, Pa., in this town yesterday morning, who intends making this his home. The Doctor proposes to resume the practice of medicine immediately, when he will doubtless be at the service of all who may call at his office on William Street, east of King."

Martin Delany certainly had four good reasons for leaving the United States: Toussaint who was now nine, five-year-old Charles, and their baby brothers, Alexander Dumas and St.

Cyprian. In his writings Delany had warned that American racism had a "pernicious and degrading" effect on black children. "How could it otherwise be when they see . . . every situation of respectability, honor, profit or trust filled by white men, and [blacks] existing among them merely as a thing of convenience? . . . They cannot be raised in this country without being stoop shouldered."

He and Catherine had done their best to insulate the boys against the soul-deadening effects of discrimination. The walls of their home were decorated with pictures of black heroes, living and dead, and Toussaint and Charles knew the stories of their namesakes long before they could read. But pride in their race could not conceal the fact that they lived in a run-down segregated neighborhood and attended an inferior segregated school.

While attending a convention in Toronto in 1851, Delany had been favorably impressed with Canada West, the southwestern part of the present province of Ontario. Runaway slaves and free blacks from the United States had been clearing the forest and tilling the fertile soil north of Lake Erie for two decades. Since his visit, the Fugitive Slave Law had driven more than ten thousand black Americans across the border. Some had joined all-black communities where, with help from United States and British philanthropists, they purchased land and sold their crops communally. Others had settled in Chatham, a market town on the Thames River which was only a few hours from Detroit by steamboat or rail and a dozen buggy miles from Dawn and Elgin, the most successful of the black farming communities.

When the Delany family got off the train at the Great Western depot in February 1856, Chatham was known as the colored man's Paris. Fugitives from the United States, who made up a third of the town's population of 4000, had established two churches, a school, and a colored fire engine company. Wherever the boys looked they could see signs of black achievement. Black Sherwood Barber owned the Villa Mansion Hotel where the Delanys lived during their first months in Canada. Black James Charity owned a shoe store near by and a block of brick shops on King Street. Black James M. Jones, a graduate of Oberlin, was the best gunsmith in town, Isaac Holden was a surveyor, and Mansfield Johnson a skilled ironworker. Israel Shadd, publisher of the *Provincial Freeman,* was a black man from Delaware and his niece, Mary Ann Shadd, was the first black "editress" in North America.

The Delanys never had time to feel lonely in their adopted home. Martin had met Mary Ann Shadd years earlier when he visited her home town of Wilmington on behalf of *The North Star.* Through the Shadds and Mary Ann's husband-to-be, Thomas Cary, they were quickly caught up in Chatham's social and political life. Martin became a contributor to the *Provincial Freeman,* lectured on anatomy at local churches, and was the principal speaker at a Queen's Birthday celebration at Town Hall.

Familiar faces from the States turned up almost every month. The teacher at Chatham's King Street School was Alfred Whipper of Pennsylvania. The pastor of the Colored Baptist Church was William C. Munroe of Detroit who had been president of the first Emigration Convention. William Day gave up newspaper work in Cleveland to teach at the Elgin Colony and H. Ford Douglass joined the staff of the *Provincial Freeman.*

When Amelia Freeman, formerly a "professoress" at Avery College in Pittsburgh, moved to Chatham to give painting and music lessons, her arrival was the occasion for a party. "At the Villa Mansion in the apartment of Dr. M. R. Delany,

Miss Freeman was greeted with some welcome tunes from the Union Brass Band," the *Provincial Freeman* reported. "The Band played several beautiful pieces and were responded to by some choice pieces from Miss Freeman on the Melodian."

Saint and Charles went ice skating on the frozen Thames, learned to plod down King Street on snowshoes and to sing "God Save the Queen" instead of "My Country, 'Tis of Thee" at school assemblies. Although the school in Chatham was segregated, black youngsters were accepted at Knox College in Toronto and there was little discrimination in public places throughout Canada West.

After the snow melted and the spring floods subsided, the Delanys moved to a rented cottage on Murray Street, close to the Colored Baptist Church. Known as "the Hut," because it had low eaves and small windows, the cottage was surrounded by fields and woods that reached to the banks of the Thames. While the boys explored the woods, Martin paid sick calls in a new horse and buggy or saw patients in his dispensary in the Villa Mansion. At the end of their first year in Chatham, he was able to buy the Hut and a quarter acre of the land on which it stood for $1800.

Catherine sewed curtains for their home, glorying in the absence of Pittsburgh's soot and grime, and dared to hope that Martin would be content to remain in Chatham. He had already won the respect of the community and a modicum of political power. Black Americans could become naturalized citizens after three years of residence in Canada. Although Martin could not yet vote, hundreds of other black men could. In the fall of 1856 he canvassed the district for Archibald McKellar, a white liberal who was running for Parliament on the Reform Party ticket. When the black vote helped McKellar win the election, he invited Martin to become a member of his executive committee.

The contrast between life in Canada and the United States was sharpened when, only weeks after Martin's purchase of the Hut, the U. S. Supreme Court handed down its decision in the Dred Scott case. Scott, a slave, had sued for his freedom after his master took him to live in a free state. Scott's plea was rejected, Chief Justice Roger Taney announced, because slaves and their descendants were not and could never become citizens of the United States. It was his opinion, supported by a majority of the Supreme Court, that they were "regarded as beings of an inferior order and altogether unfit to associate with the white race . . . so far inferior that they had no rights which the white man was bound to respect."

Speaking at a meeting in New York, Frederick Douglass saw reasons why "we, the abolitionists and colored people, should meet this decision in a cheerful spirit. This very attempt to blot out forever the hopes of an enslaved people may be one necessary link in the chain of events preparatory to the downfall and complete overthrow of the whole slave system."

From his vantage point in Canada, Martin was less optimistic. The Dred Scott decision only strengthened his belief in the need for a black homeland. Although he was still corresponding with officials in Central and South America, he had begun to move in a new direction. At the time of the first Emigration Convention no black militant dared to mention Africa for fear of being attacked as a supporter of the American Colonization Society. But in the convention's secret sessions he had tentatively broached a scheme for an expedition to the "Dark Continent." There had been no takers for his proposal then, but in the spring of 1857 his dream of resettlement in Africa received support from an unlikely source.

Thomas Jefferson Bowen, a white Baptist minister from

Georgia, published *Central Africa,* an account of his missionary labors in the kingdom of the Yorubas, which lay between Dahomey and Benin on Africa's west coast. Martin sent away to the States for the book. Flipping through its pages while he walked home from the post office he saw names, phrases, that he had not thought about for forty years. He read with mounting excitement, skipping dinner, shushing the boys, forgetting sleep. Thomas Jefferson Bowen, a white man from Georgia, was telling about the land of Grandmother Graci!

All her stories were in the book—reported in the dry language of a Baptist minister, but still unmistakably the tales he remembered from childhood. The Yolla Ba was the Mandingo name for the Niger River—"the Mississippi of Africa," Bowen called it. Graci had grown up in the Niger Valley where people worshiped Shango, the storm god—"and certain old hatchets like those found in America are picked up in the fields and venerated as thunder-bolts."

Even Graci's rain song was included. The boys crowded around to hear

> Ojo pa, batta, batta,
> Ojo pa, batta, batta . . .

When Martin closed his eyes the better to recall the tune, Catherine knew that he was lost to Canada.

The Africa that Bowen described was not the Africa of the geography books. Bowen found the land fertile, the people healthy, cleanly, and industrious. He devoted page after page to descriptions of clay-walled cities and market places where not only farm produce but cotton cloth and iron, paper and raw silk could be purchased. In his concluding chapters he proposed that the United States government sign treaties with

Yoruban kings and chiefs in order to explore the upper reaches of the Niger and establish commercial relations with its people. As a missionary he was interested in bringing Christianity to the natives, but he saw commerce as a necessary first step.

While Bowen gave lectures in the principal cities of the North and South, Delany sent copies of *Central Africa* to members of the National Board of Commissioners set up by the Emigration Convention. The convention was scheduled to meet again in the summer of 1858, but he hoped for tentative approval of an African expedition before then.

Interest in Africa was further stimulated by the publication, late in 1857, of David Livingstone's *Missionary Travels and Researches in South Africa.* A Scottish medical missionary, Dr. Livingstone had traveled from Bechuanaland to Angola on the west coast and had then followed the Zambezi River to the shores of the Indian Ocean. Like Bowen, he described the people as intelligent and friendly, the countryside rich in plant and animal life, and the opportunities for Christian commerce unlimited.

American black men were at last able to read accounts of Africa that did not stress the naked-cannibal, snakes-and-tropical-fevers stereotypes. For the first time they could discuss the land of their forefathers without feeling shame.

"I have read Bowen's work, and shall today purchase Livingstone's," the principal of Avery College wrote to Martin. "I am more and more convinced that Africa is the country to which all colored men who wish to attain the full stature of manhood, and bring up their children to be men and not creeping things should turn their steps. I made a great mistake in not going there, when I was untrammeled by family ties."

Even more encouraging was the response from strangers.

After a group of Wisconsin blacks who wanted to settle in Africa sent a spokesman to Chatham to consult with Delany, he decided not to wait for the National Board meeting but to push ahead as speedily as possible. In April 1858 he was making plans to raise money and personnel for an expedition when an elderly white man called to see him.

Martin was away, but Catherine talked to the stranger. She described him as tall, with white hair and beard, and a peculiarly solemn way of speaking.

"He looked for all the world like one of the Old Testament prophets," she reported.

Although he would not leave his name, he promised to come back in two weeks. He returned at the appointed time but once again Martin was absent.

"Tell him that I'll call again in four days," the old man instructed Catherine. *"And I must see him then."*

Four days later Martin was in Chatham posting some letters when he saw a man who fitted Catherine's description leaving the office of the *Provincial Freeman*. He walked over to introduce himself.

The old man, ramrod tall, inclined his head to acknowledge the introduction. "I am John Brown," he said.

"Not Captain John Brown of Kansas?" Martin's face expressed his bewilderment.

For several years Free-Soil men from the East and slave-owners from the South had been fighting on the prairies to determine whether Kansas Territory would be free or slave. No one had played a more important role in the bloody struggle to keep Kansas free than John Brown. What was he doing in Canada?

"I have come to Chatham expressly to see you," the stranger replied. "I must talk to you at once, sir, in private, as I have much to do and but little time."

There was no milk and water sentimentality—no offensive contempt for
the Negro, while working in his
cause . . . In John Brown's house, and
in John Brown's presence, men from
widely different parts of the continent
met and united into one company,
wherein no hateful prejudice dared
intrude its ugly self."
    —OSBORNE ANDERSON *of Chatham,*
one of John Brown's black lieutenants,
in "A Voice from Harper's Ferry,"
1861

16

JOHN BROWN IN CANADA

Behind a locked door in Dr. Delany's office in the Villa
Mansion, John Brown disclosed his plans. With a small band
of picked men he proposed to set up armed camps in the
Appalachians. From time to time his guerrillas would go
down to the plantations to induce slaves to join them. As slaves
and free blacks flocked to his standard, they would gradually
extend their holdings until a continuous chain of camps ran
from the Pennsylvania border to the swamps of South Carolina and Georgia. In the heart of the slave states he would
establish a free land.

"The mountains and swamps of the South were intended
by the Almighty for a refuge for the slave." The old man's
blue-gray eyes darkened almost to blackness as he talked.

"They are full of natural forts and hiding places where large numbers of men could elude pursuit for a long time."

For two decades, Brown had been studying the history of guerrilla warfare. On a journey to Europe nine years earlier he had inspected fortifications, particularly earthen breast-works that could be built without the aid of draft animals or machines. Using a pen that lay on Martin's desk he sketched a fort that he had devised for mountain operations.

"Twenty men could build one in a day. And it will defy all the artillery that can be brought to bear against it."

In addition to his military program, Brown had drawn up a "Provisional Constitution for the Oppressed People of the United States" as a framework for civil government in the liberated zones. His guerrilla fighters would organize schools, churches, courts while the fighting was going on.

In recent months he had been conferring with black men like Frederick Douglass, Henry Highland Garnet, and William Still who was in charge of Underground Railroad operations in Pennsylvania. In Canada he had met with William Day and Harriet Tubman, the Underground Railroad leader. Of the latter, Brown said, "She is the most of a man I ever met with. She hooked on her whole team at once."

The old man's manner was so compelling that Martin, ordinarily skeptical of white saviors, found his doubts melting away. Besides, if Harriet Tubman had "hooked on her whole team" could Martin do less?

"How can I help?" he asked.

"It's men I want," said Brown.

Feeling almost apologetic, Delany told Brown of his plan for an expedition to Africa.

Brown's bushy eyebrows rose. Africa was no concern of his. He intended to free blacks in the United States. And he had a specific task in mind for Martin Delany. Before he made his first foray into slave territory, he wanted a responsible body of men to consider and ratify the constitution he had prepared. The government in the mountains must not only be *for* the oppressed people but *of* and *by* them as well.

The need for secrecy made it impossible to hold a convention in the United States. Would Martin convene one in Canada?

He would. Day after day he rode out into the country, visiting Elgin, Dawn, and the other settlements to round up men for the meeting. On April 29 the morning train from Detroit brought a party of strangers to Chatham. Twelve young white men who had fought with John Brown in Kansas took rooms at the Villa Mansion Hotel.

"Here we intend to remain till we have perfected our plans, which will be in about ten days," one wrote to a friend in the United States. "After which we start for *China.* Yesterday and this morning we have been busy in writing to Gerrit Smith and Wendell Phillips and others of like kin to meet us in this place on Saturday, the 8th of May, to adopt our Constitution, decide a few matters and bid us goodbye. Then we start. Remember me to all who know our business, but to all others be as dumb as death."

Early in the morning on Saturday, May 8, 1858, Alfred Whipper unlocked the door of the little frame building on Princess Street which housed the colored school. Men strolled by in groups of two or three and casually crossed the school yard. Martin had let it be known that he was organizing a Masonic lodge so that passers-by who noticed the gathering would have little reason to be curious.

None of the white abolitionists who had been invited had come from the States, but all of the leading colored men of Chatham and its vicinity were present. When the meeting was called to order, forty-seven men were seated on the

wooden benches of the schoolroom, thirty-four blacks and
John Brown and his Kansas followers.

After the election of Reverend William Munroe as president
and John Kagi, one of Brown's men, as secretary, Martin
Delany introduced Captain Brown. The room fell silent as the
old man spoke.

"Mr. Brown proceeded to state the object of the convention
at length, and to explain the general features of the plan of
action in the execution of the project. Mr. Delany and others
spoke in favor of the project and the plan, and both were
agreed to by general consent," Kagi noted in his minutes.

Brown intended to print the journal of the convention so
that it could be made public at the proper time. Meanwhile it
must contain no explanation of "the plan of action" lest it
fall into unfriendly hands.

"Mr. Brown then presented a plan entitled 'Provisional
Constitution and Ordinances for the people of the United
States,' and moved the reading of the same," Secretary
Kagi continued. "Mr. Kinnard objected to the reading until
an oath of secrecy be taken by each member of the Convention. Whereupon, Mr. Delany moved that the following
parole be taken by all members of the Convention: 'I solemnly
affirm that I will not in any way divulge any of the secrets of
this convention, except to persons entitled to know the same
on the pain of forfeiting the respect and protection of this
Organization,' which motion was carried."

After each man affirmed his willingness to keep the pro-
ceedings secret—even from your wives, Brown warned—the
Provisional Constitution was taken up, section by section.
Heads nodded agreement as Kagi read the preamble:

"Whereas, slavery throughout its entire existence in the
United States, is none other than a most barbarous, unpro-
voked, and unjustifiable war of one portion of its citizens

upon another portion . . . in utter disregard and violation of those eternal and self-evident truths set forth in our Declaration of Independence: Therefore

"We, citizens of the United States, and the Oppressed People, who, by a recent decision of the Supreme Court are declared to have no rights which the White Man is bound to respect; together with all other people degraded by the laws thereof, Do, for the time being ordain and establish ourselves, the following PROVISIONAL CONSTITUTION and ORDINANCES, the better to protect our Persons, Property, Lives, and Liberties, and to govern our actions."

The forty-eight articles that followed proposed a framework of government patterned on that of the United States, but adapted to the special conditions of guerrilla life. "All persons of mature age, whether Proscribed, oppressed and enslaved" had the right to vote. All were required "to labor for the common good." Property, including that captured or confiscated, was "the property of the whole, equally, without distinction." No one was to receive pay beyond support for his family "unless it be from an equal dividend of public property on the establishment of peace."

Brown had laid great stress on the need for honesty and sobriety. Only "men of integrity, intelligence, good business habits and above all of first-rate moral and religious character [were] to act as civil officers . . . teachers, chaplains, physicians, clerks." Those who were "habitually intoxicated" were to be removed from office and "profane swearing, filthy conversation, indecent behavior or quarreling" were strictly forbidden.

In his dealings with the enemy, he proposed to be merciful. Although the slaveholders' property was to be confiscated, prisoners were to be accorded "every degree of respect and kindness the circumstances will admit of." Rape of a female prisoner would be punishable by death and those who voluntarily gave up their slaves were to be treated as friends.

The United States Constitution guaranteed the right of people to bear arms, but state law and custom denied this right to blacks. In John Brown's constitution, "All persons known to be of good character, and of sound mind and suitable age, who are connected with this organization, whether male or female, shall be encouraged to carry arms openly."

Only one article provoked debate: "The foregoing shall not be construed so as in any way to encourage the overthrow of any State Government of the United States: and look to no dissolution of the Union, but simply to Amendment and Repeal. And our flag shall be the same that our Fathers fought under in the Revolution."

When an ex-slave protested that he owed no allegiance to the Stars and Stripes, Brown shook his head. Nothing was wrong with the principles on which the United States was founded, he explained. Slavery had subverted these principles and must be overthrown. "The old flag is good enough for me," he said. "Under it, freedom was won from the tyrants of the old world, for white men. Now I intend to make it do duty for black men."

Delany, too, agreed that the Provisional Constitution did not threaten the government of the United States. "The independent community that Captain Brown proposes to establish will be similar to the Cherokee Nation of Indians or the Mormons in Utah Territory," he pointed out.

After several other speakers sided with Brown, the article was adopted with one dissenting vote.

"On motion of Mr. Delany it was then ordered that those approving of the Constitution sign the same," Kagi's minutes noted. "Whereupon the names of all the members were appended. After congratulatory remarks by Messrs. Kinnard and Delany, the convention adjourned at a quarter to 4."

Brown's "Constitution for the 'proscribed and oppressed people' of the United States" would later be called absurd, utopian, or "a piece of insanity in the literal sense of the word." To the blacks in the little schoolroom on Princess Street, it seemed eminently reasonable and right. Brown was not only proposing to free their brothers in slavery, but he had demonstrated in section after section of the document, his respect for the capabilities of black men.

They met again that night in the engine house of the colored fire company to elect John Brown commander-in-chief of the guerrilla forces and John Kagi his secretary of war. Sunday, Brown's fifty-ninth birthday, was a day for churchgoing. On Monday the convention reconvened to fill the other offices established by the constitution. Two black men were chosen as members of Congress, but no one could be found to be President of the future state.

Martin Delany shook his head when eyes turned to him. Since Brown's arrival in Chatham his own plans had been in disarray. Should he give up his African expedition to join Brown's band of liberators? There was a new baby, Faustin Soulouque, in the house on Murray Street. Did Faustin's future lie in a free United States or with his 200 million brothers in Africa? And what if Brown failed? Prevented by his vow of secrecy from discussing his decision with Catherine, Delany spent sleepless nights struggling with the problem.

Ultimately one Hugh Forbes, a soldier of fortune hired by Brown to instruct his band in the art of guerrilla warfare, made the decision for Martin. Disgruntled because Brown had not been able to pay him adequately, Forbes betrayed the old man. While the Constitutional Convention was meeting in Chatham, Forbes was in Washington. Forcing his way onto the floor of the Senate, he disclosed Brown's plans to Senator Henry Wilson of Massachusetts and other antislavery senators. His disclosure had little effect in the capital, where the scheme sounded too fantastic to be believed, but it alarmed Brown's Boston friends who had been supplying him with guns and money.

"I have only received $15 from the east," Brown wrote to his son Owen in late May. "Such has been the effect of the course taken by F. on our eastern friends that I have some fears that we shall be compelled to delay further action for the present. I am in hourly expectation of help sufficient to pay off our board bills here and to take us to Cleveland, to see and advise with you."

The money for the board bills finally arrived, but Brown's supporters insisted that he go to Kansas at once, in order to allay suspicion. Regretfully he agreed.

"Wait," he told the men of Chatham. "I'll send word when to turn loose the flock."

On the twenty-ninth of May, Martin Delany went to the depot to say good-by to John Brown. It was the last time he saw the old man.

In June, Brown wrote to Delany from Rochester. He had visited his family and was heading west. In July, letters came from Charles Tidd and other members of the band. In August John Kagi wrote from Kansas where Brown was "laid up with Ague and Chill fever."

"I am pleased to hear from you, 'Uncle' and Mr. Tidd," Delany replied on August 16. "I hope ere this reaches you that 'Uncle' will have recovered from his febrile attack. Say to Mr. Tidd that I have sent the letter on to Mr. Real,* New York State, which he sent in my care for him. I also enclose one that I have for some time had from Mr. Moffit* for you, but did not know where to send it until now.

"I have not seen Richardson* since I received your letter

* Men that John Brown had brought to the Chatham convention.

today, but have seen Bell, Shadd, Jackson and Thomas
[black Canadians]. W. H. Day is now here and will be for
some days. Tell 'Uncle' I received his letter dated at Syracuse
and postmarked Rochester.

"There is nothing new here, nor worthy of note. I have
been anxiously looking and expecting to see something of
'Uncle's' movements in the papers, but as yet have seen
nothing. Please send me any paper which may mention your
doings. All are in good spirits here, hoping and waiting the
'good time coming!' "

The "good time coming" was still more than a year away.
John Brown had said "Wait," but Martin Delany was not
good at waiting. When the "good time" came, he was in
Africa.

> In the many struggles black Americans
> carried on with white people, we
> found all too often that well-meaning
> whites assigned to us the role of
> strangers in our own struggle; and
> thus well-meaning white people knew
> what was good for us better than we
> did.
> —MAYOR RICHARD G. HATCHER *of*
> *Gary, Indiana, in* Freedomways, *1969*

17

INTERLUDE

The year following the Chatham convention was one of high hopes and deep frustrations for Martin. As soon as John Brown's action was postponed, Delany started to line up men for his exploring party.

"I think very highly of the intended Expedition to the Valley of the Niger," Robert Douglass replied when he was asked to become official artist for the expedition. "I would be pleased to accompany it professionally, if I were to receive a proper outfit and salary. Mr. Robert Campbell of the Institute for Colored Youth, a very accomplished Chemist &c., says he will gladly accompany the Expedition, if a proper support for his family in his absence were assured."

When others recommended Campbell, a young West Indian who had been teaching in Philadelphia for several years, Delany appointed him Naturalist. By the time the Emigra-

tion Convention held its biennial meeting in August, two
others had accepted posts—Dr. Amos Aray of Chatham as
Surgeon and James W. Purnell, a youngster who had attended
the John Brown convention, as Secretary and Commercial
Reporter. After resigning as President of the Emigration Convention in favor of William Day, Delany was appointed Chief
Commissioner of the Niger Valley Exploring Party.

"The object of this Expedition," his formal commission
stated, "is to make a Topographical, Geological and Geographical Examination of the Valley of the River Niger, in
Africa, and an inquiry into the state and condition of the
people of that Valley, and other parts of Africa, together with
such other scientific inquiries as may by them be deemed
expedient, for the purpose of science and for general information."

However, the convention officers noted, they were "entirely
opposed to any Emigration there as such" although they
would not "interfere with the right of the Commissioners to
negotiate in their own behalf for territory." Commissioner
Delany was further empowered to appoint his own assistants
—"it being agreed that this organization is to be exempted
from the pecuniary responsibility of sending out this Expedition."

With this halfhearted acceptance of his project, Martin
undertook to finance the expedition himself. It proved to be a
difficult task. The problem was not so much that Americans
were opposed to black emigration. More people than ever
were in favor of it—but they were the wrong kind of people.

T. J. Bowen's book and lectures had touched off a wave
of commercial interest in Africa. British and American textile
mill owners were impressed with the possibility of cultivating
African cotton on a large scale. Africa's climate permitted
two crops a year and its plants bore cotton for seven years

instead of only one, as in the United States. If American blacks were to go to Africa to teach modern methods of cotton culture, Africa might be able to capture the world cotton market and put the Southern slaveholders out of business. All the mill owners and their bankers had to do was to create more African cotton fields while ending slavery in the States and bringing Christian enlightenment to the "Dark Continent." Thus morality and profit would walk hand in hand.

Martin Delany saw little wrong with this program, but he wanted it to be black-financed and black-led, with the profits accruing to blacks. The object of *his* expedition was "the Moral, Social and Political Elevation of Ourselves and the Regeneration of Africa." And this could be accomplished only by "men of African descent, properly qualified and of pure and fixed principles," he wrote.

He soon found himself in competition with a newly formed African Civilization Society which also planned an expedition to Yoruba to seek land for black settlers. Although the society was headed by his old acquaintance, Henry Highland Garnet, now pastor of a church in New York, its chief support came from Quaker businessmen, middle-of-the-road abolitionists, and members of the American Colonization Society.

The businessmen backers of the African Civilization Society warned young Robert Campbell against Delany. "Mistaken persons (white), presuming to know more about us (the blacks) than we did ourselves, went so far as to speak to one of our party, and tell him that we were *not ready* for any such *important* undertaking, nor could be in *three years yet to come,*" Martin angrily related. "This was followed up with a dissertation on the disqualification of the Chief of the Party, mentally and physically, *external* appearances and all."

Apparently, the white supporters of the emigration movement thought Delany was too black to lead an expedition to Africa!

Their opposition only strengthened Martin's determination to go it alone. He would have to fall back on his own slender resources. With Catherine's tremulous assent he sold the Hut to its original owner for the price he had paid for it the year before. The purchaser agreed that Catherine and the boys could live there as tenants until Martin's return from Africa.

He spent the winter of 1858–59 in New York, lecturing, speaking at church meetings, soliciting from friends. James Purnell, who had come from Chatham to help, wrote letters at his dictation to black men across the country. Money dribbled in—dimes, quarters, dollar bills. But thousands of dollars were needed to pay for the passage of five men across the Atlantic, to buy supplies, and to support five families for the years they would be away.

Once before when he was living in a boardinghouse in New York Martin had tried to make a living with his pen. While struggling to gain attention for *Condition, Elevation, Emigration,* he had started a novel of slave life. He had put it aside after writing a few chapters. Now he brought it out again.

Working on the book nights, Sundays, whenever he had a spare hour, he finished it just before Christmas 1858. Titled *Blake; or The Huts of America,* it was a black man's answer to Harriet Beecher Stowe. Her Uncle Tom was elderly, pious, and ignorant. His hero, Henry Blake, was young, educated, black, and proud. Although he was a slave on a Mississippi plantation, he came originally from Cuba where he had been kidnaped as a boy.

In *Uncle Tom's Cabin,* Tom refused to run away when he had the chance. Instead he put his faith in the Lord and prayed for the soul of the slave trader who was taking him from his wife and children.

"Religion! That's always the cry with black people," Henry Blake exploded when *his* wife was sold. "Put my trust in the Lord! I've done so all my life and of what use is it? I want something on this earth as well as a promise of things in another world."

Mrs. Stowe was a far more skillful writer than Martin Delany, but she had never been further South than Kentucky. The only slaves she had talked to were fugitives she met in the North. She described Uncle Tom's cabin as a snug log building, its outer walls covered with roses and trumpet flowers. Inside was a bed with a snowy spread, a well-set table, and a comfortable seat by the fire. Pictures adorned the walls and a piece of carpeting "of some considerable size" lay on the floor.

Delany had slept in slave cabins in Louisiana and Mississippi. The quarters he described were real—dark and roach-infested, with logs and inverted buckets serving as furniture. Drawing on his recollections of the trip he had made two decades earlier, he depicted slavery as it still was—cheerless, brutal, ugly. Even his awkward attempts to reproduce the speech of the slaves was more realistic than Mrs. Stowe's.

As the book unfolded, Henry Blake ran away from his master. Traveling through the South and up to Canada, he laid the groundwork for a general insurrection of the slaves. Martin, who was still waiting to hear from John Brown, was careful not to reveal the details of Henry's plan for a slave rebellion. Urging the slaves to "organize continually," his hero said: "All you have to do is to find one good man or woman on a single plantation. Make them the organizers for their own plantation and they in like manner impart it to some other next to them and so on. In this way it will spread like smallpox." Then, when he gave the signal, thousands would be ready "to make a strike."

The second part of the novel followed Henry back to Cuba. In 1858 Cuba was the only Spanish-American country where blacks were still enslaved. Ninety miles from Florida, the island served as a source of slave labor for southern planters who hoped to annex it to the United States. In the novel, Henry joined with black Cubans to organize a revolt against their Spanish masters and thwart the schemes of the Southerners. Here, also, there were echoes of the John Brown convention, as the Rebels drew up plans for a Provisional Government and elected Henry Blake commander-in-chief.

One of Blake's co-conspirators was his cousin, Placido, a black poet. Placido, too, was drawn from life. The real Placido was a poet and revolutionary leader who was executed by the Spanish after an abortive revolt in 1844. In *Blake*, however, the poetry that Placido read sounded suspiciously like Martin Delany's:

Were I a slave I would be free!
   I would not live to live a slave;
But rise and strike for liberty,
   For Freedom, or a martyr's grave!

One look upon the bloody scourge,
   Would rouse my soul to brave the fight,
And all that's human in me urge,
   To battle for my innate right!

One look upon the tyrant's chains,
   Would draw my sabre from its sheath,
And drive the hot blood through my veins,
   To rush for liberty or death!

> One look upon my tortured wife,
>   Shrieking beneath the driver's blows,
> Would nerve me on to desp'rate strife,
>   Nor would I spare her dastard foes!
>
> Arm'd with the vindicating brand,
>   For once the tyrant's heart should feel;
> No milk-sop plea should stay my hand,
>   The slave's great wrong would drive the steel!
>
> Away the unavailing plea!
>   Of peace, the tyrant's blood to spare;
> If you would set the captive free,
>   Teach him for freedom bold to dare!
>
> To throw his galling fetters by,
>   To wing the cry on every breath,
> Determined manhood's conquering cry,
>   For Justice, Liberty or death!

Into the book's eighty chapters, Martin had put something of everything that he had experienced, read, or thought about. The sorrow songs of the Mississippi boatmen were there. So was a section on slave conjurers, an account of the voyage of a slave ship from Africa, and descriptions of free black society in New Orleans and South Carolina. *Blake* was wordy and preachy, full of the plots-within-plots and improbable co-incidences so dear to the hearts of nineteenth-century writers. But as Martin read it over, it seemed to him no worse than other novels then in print, and perhaps a bit better than some.

Would anybody publish it? Only two other black Americans had attempted fiction and neither had found publishers in the United States. William Wells Brown's *Clotel: or The*

President's Daughter was printed in England in 1853 and Frank Webb's *The Garies and Their Friends* appeared there four years later.*

Nevertheless Martin hopefully made the rounds of publishers in New York with his manuscript. Those who took the trouble to read it may have boggled at the antiwhite and anti-American sentiments expressed. In the Cuban section of the book, the rebels referred to their white overlords as "the alabasters" or "the candle-faces" and one chapter ended "Woe be unto those devils of whites!"

The black crew of the slave ship sang a parody of "America":

> O Cuba! tis in thee
> Dark land of slavery,
> In thee we groan!
>
> Long have our chains been worn,
> Long has our grief been borne,
> Our flesh has long been torn,
> Even from our bones!
>
> The white man rules the day,
> He bears despotic sway,
> O'er all the land;
>
> He wields the tyrant's rod,
> Fearless of man or God,
> And at his impious nod,
> We fall or stand!

---

* A revised version of *Clotel* was published in the United States during the Civil War, but *The Garies and Their Friends* waited until 1969 for an American publisher.

There was also a sea chanty that began:

> My country, the land of my birth,
>   Farewell to thy fetters and thee!
> The by-word of tyrants—the scorn of the earth,
>   A mockery to all thou shalt be!

Thomas Hamilton, a black New Yorker, was the only pub-lisher interested in *Blake*. Editor of *The Weekly Anglo-African,* he was gathering material for a monthly magazine "to uphold and encourage the now depressed hopes of thinking black men in the United States." Would Martin let him have a few chapters of the novel for the first issue of his new venture? Of course he couldn't pay his contributors, but perhaps someone seeing the work in the magazine would want to bring it out in book form.

The Anglo-African Magazine appeared in January 1859 with three chapters from *Blake*. "This work differs essentially from all others heretofore published," Hamilton wrote in an introduction. "It not only shows the combined political and commercial interests that unite the North and South, but gives in the most familiar manner the formidable under-standing among the slaves throughout the United States and Cuba. We commend these chapters to our readers and hope that the author may place the work into the hands of a pub-lisher before he departs to Africa."

For the next six months *The Anglo-African Magazine* continued to print installments from *Blake,* as well as essays, poems, and historical studies by Dr. James McCune Smith, William Nell, George Vashon, John Mercer Langston. Delany also contributed scientific articles—"Comets" and "The At-tractions of Planets." Although *The Anglo-African* was praised as the first literary journal by and for black people, it remained as Hamilton said, "a labor of love" for him and his authors.

In February 1859 Delany wrote to William Lloyd Garrison to ask him to read the installments of *Blake* in the magazine: "I am anxious to get a good publishing house to take it, as I know I could make a penny by it, and the chances for a Negro in this department are so small, that unless some disinterested competent persons would indirectly aid in such a step, I almost despair of any change. The Story as it proceeds, increases noticeably in interest, there being no dull nor tame sameness to it, and whilst I have studiously guarded against harshness and offensiveness, I have given truth its full force in the pictures drawn. I hope that it may so far meet your approbation and approval, that you may recommend it to the consideration of some publisher. I would like to see your criticism of it in the columns of the 'Liberator.' It is written in Parts 2, pp about 550 of Fools Cap."

When nothing came of this effort, he put the manuscript aside. The problems connected with his African expedition were escalating. Impatient at the delay, Robert Campbell was accepting assistance from the African Civilization Society. With James Purnell, he had also gone to Washington to ask the American Colonization Society for help. In April he sailed to England with letters of introduction from the Colonization Society. There he was approaching businessmen interested in African cotton, in the name of Martin Delany and the Niger Valley Exploring Party.

Delany looked on his young colleague's actions as a betrayal. Hurt and angry, he reproached him for saying in effect that the expedition "was too great an undertaking for Negroes and therefore they *must* go *under* the auspices of some white American Christians." Although he later forgave "my young brother Campbell who, being a West Indian, probably did not understand white Americans," he saw that he would have to move quickly if his dream of a lifetime were to remain in black hands.

Regretfully he scaled down his plans. Instead of spending three years to explore the Niger Valley, he would spend only one. Instead of five commissioners, there would be only two. With Campbell already on the way, he completed his own arrangements for the trip.

Once more he made the rounds of churches and ladies' fairs in New York. This time the urgency of his appeal brought him books, charts, instruments, and some hundred-dollar contributions. After a flying trip to Canada to leave money for Catherine and the boys, he booked passage on the bark *Mendi*. On the afternoon of May 24, 1859, the *Mendi* stood out to sea, bound for Liberia.

> For five years the Universal Negro
> Improvement Association has been
> advocating the cause of Africa for the
> Africans—that is, that the Negro
> peoples of the world should concen-
> trate upon the object of building up
> for themselves a great nation in
> Africa.
> —MARCUS GARVEY, *1923*

18

ON BEHALF OF THE AFRICAN RACE IN AMERICA

A day out of New York Martin paced the deck restlessly. He found it hard to unwind, but slowly sunshine and salt air began to work their magic. The tensions of the past months fell away and for the first time in his life he enjoyed a vacation.

He spent hours leaning over the rail to watch dolphins leap and dive around the ship. Then a school of whales was sighted—"probably five hundred sperm whales blowing and spouting, filling the air with spray to our amusement and delight," he wrote in his diary. "Other whales were also seen frequently—lazy, shy 'old bulls' which floated with their huge backs and part of their heads out of water." Equally fascinating were the squid, "the peculiar *mollusca* upon which the sperm whale feeds."

The first mate had served on a whaling vessel and was now collecting scientific information for the Naval Observatory in Washington. On windless days when the sails hung limp and the ship seemed to stand still in mid-ocean, the mate trawled for squid and other sea creatures so that Martin could examine them under the microscope that he was bringing to Africa.

The *Mendi* had recently been purchased by three black New Yorkers who had pooled their resources to open up trade between the United States and Liberia. Along with a cargo valued at more than $20,000, the partners were bringing their families to Monrovia, capital of the African republic. Also aboard was the Reverend William C. Munroe who had presided over both the emigration and the John Brown conventions. With his wife and two children, he now planned to settle in Liberia. Below deck in crowded quarters in the steerage were twenty-five more emigrants, their passage paid by the New York State Colonization Society. Aside from the officers and some of the crew, the only white man aboard was "a German gentleman traveling for pleasure," Martin noted.

In the after-cabin and in the little saloon where meals were served, the passengers played chess and backgammon, sang and read. Although Martin's boundless curiosity kept him from boredom, time passed slowly. The days were set apart from one another only by remembered events—"the day the sailor caught the dolphin . . . the day the Portuguese vessel was sighted." On the forty-seventh day out of New York, the lookout gave the long-awaited cry, "Land ho!" Cape Mount, the green headland that marked Liberia's northern border, was in view.

The *Mendi* dropped anchor in the harbor of Monrovia

on July 12. In the roadstead alongside her was a trading vessel owned by a firm of black men and a schooner-of-war belonging to the Liberian Navy. The *Mendi*'s passengers were carried to shore on great ten-oared barges manned by Kru men, a people who traditionally followed the sea. Delany listened to them sing as they bent to their oars. The words were in a strange tongue, but the songs were hauntingly familiar. Melody, beat, intonation belonged to music he had experienced before. Grandmother Graci at her spinning wheel . . . the stevedores on the Mississippi . . . the sweet, sorrowful, joyful singing in churches.

Suddenly the world was black. Black naval officers and sailors, customs officials and shipping agents; black clerks checking bills of lading and black stevedores balancing boxes of merchandise on their heads. A black policeman directed Martin to the home of Widow Moore where he took lodgings. John Seys, the United States Consular Agent, also boarded there. On the other side of the Atlantic an agent of the United States government would have refused to share a table with Martin Delany. In Africa, Seys was obliged to treat black Americans quite differently. He could not put on the airs of white superiority that were customary in the States.

In his room that night Delany wrestled with a delicate problem in diplomacy. For almost two decades he had attacked Liberia and the Liberians. Although he had been less critical since the country declared its independence, only four years earlier he had written the introduction to a pamphlet titled "Four Months in Liberia or African Colonization Exposed." In the polemic style familiar to readers of abolitionist papers, he had called Liberians "the servants and slaves" of "that most pernicious of all schemes for the degradation of our race, the American Colonization Society" and had described the country as a "tide-swamp" that was daily flooded with water from the ocean.

After a day in Monrovia, he had to admit that this description was somewhat overstated. The relaxed weeks at sea had permitted him to look with less tension at the organizational battles that preoccupied black leaders in the United States. But would Liberian officials be similarly disposed to forgive and forget?

Somewhat uneasily he wrote to Stephen Benson, President of the republic, to ask for an interview and "any aid which you may please to give to facilitate the mission in Liberia."

He need not have worried. President Benson's secretary brought a reply the next day. Although Benson was leaving Monrovia for an official trip down the coast, his Secretary of State would be pleased to assist Delany in achieving "the highly important objects" of his mission. Along with Benson's answer came a letter from a group of Liberian citizens:

"The undersigned, having long heard of you and your efforts to elevate our down-trodden race, though those efforts were not unfrequently directed against Liberia, are glad to welcome you, in behalf of the community, to these shores; recognizing as they do in you, an ardent and devoted lover of the African race, and an industrious agent in promoting their interest.

"The undersigned, further, in the name and behalf of the members of this community, respectfully request that you would favor the citizens with a lecture tomorrow evening or any other evening you may choose to appoint, on any subject you may be pleased to select."

Accepting their invitation to lecture, Delany replied: "You are mistaken, gentlemen, in supposing that I have ever spoken directly 'against Liberia,' as wherever I have been I have always acknowledged a unity of interests in our race wherever located; and any seeming opposition to Liberia could only be constructively such."

Well and good. He had made his peace with Liberians and they with him. His next weeks were almost a triumphal tour. Sightseeing with official escorts by day, he spoke to crowded meetings at night on subjects ranging from "Physiology" to "The Political Condition and Destiny of the African Race." On Liberia's Independence Day he reviewed the troops as they marched to Palm Palace, the President's residence, and at a First of August celebration he was a leading speaker.

Everywhere he went he saw familiar faces. During one trip to the interior he stayed with Dr. Daniel Laing, his ex-classmate at Harvard Medical School. On another he visited the Reverend Alexander Crummell, a former New Yorker who was now in charge of a high school and mission near Cape Palmas.

For the six thousand black American settlers in Liberia, Delany's presence was a vindication of their move. They had been called traitors to the cause of the slave. Now one of their loudest critics had come with the hand of friendship extended. In the columns of the *Liberia Herald* young Edward Blyden, who had left the United States after three colleges refused to accept him as a student, described the impact of Delany's visit, calling him the "Moses who would lead the exodus of his people from the house of bondage."

Accompanied by Seys and a Liberian official, Delany made a trip up-river to the planting districts. "Six jolly Krumen rowed up the beautiful St. Paul river in a canvas-covered boat, loaned for my especial use by Colonel Yates, Vice President of the Republic," he wrote. "They are without doubt the best watermen in the world. They swim like fish and will dive and fix anything at the hull of a vessel or of an anchor cast—their heads all the time under water."

As they stopped each day to visit farms, he made notes in his journal. "Palm oil and camwood are abundant . . . Fowls of various kinds—as chickens, ducks, Guinea fowls, turkeys. Cattle are handsome and well-built . . . also swine, goats and sheep are plentiful . . . extensive farms of coffee and sugar; also producing rice, ginger, arrowroot and pepper . . . Sugar mills and machinery for the manufacture of sugar and molasses . . . no improvement introduced in the hulling and drying of coffee."

Although he had never farmed, Martin had acquired an astonishing amount of practical information on cattle-breeding and the cultivation of crops. At one coffee plantation he showed the workers how to prune their trees to keep them low and spreading. "The tree should never be permitted to grow too high to admit of the berry being picked from the ground," he explained. "I had the satisfaction of seeing them immediately commence the execution of the work."

Most of the farmers were American settlers who sent their children to the mission schools and were described as "civilized," to distinguish them from native-born Africans. But Delany had nothing but praise for the latter, whom he found "industrious, noble-hearted and willing-headed fellows to work. Treat them well and they'll die for you."

Despite his euphoric mood, not everything pleased him. Although he enjoyed his trip with the Kru boatmen, he thought that "a suitable little steamer is much needed on the St. Paul River and I know of nothing which would pay better now and for time to come. Vessels could take in sugar at the planters' doors who now have to transport it, *one barrel at a time in a canoe* down to the city of Monrovia."

Monrovia, which had been named after President James Monroe and modeled on Washington, D.C., lacked paved streets, public buildings, and market house. Its location was "much better than I had supposed, both in point of land and water," but a breakwater would make its harbor "a safe and convenient roadstead for vessels. This could be done at comparatively small expense," he pointed out.

On August 5 he again boarded the *Mendi,* to sail down the coast to Cape Palmas, Liberia's southernmost promontory, and then on to Lagos, where Robert Campbell was waiting for him. However, on the day he left he was stricken with an illness known as "acclimating fever," a sickness that felled every newcomer to Africa, no matter what the color of his skin. For almost a month he stayed in Cape Palmas with Alexander Crummell.

In a curiously subjective account of the disease which might be taken as a report on his own emotions, he described its early symptoms as exhilarating: "The first sight and impressions of the coast of Africa are always inspiring. These pleasing sensations continue for several days, until they gradually merge into feelings of almost intense excitement, a hilarity of feeling almost akin to intoxication; or as I imagine like the sensation produced by champagne wine. Never having enjoyed the taste of it, I cannot say from experience."

This was followed by "a disposition to stretch, gape and yawn with fatigue" and then "febrile attacks, with nausea, chills or violent headache."

"[The fever was accompanied by] a feeling of regret that you left your native country for a strange one; an almost frantic desire to see friends and nativity; a despondency and loss of the hope of ever seeing those you love at home again.

"These feelings, of course, must be resisted, and regarded as a mere morbid affection of the mind, arising from disease. It is generally while laboring under this last-described symptom, that persons send from Africa such despairing accounts of their disappointments and sufferings.

"When an entire recovery takes place, the love of the country is most ardent and abiding," he concluded.

Prescribing for himself, Dr. Delany battled homesickness and fever with doses of quinine and Dover's powder. On days when he felt well enough he toured the interior with Crummell and spoke at meetings in near-by towns. By mid-September he had recovered sufficiently to resume his trip.

On the British Royal Mail steamer *Armenian* he traveled down the coast to Lagos. An island in the Gulf of Guinea, and the capital of present-day Nigeria, Lagos was the port of entry to the Niger Valley and the land of the Yorubas. In the eighteenth century, the Yoruba peoples had been united in the Old Oyo Empire, but a series of wars in the nineteenth century had divided them into separate states, each with its own capital town, king, and council of chiefs.

Lagos was not typical of the Yoruba city-states. Formerly a slave-trading post, it was now a commercial city, exporting millions of dollars worth of palm oil and ivory each year. Many of its inhabitants were former slaves who had returned to Africa from Brazil or Cuba. Others had been repatriated by the British Slaving Squadron which patrolled West African waters in an effort to end the slave trade. "The merchants and business men of Lagos are principally native black gentlemen," Delany noted approvingly in his journal, "and all of the clerks are native blacks."

Still suffering from bouts of fever, he spent five weeks

in Lagos, making trips to the nearby mainland and meeting with chiefs and businessmen. The high point of his stay came in late October when, after an audience with King Docemo, he was presented with a plot of land close to the center of the city. In a jubilant letter to Catherine, he sent her a copy of the deed:

Lagos, October 25, 1859

Know all Men by these Presents:

That I DOCEMO, King of Lagos and the Territories thereunto belonging, have this day granted, assigned, and made over, unto Doctor Martin R. Delany, for his use and the use of his Heirs and Assigns forever, All that Piece of Ground, situated on the South of the Premises and Ground occupied by Fernando, in the field at Okai Po, Po, measuring as follows, Three Hundred and Thirty Feet square.

Witness my Stamp hereunto affixed and the Day and Year above written.

KING

DOCEMO

OF LAGOS

Leaving Lagos on October 30, he traveled up the Ogun River to Abbeokuta. The six-day journey up the Ogun was made in an open canoe. Martin slept on the river bank at night and dined on fish that his guides netted in the water. In Abbeokuta where he at last caught up with Robert Campbell, he felt that all that had gone before was merely prelude. This walled city, which housed more than a hundred thousand people, was the Africa he had dreamed of.

Built by the Egba people after the dissolution of the Old Oyo Empire, its homes of clay with thatched roofs opened onto inner courtyards. Streets were narrow and irregular, but there were trees and flowers everywhere. To Martin it presented "a scene so romantic and antiquated in appearance that you cannot resist the association with Babylon, Nineveh, Tyre and Thebes."

In the market place, which covered twelve acres in the center of the city, he sampled the riches of the countryside: "Pineapples, the most delicious in flavor and taste conceivable, oranges the same, bananas the finest, plaintains equally so, mangrove plums, guavas and soursops . . . Indian corn, the finest in the world, chickens, the sweetest and tenderest . . . The goats are the most beautiful, shiny, plump, active, saucy creatures . . ." Horses and hogs, pigeons and squabs, sheep and wild game—everything seemed worthy of superlatives.

The women vendors who tended the market stalls also sold earthen vessels—"some of them quite handsome"—raw cotton and cloth colored with native dyes, implements of iron and brass, "excellent razors which shave quite well," steel-bladed knives and leather sandals and boots.

Delany and Campbell were welcomed by the small group of "civilized natives" who lived in the walled city. During their two months in Abbeokuta, they stayed with the Reverend Samuel Adjai Crowther, a Yoruban who later became bishop of the Niger, the Church of England's first black bishop. Crowther's sons had been educated in England and were in charge of a church-led venture to encourage the cultivation of cotton.

When native cotton traders and chiefs held a meeting to set a price for their produce, Delany and Campbell were invited to attend because they "knew how things ought to be done." "The meeting went off well, we making many suggestions which were always received with approbation," Delany wrote. They also became members of the Abbeokuta Road Improving Society, which was widening the footpath leading from the city, to permit carriages to pass over it.

Delany was flattered when Princess Tinuba, a formidable woman trader who traveled with a retinue of sixty, asked his advice. Expelled from Lagos five years earlier because she had been implicated in a plot to assassinate the British consul, she wanted Delany's help in marketing her goods on the coast. "She promised to place the entire management of her extensive business in my hands, as much advantage was taken of her by foreigners," he wrote.

Although pleased by her confidence in him, Martin was shocked when he later learned that she was supplying guns to the King of Ijaye to use in waging war against neighboring cities. But when he charged her with gunrunning, the princess smilingly denied the accusation.

"I can assure you that all what you heard is false respecting my sending guns and powder to Arie, the Chief of Ijaye," she reiterated in a letter that her male secretary delivered to him the next day. "You must not forget to find the Clerk who will stop at Lagos to ship my cargo and make agreement with him before you send him here."

Delany did not know that some of Princess Tinuba's hostility toward the British had to do with her heavy involvement in the slave trade which the British had brought to a halt. Although she had turned to palm oil and ivory instead, she was still suspected of smuggling slaves to secluded places on the coast.

Delany was a long way from home. Despite his warm feelings toward Africans, he did not always understand their ways. Occasionally he felt alien. During his first week in Abbeokuta he was riding at night with a missionary from Oyo when a sudden thunderstorm frightened their horses and the men were separated. Soaked to the skin by the torrential rain, Delany spent hours wandering through the inky-black city in an effort to find his way home.

Once he saw lights in a native compound. Bellowing "Acushe! Acushe!," a term of greeting and one of the few Yoruba words he knew, he tried to call attention to his plight. His stentorian shouts only succeeded in alarming the Africans. They hastily blew out their lamps and fled to the far recesses of their dwellings. It was close to dawn before he found a man who led him to the Crowthers' house.

Although Robert Campbell described the incident in his account of their trip, Martin Delany never mentioned it. However, the two men noted their disapproval of some aspects of African life. Both deplored polygamy and "its sister evil," domestic slavery, though the latter, they defensively reported, was far milder than slavery in the United States. And, as good Protestants, they could not fail to take notice, disapproving, of the bare-breasted women they encountered everywhere.

In this respect, Delany remained more American than African. The missionaries, he suggested, should insist that their servants "eat at a table instead of on the ground and wear some sort of garment to cover the entire person above the knees, instead of a loose native cloth thrown around them, to be dropped at pleasure, at any moment exposing the entire upper part of the person. I am certain that it would go far toward impressing them with some of the habits of civilized life."

For the rest, he thought that the missionaries had gone as far as they could in "civilizing" Africa. They had brought the Bible, but they had failed to raise the Africans' standard of living or train them to use modern tools and machinery. "Of what use is the white man's religion," an African had asked him, "since it does not give me the knowledge and wisdom nor the wealth and power of the white man? Our young men and women talk to God like white man, but God no hear 'em like He hear white man!"

Delany was sharply critical of the missionaries' practice of changing the names of Africans who embraced Christianity—"as though their own were not good enough for them." Not only were native names "more significant and euphonious" than the English names they were given, but the custom encouraged "the impression that to embrace the Christian faith implies a loss of name and loss of identity."

Far-reaching changes could never be wrought in Africa by white men. Only "the descendants of Africa . . . a part of the most enlightened of that race in America, [could] introduce all the well-regulated pursuits of civilized life," Delany wrote. "Our policy must be *Africa for the African race, and black men to rule them.*"

In this spirit, he and Campbell opened negotiations with the chiefs and Alake (king) of Abbeokuta for permission to bring a select group of blacks from the United States to their walled city. Unlike Lagos, where the British had succeeded in changing local customs, land in Abbeokuta could not be sold or given away. As in most African kingdoms, the land belonged to the community as a whole. Any citizen could use unoccupied land, but when he stopped using it, it again became common property. Although the Alake could not give them a specific plot of land, he agreed to admit a limited number of settlers who would have the same rights that his own people enjoyed.

They hammered out an agreement in a series of formal conferences, with the Americans occupying the only chairs in the royal establishment while the Alake sat cross-legged on a mat with one of his wives fanning him. Witnessed by the

Crowthers and ratified by the council of chiefs and elders,
the treaty said:

> This Treaty, made between His Majesty, OKUKENU,
> Alake; SOMOYE, Ibashorun; SOKENU, OGUBONNA,
> and ATAMBALA, Chiefs and Balaguns, of Abbeokuta, on
> the first part; and MARTIN ROBISON DELANY, and
> ROBERT CAMPBELL, of the Niger Valley Exploring
> Party, Commissioners from the African race, of the United
> States and the Canadas in America, on the second part
> covenants:
>
> ART. 1. That the King and Chiefs on their part, agree to
> grant and assign unto the said Commissioners, on behalf
> of the African race in America, the right and privilege of
> settling in common with the Egba people, on any part of
> the territory belonging to Abbeokuta, not otherwise oc-
> cupied.
>
> ART. 2. That all matters, requiring legal investigation
> among the settlers, be left to themselves, to be disposed
> of according to their own custom.
>
> ART. 3. That the Commissioners, on their part, also agree
> that the settlers shall bring with them, as an equivalent for
> the privileges above accorded, Intelligence, Education, a
> Knowledge of the Arts and Sciences, Agriculture, and
> other Mechanical and Industrial Occupations, which they
> shall put into immediate operation, by improving the lands
> and in other useful vocations.
>
> ART. 4. That the laws of the Egba people shall be strictly
> respected by the settlers; and, in all matters in which both
> parties are concerned, an equal number of commissioners
> mutually agreed upon, shall be appointed, who shall have
> the power to settle such matters.
>
> As a pledge of our faith, and the sincerity of our hearts,

we each of us hereunto affix our hand and seal this Twenty-seventh day of December, ANNO DOMINI, One Thousand Eight Hundred and Fifty-nine.

His Mark, + OKUKENU, Alake
His Mark, + SOMOYE, Ibashorum
His Mark, + SOKENU, Balagun
His Mark, + OGUBONNA, Balagun
His Mark, + ATAMBALA, Balagun
His Mark, + OGUSEYE, Anaba
His Mark, + NGTABO, Balagun, O.S.O.
His Mark, + OGUDEMU, Ageoko
                    M. R. DELANY
                ROBERT CAMPBELL
Witness—SAMUEL CROWTHER, Jun.
Attest—SAMUEL CROWTHER, Sen.

"I am happy to inform you that we yesterday concluded a treaty with the King and chiefs of Abbeokuta by which we secure the right of locating in common with the natives in any part of their territory not otherwise occupied," Robert Campbell wrote to Henry Highland Garnet in New York.

Garnet immediately called a meeting of the African Civilization Society to raise men and money for the settlement in Abbeokuta. "Our plan is not to subvert the government and overthrow the reigning powers but to teach them by the power of example those things that will elevate their manhood and to make them feel that we are part of them-selves—interested in everything which promises to promote their happiness and increase their prosperity," he promised. "We have now a number of men who are willing to embark on this glorious enterprise and who believe as I do—that there is a glorious future before Africa." The meeting concluded with a song composed for the occasion, "Once poor Afric's day is dawning."

Meanwhile, there was news from the United States. When their mail finally caught up with them, Martin unfolded a copy of a New York newspaper. The headlines leaped out at him: UNITED STATES ARSENAL ATTACKED AT HARPERS FERRY. SLAVE UPRISING. KANSAS JOHN BROWN HOLDS FEDERAL ARSENAL.

On October 16 John Brown and his Provisional Army had seized the government arsenal at Harper's Ferry, Virginia. The Marines and cavalry had been called out. After a terrible day of fighting, Brown and his men had been captured. Beaten about the head by a Marine lieutenant's sword, Brown lay wounded in a jail in Charles Town—the same brick jailhouse at the corner of George and Washington streets where Samuel Delany had been imprisoned so long before.

Martin rode out in the bush beyond the walls of Abbeokuta, trying to digest the news. Kagi was dead, Tidd in hiding. Of all the black men at the Chatham convention, only Osborne Anderson, printer of the *Provincial Freeman,* had taken part in the raid. Anderson had somehow managed to escape and get back to Canada.

When a trader came up the Ogun from Lagos with a second batch of newspapers, Delany followed the story through to its finale.

Brown in the courtroom defending his design to free the slaves: "I did no wrong, but right. If it is deemed necessary that I should forfeit my life for the furtherance of the ends of justice, and mingle my blood with the blood of millions in this slave country whose rights are disregarded by wicked, cruel and unjust enactments, I say, let it be done."

Brown refusing offers of rescue: "I am worth now infinitely more to die than to live. In no other possible way could I be used to so much advantage to the cause of God and humanity."

Brown calmly following the windings of the Blue Ridge Mountains as he rode to the gallows outside of Charles Town: "This is a beautiful country. I never had the pleasure of seeing it before."

Brown on the scaffold bidding good-by to the jailer, his last words: "Be quick!"

For an hour, for a day, Martin wished he were back in the United States. By a strange coincidence, Brown's jailer and constant companion in his last weeks of life was Martin's boyhood friend John Avis. As a captain in Charles Town's militia, Avis had helped to capture Brown. As deputy sheriff and jailer for Jefferson County he had put him behind bars. He had read Brown's mail, supervised his visitors, and ridden in the wagon that carried Brown to the gallows. Yet despite the fear and hatred of Brown in Virginia, John Avis had become his confidant and protector.

On the eve of Brown's execution when Mrs. Brown came for a last good-by, Avis broke all prison rules by permitting the two to meet in his own apartment. There Mrs. Avis served them supper while they made plans for the education of their children and the disposition of Brown's small estate. In the will that Brown drew up on that same sad day, he bequeathed "a Sharp-rifle of those belonging to me" to "my friend John Avis."

Nor was Brown the only one to praise Avis. "I have been treated exceedingly well," John A. Copeland, a black member of Brown's band, wrote in a farewell letter. "My jailer, Captain John Avis, is a gentleman who has a heart in his bosom as brave as any other. Since we have been in his power he has protected us from insult and abuse which cowards would have heaped upon us. He has done as a brave man and gentleman would do."

A newspaperman described Captain Avis as "a man approaching middle age, short and stout, with a humorous-looking pleasant face." Yes, that would be him. Martin could still see John's friendly face, the corners of his mouth turned up. And even as a boy, John had tended to be plump.

What had the jailer and his prisoners talked about in the weeks before the execution? Had his own name been mentioned? Martin liked to think so—nor was this an unreasonable conjecture. His name had appeared in the newspapers during Brown's trial and the Senate investigation that followed. The proceedings of the Chatham convention were published and even his letter to Kagi became part of the official record.

In the last of the newspapers, Martin read of the memorial meetings held all over the North to honor John Brown. "Marvelous old man!" Wendell Phillips said at his grave. "He has abolished slavery."

Perhaps it was true, as the abolitionists were saying, that John Brown had not died in vain, that his death marked the beginning of the end of slavery. At any rate, a chapter in Martin's own life had ended, and a new one was beginning.

Leaving Abbeokuta in January 1860, Delany and Campbell spent almost three months touring the Yoruba cities of the Niger Valley. This part of their trip was a real safari. Traveling on horseback, they were accompanied by an interpreter, a cook, and half a dozen carriers. On the road they camped out in forest and field, their bedding a woven mat with a calico sheet for covering. In towns they sometimes found shelter at mission houses. More often they slept in the courtyards of compounds or in public market places.

The geography books that Martin had read described

London and the Cotton Supply Association of Manchester sent them money, they decided to visit Great Britain before returning home.

Troubles continued to beset them as they headed for the coast. After riding through burned-out villages and aiding refugees who were fleeing from the enemy, they reached Abbeokuta at the end of March. Using their last bags of cowries, they hired a new team of carriers for the trip to Lagos. Outside the walls of Abbeokuta their carriers staged a sit-down strike, refusing to go on unless they received extra pay. "The semicivilized natives," Campbell mourned, have acquired "all the vices of the white man [but] less of his virtues."

By now the travelers were racing against time, for they had booked passage on a ship scheduled to leave Lagos for Liverpool in a few days. Anxiously they pushed on, Delany on horseback accompanied by the cook, while Campbell and "an intelligent young native" paddled down the Ogun River in a canoe piled high with luggage. Weary and travel-stained, they met in Lagos again.

On April 10 a native sailboat carried them through the rolling surf of the harbor to the Royal Mail steamship *Athenian*. As the sailboat pitched in the heavy seas, Delany jotted down a note about the need for a proper boat for harbor crossings. A steam tender would be one of the first improvements made by the American settlers when they reached Lagos.

There was no doubt in his mind that he would be back.

The white man told Sam he was going
to put him on the radio. "You been a
mighty good Nigra and we gonna give
you a chance to tell how fine we treat
your people here in Mississippi. Now,
you just talk into this microphone,
Sam. The world's gonna hear you."
   "The whole world, boss?"
   "That's right, Sam. The whole
world."
   So Sam walked over to the microphone, grabbed on to it with both
hands and hollered: "H-E-E-L-P!"
   —*Popular story, circa 1960*

19

LISTEN WORLD!

"Mr. Campbell and myself left Lagos on the 10th of April,
arriving in Liverpool May 12th, and in London on the 16th.
On Thursday, the 17th, by a note of invitation, we met a
number of noblemen and gentlemen interested in the progress
of African regeneration. By request of the noble chairman, I
made a statement of our Mission to Africa."

Martin Delany's terse account of his arrival in England
gave no report of his own emotions. Sixty years earlier it had
been widely said that the bricks of Liverpool were cemented
with the blood of African slaves. England had dominated
the slave trade for more than 200 years. The profits derived
from the despoilment of Africa had financed Great Britain's

industrial revolution and made it the leading commercial power in the world. Only comparatively recently Parliament had outlawed the slave trade and abolished slavery in its West Indian islands (although not in India).

As a student of history, Delany was aware of England's role. Speaking at Liberia's First of August celebration a year earlier he had said that "the sublime act of Great Britain—the emancipation of 800,000 Negroes—was extorted from the English crown by black men." Yet when he walked the streets of Liverpool and London he saw not bloodstained bricks but outstretched hands.

During a half century of antislavery agitation the country had opened its doors to black Americans. At the University of Glasgow, Dr. James McCune Smith had received the medical education denied him in his native land. Robert Douglass had studied painting at the Royal Academy in London. The British people had purchased Frederick Douglass' freedom. They had flocked to Henry Highland Garnet's lectures, bought William Wells Brown's books, and offered a refuge to William and Ellen Craft.

Delany was the last of a long series of black abolitionists to come to Great Britain for help. Although he had come reluctantly, forced by necessity to ask for "white" money for his African settlement, he could not fail to be disarmed by the differences between Great Britain and America.

Delany and Campbell scarcely had time to unpack their bags in London when a note delivered to their lodgings invited them to a gathering at the home of Dr. Thomas Hodgkin on fashionable Bedford Square. Hodgkin was a Quaker physician who has come down in history as the discoverer of Hodgkin's disease. Long interested in the movement to "civilize" Africa with the help of freed slaves, he brought together a distinguished group of men to hear the two explorers.

The gathering at Dr. Hodgkin's home was only the beginning. In the weeks that followed the two Americans were besieged with invitations to speak. On June 11 Martin Delany, the self-taught son of a slave, read a paper entitled "Geographical Observation on Western Africa" before the members of the Royal Geographical Society. Two weeks later he spoke on the "Conditions and Prospects of the African Race" at a soiree at the National Club.

The meeting at the National Club resulted in the formation of an African Aid Society "to develop the material resources of Africa, Madagascar and the Adjacent Islands; and to promote the Christian civilization of the African races." Headed by Lord Alfred Churchill, an Oriental scholar and philanthropist, its vice-presidents were Lord Calthorpe, a member of Queen Victoria's Privy Council, and the Bishop of Sierra Leone. Other founders included members of Parliament, church officials, and merchants interested in Africa as a source of raw cotton.

In a "Statement of Objects," the society proposed to:

1. Encourage the production of cotton, silk, indigo, sugar, palm oil etc. by the introduction of skilled labor, African or European.

2. Assist Africans willing to emigrate from Canada and other parts.

3. Form Industrial Missions for the extension of Christianity in Africa.

4. Procure samples of every kind of native produce, for the promotion of legitimate commerce.

5. Encourage . . . exploring expeditions into the interior of Africa and Madagascar.

As a first step, the statement concluded, "The Executive Committee with the generous aid of friends to this movement, have already assisted Dr. Delany and Professor Campbell (two colored gentlemen from America) with funds to enable them to continue their labors and to lay before the colored people of America, the reports of the Pioneer Exploration into Abbeokuta from which they have lately returned."

Martin's worries about money were over for the time being. After sending a postal order to Catherine, he agreed to spend the next months touring the British Isles on behalf of the African Aid Society.

Despite the illustrious company he was keeping, he struggled mightily to remain his own man. At the society's first public meeting at the Caledonian Hotel in July, he took the floor to explain that the Africo-American settlers wanted not charity but loans.

"I wouldn't give one cent for all the assistance afforded to the colored people by sending them out gratuitously. Make us find a part of the money ourselves, and afterwards repay what was advanced, so that we might retain our self-respect and feel ourselves responsible."

While his listeners showed their approval with shouts of "Hear, hear!" he went on to another topic. With a sidelong glance at the church leaders seated on the platform, Delany urged the society "to make the present movement purely secular. Settlers must go to Africa with the Bible in one hand and Wayland's 'Political Economy' in the other."

Dr. Delany's proposal was greeted with "laughter and applause," the *Morning Chronicle* reported the next day.

This was not the only time his name appeared in the London papers that week. On July 16 he attended the opening session of the International Statistical Congress, an organization of social scientists—university professors, statisticians, and medical men from Europe, Asia, the Americas, and faraway Australia. In addition to the official delegates, specialists like Florence Nightingale, who had opened England's first school of nursing that year, were invited to take part in the discussions. Delany had been asked to report on sickness and health in Africa.

The great hall of King's College was well filled. On the platform sat some of England's greatest dignitaries—His Royal Highness Prince Albert, husband of Queen Victoria, the British foreign minister, and state officials. Sharing these seats of honor with their hosts were high-ranking representatives of other nations including the United States minister, George Mifflin Dallas. The congress president was Lord Brougham, former chancellor of Great Britain and a pioneer in the movement to end slavery in the West Indies. Now eighty-two, Lord Brougham was the grand old man of British reform.

As part of the opening ceremonies, Lord Brougham introduced a number of the personages from overseas, with the usual exchange of dignified pleasantries. In the case of the American minister, however, he could not resist an antislavery taunt.

"I beg my friend Mr. Dallas to observe," he said, "that there is in the assemblage before us a Negro, and hope that fact will not offend his scruples."

Though Lord Brougham may not have realized it, his remark was as much of a challenge to Martin Delany as it was to George Dallas. All eyes were now on the black American. How should he respond? Or should he remain silent?

Rising—"with all his blackness, as quick and graceful as an African lion," Frederick Douglass wrote in *Douglass' Monthly*—he addressed Prince Albert: "I pray your Royal Highness will allow me to thank his Lordship for the observation he has made. I assure your Royal Highness and his Lordship that *I am a man*."

"ALL RIGHT!"

A cartoon that appeared in *Vanity Fair* on August 11, 1860, spoofing the international incident caused by the outraged reaction of George Dallas, American minister to Great Britain, to Lord Brougham's introduction of Martin Delany and Delany's own remarks, made before the International Statistical Congress. The caption reads: Mr. Dallas—"I accept your apology, my lord—you need not have brought your friend." (Courtesy of The New-York Historical Society)

It was the shortest speech Martin Delany ever made, and one of his most effective. Dallas sat, flushed and frowning, while the notables on the platform and the delegates in the auditorium burst into cheers.

Delany woke the next morning to find himself a celebrity. The mere presence of a black man at a congress of scientists was news in 1860. An account of his interchange with Lord Brougham appeared in every London newspaper. Within weeks the story had traveled around the world.

Most U.S. papers carried headlines lamenting the "Public humiliation of an American minister." But Frederick Douglass applauded: "Never was there a more telling rebuke administered to the pride, prejudice and hypocrisy of a nation. It was saying: Mr. Dallas, we make members of the International Statistical Society out of the sort of men you make merchandise of in America. Truth is of no color, Mr. Dallas, and to the eye of science a man is not a man because of his color, but because he is a man and nothing else. Delany's presence in that meeting was an answer to a thousand humiliating inquiries respecting the character and qualifications of the colored race. Lord Brougham, in calling attention to him, performed a noble act."

Augustus B. Longstreet, the Georgia-born judge and college president who headed the American delegation, stalked out of the Congress, packed his bags, and went home. In two long letters to the London *Morning Chronicle,* he explained the reasons for his departure.

Lord Brougham's remark "was meant as a cutting reflection upon that country where Negroes are not admitted to the councils of white men. Had the delegates received his lordship's remarks with a silent smile, and Dr. Delany's response in the same way, I never should have left the Congress. But the plaudits came like a tempest of hail upon my spirit. The

signs were infallible that I could not be received as an equal while the Negro was received with open arms."

George Mifflin Dallas, a Pennsylvanian who had been Vice President of the United States from 1845 to 1849, was similarly incensed. As he wrote to Lewis Cass, the Secretary of State: "The act of Lord Brougham was a premeditated contrivance to insult the country which I represented and to provoke an unseemly discussion between the American Minister and the Negro . . . The convocation energetically applauded both Lord Brougham's annunciation to me, and the Negro's speech to the Prince Consort . . . You will, of course, perceive the extremely unpleasant position in which this matter places me socially here . . ."

In Washington President Buchanan and his Cabinet met to consider what action to take. Secretary Cass thought that Dallas should be instructed to ask the British government for an official disavowal of Lord Brougham's remark. His Lordship had insulted not only slaveowners, but "a still larger portion of the American people, of whom I am one, who consider the Negro race as an inferior one and who repudiate all political equality and social connection with its descendants," Cass argued.

In the end, the Cabinet decided not to press for an apology. "I am compelled to inform you that there is one point upon which the opinion of the President and of the Cabinet does not concur with your decisions," Cass wrote Dallas. "This regards your retaining your seat after Lord Brougham had made his appeal to you . . . Your true proceeding would have been immediately to address the Prince and to announce to him that finding your Country through you exposed to insult . . . you would quit the meeting; and to have followed this annunciation by an immediate departure."

Meanwhile the team of Brougham and Delany had acquired a new recruit. Dr. Edward Jarvis, Massachusetts' delegate to the International Statistical Congress, differed from Judge Longstreet on what the honor of his country required. He had jousted with the scientists and statesmen of the South before. As a young doctor interested in the new science of vital statistics, he had been puzzled by the United States census of 1840. Enumerating the "insane and idiots" for the first time, the census had revealed a far greater incidence of insanity among free blacks in the North than among slaves. Southerners pounced on the statistics as proof that slavery benefited blacks while freedom drove them mad. However, Jarvis found that the census reports were full of glaring errors. In 115 instances, insane blacks were listed for towns where no black lived. In other localities, the number of insane blacks exceeded the total black population. And, in at least one town, the white patients in a mental hospital were reported by the census taker as black.

Publishing his findings in the *American Journal of the Medical Sciences,* Jarvis declared that a correction was "due to the honor of our country, to medical science and to truth." But more than a decade of protests by Jarvis and by black men like Dr. James McCune Smith had not brought a correction.

Taking his stand alongside Martin Delany, Dr. Jarvis pointedly attended all of the congress sessions and social gatherings. Both men were welcomed at a reception for the delegates at Buckingham Palace and a farewell *déjeuner* at the Crystal Palace.

When Jarvis was called on to read his paper "On a Uniform System of Reports for Lunatic Asylums," Lord Brougham seized the occasion to underline his earlier comment. Regretting that he had pained "our kinsmen in the United States for whom I have the greatest respect, though

here are subjects on which I and they differ," his Lordship
said: "When I saw Dr. Delany, a respectable colored gentleman, in the room, I merely mentioned it as a statistical fact,
which it was, and a fact, I might be permitted to add, of no
small importance."

At the end of that session, Dr. Jarvis went to the United
States Legation to present Lord Brougham's backhanded
apology. But George Dallas was in no mood for peace makers.
When Brougham, who was under pressure from his own
government, also called at the Legation, Dallas instructed his
servant to turn him away.

On the final day of the congress, the irrepressible Brougham
invited Delany to attend the Congress of the National Association for the Promotion of Social Science, to be held in Scotland
in September. As the audience applauded, Delany again rose
to the occasion, saying, "I am not foolish enough to suppose
that the reception which has been given me was intended for
myself individually. I know that that outburst of sentiment
was an expression of sympathy for the race to which I belong."

With "loud cheering" for Dr. Delany and "three hearty
and prolonged cheers" for Lord Brougham, the International
Statistical Congress ended. The issues raised there continued
to be debated throughout the summer. Despite the degrading
caricatures of himself that appeared in the American press,
Delany, with Lord Brougham's help, had brought American
racism to the bar of world public opinion.

While Campbell returned home, Delany lectured to anti-
slavery societies and meetings of industrialists to raise money
for their Abbeokuta settlement. He gave a series of talks at
Brighton, a seaside resort, and spoke in Manchester, Leeds,
and Newcastle upon Tyne.

September found him in Scotland. After attending the Congress of Social Science, he spent almost two months conferring with Glasgow businessmen. They were impressed with the samples of African weaving and carving that he had brought back with him. By the time he was ready to leave he had signed agreements with three leading export-import firms. As soon as the Yoruba settlement was under way, they would buy not only cotton but many other African products.

"The Scottish houses deal with us as men, and not as children," he wrote in his report of the trip. "The British people have the fullest confidence in our integrity to carry out these enterprises successfully, and now only await our advent there."

Preoccupied with his business negotiations, he paid scant attention to the news from the United States. In Glasgow he read that Abraham Lincoln had been elected President. He was at sea heading for home in December 1860 when South Carolina seceded from the Union.

In God's name, must we ever be
subordinate to those of another race
both in as well as out of Africa? Have
we no other destiny in prospect as an
inheritance for our children? It is for
us to determine whether or not this
shall be so.
—MARTIN R. DELANY *to Dr. James
McCune Smith, January 4, 1862*

20

NO TIME TO LEAVE THE COUNTRY

The Delany family had a belated Christmas on December 29
when Martin reached home laden with gifts from Africa—
toys for the children, cloth and women's finery from the
market in Abbeokuta for Catherine. He brought back African
garments for himself, too, a loose trouserlike *shocoto* and a
long overblouse with a high embroidered collar that the
Yorubans called a *dashiki*.

Delany's dashiki became a familiar sight in Chatham as
he wore it to lecture on Africa at Town Hall, the Baptist
Church, and the colored school. Between public appearances
he was hard at work on the official report of his expedition.
A rambling account of West Africa's climate, topography,
agricultural and mineral resources, along with a summary of
his own adventures there and in England, it was completed
in February and published in New York and London the

following summer. Dedicated to the Board of Commissioners of the Emigration Convention, the report's final sentence read, "I return of course, to Africa, with my family."

A letter to the *Weekly Anglo-African* in New York announced that he was organizing "a select emigration of intelligent persons (male and female) of various vocations . . . Cotton cultivators (such as can direct and manage the planting) and mechanics, by sending me their names, age, occupations, and the recommendation of the pastor of their standing, can have aid secured to them at once to go out with myself and party in the first adventure."

Emigration was in the air of American black communities in the winter of 1860–61. While the Southern states were forming the Confederacy, politicians in the North cried for peace at any price—or, rather at any price which the slave-holding South would accept. One "compromise" sponsored by Senator John Crittenden of Kentucky would have guaranteed slavery forever in the states and territories south of the Mason-Dixon line through a series of amendments to the Constitution which could never be repealed. As an added bonus, Crittenden proposed expelling free blacks from the country, as well as disfranchising them in the few states where they were allowed to vote.

The Crittenden Compromise failed, but the inauguration of Abraham Lincoln on March 4 did little to lull black people's fears. After Chief Justice Taney, author of the Dred Scott decision, administered the oath of office, the new President also attempted to conciliate the South in his inaugural address, by promising not to interfere with slavery or with the enforcement of the Fugitive Slave Law.

Afraid that their limited liberties would be sacrificed in order to save the Union, many free blacks made plans to leave the country. Most looked toward Haiti rather than Africa

as a homeland. The Haitian government, headed by Fabre
Geffrard who had taken office in 1859, was conducting a
vigorous campaign to attract settlers to the island republic.
Geffrard had appointed white James Redpath, a friend of
John Brown's, to head the Haitian Bureau of Emigration.
With a grant of $20,000 Redpath hired such prominent
blacks as William Wells Brown, H. Ford Douglass, and James
T. Holly to popularize the Haitian cause.

Almost a decade earlier Martin Delany had proposed a
mass migration of blacks to the American tropics. Now he did
his best to convince his former associates that Haiti was the
wrong place to go. In open letters to Holly and others, he
criticized Geffrard's selection of a white man to head the
Emigration Bureau.

"Abstractly considered I have no objection to Haitian Emigration," he wrote. "My objection is to the fearful manner
in which our people are being misled into the belief that
Haiti presents the material advantages and facilities for a
great and powerful nation. Haiti is a small island, with no
prospect of additional territory, and consequently must always have a limited population.

"To these unfavorable contingencies Africa can never be
subject, being a vast continent peopled by one of the great,
enduring, fixed, reproducing, absorbing races of the earth,
only ceasing when the world shall pass away."

But his remonstrances had little effect. In 1861 and 1862,
two thousand American Negroes migrated to the black republic in the Caribbean. Even Frederick Douglass, outspoken
foe of all emigration schemes, accepted Redpath's offer of
free passage to Haiti for a six weeks' visit—"to acquire information which may be useful to those who are looking to
that country for a home."

Douglass never made the trip. Ten days before his ship

was scheduled to depart, Confederate soldiers shelled Fort Sumter in Charleston harbor and President Lincoln called for 75,000 volunteers to put down the rebellion. The time of conciliation and compromise was over. The war was on.

"This is no time for us to leave the country," Douglass wrote. "We shall stay here and watch the current of events."

Delany did his best to ignore the war news. Campbell had already returned to Lagos and Delany was corresponding regularly with the officers of the African Aid Society. He promised to bring a party of settlers to Africa in June . . . in July . . . in September.

But in the fall of 1861 he was still in America. Two disconcerting events had slowed him down. The Alake of Abbeokuta denied signing a treaty with Campbell and Delany —and the British deposed King Docemo and took over the government of Lagos.

Martin found the news of the Alake's action difficult to believe. All of the chiefs and elders had given the treaty their unanimous approval. What had happened to make them change their minds?

Months later when the secretary of the African Aid Society sent him copies of letters from the British Foreign Office, he learned the reason for the Alake's puzzling behavior. The Reverend Henry Townsend, the leading Anglican missionary in Abbeokuta had set himself up as the Alake's political advisor. Fearing that he would lose his position of influence if "civilized" blacks like Delany settled there, he had told the Alake that the Americans planned to take over his kingdom and drive the Africans away. Convinced by Townsend's stories, the Alake not only denied the existence of the treaty, but also banished its chief witness, Samuel Crowther, Jr., from the walled city.

"Whatever the treaty may be worth, there can be no doubt

that it was signed by the Alake and chiefs," William McCoskry, the British consul at Lagos, assured Earl Russell, Her Majesty's Foreign Secretary. "It was not until a powerful opposition influence had been brought to bear upon the Alake and chiefs that the treaty was denied."

In forwarding copies of the McCoskry-Russell correspondence to Delany, the African Aid Society secretary had written, "I am sure they will give pleasure." They did not. Delany was further dismayed by the news that a British naval force had entered Lagos Bay in August 1861 and had seized the city of Lagos in the name of Queen Victoria.

King Docemo was exiled and William McCoskry was appointed acting governor of the black metropolis. The action bore a startling resemblance to the landing of U. S. Marines in San Juan del Norte in 1853. And if the British could take Lagos, why not also Abbeokuta? In spite of his warm regard for the English people, Martin Delany did not want to see the land of the Yorubas become a British colony, nor himself a colonist there, subject to white European rule.

The British needed a new source of cotton for their mills—needed it with a fresh urgency since the outbreak of war in the United States. Delany dreamed of Africa for the Africans. He was no longer sure the two goals were compatible.

Not yet prepared to give up his dream, he decided on a policy of wait-and-see. There might be a way to accept British support without compromising his principles. In September he made a trip to New York. Perhaps it was time to join forces with the African Civilization Society whose leaders also planned a settlement in Abbeokuta.

Working with a committee that included Robert Hamilton, editor of *The Weekly Anglo-African,* and Richard Cain, pastor of a Brooklyn church, Delany helped to write two new articles for the society's constitution. The first explained that the organization was not encouraging a general exodus from the United States but only the migration of qualified settlers, "carefully selected and well recommended." The second said: "The basis of the Society, and ulterior objects in encouraging emigration, shall be—Self-Reliance and Self-Government, on the principle of an African Nationality, the African race being the ruling element of the nation, controlling and directing their own affairs."

They were putting their white supporters on notice that they would not accept colonial status. Whether they had the power to enforce "the principle of an African Nationality" was open to question. No one was more aware of this than Martin Delany. Priding himself on his political astuteness, he wondered if he had not been naïve in expecting more from the rulers of Great Britain than from their counterparts in the United States. Although he refrained from voicing his suspicions in public, he commented in a letter to a Pittsburgh friend that England was no different from other great powers "in the course pursued by these nations toward the black races. Their policy is changed from that of abject slavery, to reducing them to political dependents. They must be in subordinate relations."

After making his peace with the African Civilization Society, Delany spent several months in New York attending to business matters. Thomas Hamilton had recently brought out his *Official Report of the Niger Valley Exploring Party.* Now Hamilton's brother Robert wanted to serialize *Blake* in *The Weekly Anglo-African.* After making a few changes to bring the novel up to date, Delany agreed.

In the issue dated November 19, 1861, the editor announced: "In our next number we will commence the publication of a story of thrilling interest, from the able pen of Dr. Martin R. Delany. The work stands without rival, not even excepting the world wide known 'Uncle Tom's Cabin. The story as soon as known, will be sought with avidity."

For the next year, while chapters from *Blake* appeared each week on the front page of the *Anglo-African,* Martin Delany toured the East and Midwest to lecture on Africa. Speaking on two topics, "The Moral and Social Relations of Africans in Africa" and "The Commercial Advantages of Africa," largely to white audiences, he set out to destroy the stereotype of the "African savage."

Each talk was carefully stage-managed. "The dress which the Doctor wore on the platform was a long dark-colored robe, with curious scrolls upon the neck as a collar," the Chicago *Tribune* reported when he spoke in Illinois. "He said it was the wedding dress of a Chief, and that the embroidery had a specific meaning well understood in African high circles. He wore it because he thought it becoming, and fitting the occasion.

"He was sorry to say that American school-books inculcated very erroneous notions of the country, describing it as sandy and barren, the soil unproductive, the air full of pestilence, the vegetation poisonous, the very animals unusually ferocious. All this is more or less false, so far as the interior of Africa is concerned."

As his grandmother had done, Delany depicted Africa almost as a Garden of Eden. "All the staple cereals of a tropical climate were grown in abundance, and every species of fruit," the *Tribune* continued.

Defending the moral standards of the people, Delany explained away polygamy as a venerable institution of Oriental origin. "King Solomon was the arch-polygamist of the world," he reminded his audience of Bible readers. "The Africans who follow his example are no worse than he."

To illustrate the high level of African civilization, he read from a grammar of the Yoruban language—"written by a native African"—and recited African proverbs and poems. One poem quoted in the *Tribune* sang of the occupations of the people:

> The day dawns.
> The trader takes his goods,
> The spinner her distaff,
> The soldier his shield,
> The hunter his bow and quiver.

He followed this with "some pretty verses composed by African children, describing the pleasure they felt at seeing the beauty and color of African birds, no description of which, the Doctor said, has appeared in any book on ornithology.

"At the close of the lecture, various specimens of native manufacture were shown to the audience. Dr. Delany is a better specimen of his race than any we, for our part, have seen before, and he is by no means a bad lecturer," the *Tribune* account concluded.

To Frederick Douglass, who heard him deliver three lectures in Rochester in the summer of 1862, Delany was speaking not only for Africans but for Afro-Americans as well. "His coming here has been of great advantage to us all," Douglass wrote. "It has given our white fellow citizens the opportunity of seeing a brave self conscious black man, one who does not cringe and cower at the thought of his hated color, but one who if he betrays any concern about his complexion at all, errs in the opposite direction.

" 'I speak (said he) only of the pure black, uncorrupted by Caucasian blood.' This feature of his discourses is so marked as sometimes to make the impression upon those who do not know Mr. Delany, that he has gone about the same length in favor of black, as the whites have in favor of the doctrine of white superiority. He stands up so straight that he leans back a little.

"He himself, is one of the very best arguments that Africa has to offer. Fine looking, broad chested, full of life and energy, shining like polished black Italian marble, and possessing a voice which when exerted to its full capacity might cause a whole troop of African Tigers to stand and tremble, he is just the man for the great mission of African civilization to which he is devoting his life and powers.

"We gather from his lectures and conversation that he is fully determined to emigrate in the course of the present year. If we were going to Africa we should unhesitatingly enroll ourselves under his leadership. He is the intensest embodiment of black Nationality to be met with outside the valley of the Niger."

While in Rochester, Delany visited Douglass for the first time in many years. The factional disputes that had separated them were forgotten as the two speculated—hopefully, fearfully—on the changes that the war was bringing. The current of events was moving swiftly.

In April 1862 Congress had passed a bill abolishing slavery in the District of Columbia. In May the United States gave diplomatic recognition to the black republics of Haiti and Liberia. In July President Lincoln signed a Confiscation Act which said that slaves who escaped from southern masters were free when they entered Union lines.

Yet neither man felt optimistic. The war was going badly for the North but the President refused to accept blacks in the army. Rather, he appeared to be preparing the way for a general deportation of blacks from the United States. In speech after speech he recommended that slaves who were given their freedom be resettled "in a climate congenial to them."

The President's policy was based on the belief that Northerners would never accept a proclamation of emancipation unless they were assured that their states would not be overrun by ex-slaves. In the West and even in Pennsylvania and New Jersey citizens were demanding new laws to "protect" themselves against an expected "Negro invasion." White workingmen who feared black competition for jobs were rioting in Chicago, Cincinnati, Toledo that summer, killing blacks and destroying their homes.

Responding to the wave of antiblack sentiment, Congress appropriated $600,000 to settle "such free persons of African descent as may desire to emigrate beyond the limits of the United States." In July a House Committee on Emancipation and Colonization, which had spent three months investigating deportation plans, recommended that the appropriation be increased to $20,000,000.

"The retention of the Negro among us with half privileges is but a bitter mockery to him. Our duty is to find for him a congenial home and country," its report said.

To back up its findings, the committee reprinted "Political Destiny of the Colored Race on the American Continent," the speech Martin Delany had delivered at the Emigration Convention in 1854.

Lincoln had probably read this before he invited five Washington black men to the White House in August. He was trying to arrange for a black settlement in Chiriquí, a province of present-day Panama, and he wanted their support.

Reactions to Lincoln's proposal varied. Meetings of colored men in Philadelphia and New York indignantly rejected it. Frederick Douglass attacked it in an angry editorial and men like George Vashon and Robert Purvis sent letters of protest to the White House. However, the New York *Tribune* reported, "The Rev. Henry Highland Garnet and other colored men of influence at the North warmly second the plan of the President." And Lewis Douglass, a son of Frederick Douglass, was one of the five hundred men who volunteered to go to Chiriquí.

The Chiriquí project fizzled largely because Central Americans objected to the use of their territory as a dumping ground for people the United States considered undesirable.

Throughout the months-long debate, Martin Delany remained silent. He was in the West, giving lectures on Africa. His descriptions of Africa were as enthusiastic as ever, but he no longer announced that he was going there. Not now.

For on September 22 President Lincoln surprised the nation with a new statement:

"On the first day of January in the year of our Lord, one thousand eight hundred and sixty-three, all persons held as slaves within any state, or designated part of a state, the people whereof shall then be in rebellion against the United States shall be then, thenceforward and forever free."

The promise of emancipation over which Lincoln had so long hesitated, confronted America's black millions with a new situation. To a man of Delany's political experience, it was clear that it would be some time before he could win support for his African settlement. Meanwhile his black brothers in the United States had sudden, urgent business to take care of. How could he stand apart from that?

The Selective Training and Service
Act of 1940 said that there shall be
no discrimination against any person
because of race or color.

How is this principle reflected in
military practice?

The Navy has refused to commission
Negroes in any branch of the service . . . The Air Corps has discrimi-
nated against Negroes in the most
complicated and costly way, building
a segregated air base for Negroes . . .
The Army commissions colored and
white candidates without discrimination
but Jim Crow rules over every Southern camp. Colored women are ex-
cluded from every auxiliary service
but the Wacs, and here there is
segregation.

—LUCILLE B. MILNER
"Jim Crow in the Army,"
New Republic, *March 13, 194*

21

THE BLACK MAJOR

The Emancipation Proclamation, which Lincoln signed on
New Year's Day, gave freedom to the slaves of the Confederacy, but it could only be enforced if the Union won the
war. And the war might be a lot longer in the winning unless
black men were permitted to fight in the Union forces.

Martin Delany longed to see a black army of liberation

marching through the South. Even before the final Proclamation was issued, he called on Asa Mahan, a founder of Oberlin College, to propose a *Corps d'Afrique* patterned on the Zouave regiments that the French had organized in Africa. Mahan agreed to apply to the President for permission to organize a division of black troops. Although his request was turned down, the governor of Massachusetts was given authority in January 1863 to raise a regiment of "persons of African descent."

Long an abolitionist, Governor John Andrew determined to make this first black regiment in the North a model for all future regiments. "Its success or failure," he wrote, will "go far to elevate or depress the estimation in which the character of Colored Americans will be held throughout the World." Finding that there were not enough black men of military age in Massachusetts, he and his supporters lined up a team of prominent blacks to recruit men from all of the free states.

While Frederick Douglass, Henry Highland Garnet, and William Wells Brown raised companies of volunteers in the East, Martin Delany and Charles and John Langston worked in the West. Paid ten dollars a week and expenses, Delany traveled through Illinois, Indiana, and Michigan urging blacks to enlist. He also acted as examining surgeon to make sure that his would-be soldiers were physically fit before sending them on to Massachusetts.

The call to arms soon reached Canada. On his seventeenth birthday, Toussaint wrote to ask his father's permission to join the army. Torn by indecision, Martin carried the letter in his breast pocket for a day. Then, half proud, half fearful, he consented.

On March 27, 1863, Toussaint L'Ouverture Delany arrived at Readville, a few miles outside of Boston, to sign the muster roll of Company D of the Massachusetts 54th Regiment. On the muddy fields of Camp Meigs, he and a thousand other black youngsters learned to march, to shoot and clean a rifle. Two months later Private Delany, along with Lewis and Charles Douglass and the sons of other Negro notables, paraded across Boston Common. All of Boston turned out to cheer them. While their regimental band played

> John Brown's body lies a'mouldering in the grave
> But his soul goes marching on. . . .

they paraded to Battery Wharf to embark on the steamer *De-Molay,* destination South Carolina.

"Saw the first regiment of blacks march through Beacon Street," Henry Wadsworth Longfellow wrote in his diary that day. "An imposing sight, with something wild and strange about it, like a dream. At last the North consents to let the Negro fight for freedom."

Delany was in Canada in late July when the Massachusetts 54th led a night attack on Fort Wagner, one of the ring of forts guarding Charleston's harbor. The troops clawed their way to the parapet of the fort to plant their flag there, but a storm of shot and shell drove them back. Hopelessly outgunned, they rallied and tried again. By morning their colonel was dead and almost half of the enlisted men had been killed, wounded, or taken prisoner.

Anxiously, Martin and Catherine turned the pages of the Chatham *Planet* to find the list of casualties. Toussaint's name was not there. It was months before they heard that he had been wounded in a skirmish shortly before the big battle and was recuperating in an army hospital in Beaufort, South Carolina.

Delany returned to the United States aching to get into the struggle himself. At fifty he was past the military age for enlisted men. He applied for the post of surgeon in a black regiment. The War Department replied, unpromisingly, that his application was "on file." Hearing nothing further he accepted the job of recruiting a regiment of black artillerymen for the state of Rhode Island.

In a letter to Secretary of War Edwin Stanton, written in December 1863, he again offered his services to the government:

"I have been successfully engaged as a Recruiting Agent of Black Troops, first as a Recruiting Agent for Massachusetts 54th Regt. and from the commencement as the Managing Agent in the West and South-West for Rhode Island Heavy Artillery, which is now nearly full, and now have the Contract from the State Authorities of Connecticut for the entire West and South-West, in raising Colored Troops to fill her quota.

"During these engagements, I have had associated with me, Mr. John Jones, a very respectable and responsible business colored man of this city, and we have associated ourselves permanently together, in an Agency for raising Black Troops for all parts of the Country . . .

"In the event of an order from your Department giving us the Authority to recruit Colored Troops in any of the Southern or seceded states, we will be ready and able to raise a Regiment, or Brigade if required, in a shorter time than can be otherwise effected.

"With the belief sir, that this is one of the measures in which the claims of the Black Man may be officially recognised, without seemingly infringing upon those of other citizens, I confidently ask sir, that this humble request, may

BRAVERY OF COLORED TROOPS

Your enemies say, "oh, the negro won't fight; he's a coward naturally." A viler slander Satan never uttered through the lips of a traitor. A dozen bloody fields attest their valor. The President, in his letter to the Springfield Convention, bears witness to the fact, and says but for their bravery one of the most important victories of the war could not have been achieved.

And again: Major General Blunt, in his official report of the battle of Honey Springs, Ark., says the First Kansas colored regiment particularly distinguished themselves. They fought like veterans, and preserved their lines unbroken throughout the engagement. "Their coolness and bravery," adds General Blunt, "I have never seen surpassed. They were in the hottest of the fight, and opposed to Texas troops—twice their number—whom they completely routed. The Twentieth Texas Regiment, which fought against them, went into the fight with 300 men, and came out with only 60."

A young soldier of company K, Tenth Connecticut Volunteers, writing home to his mother an account of the late fight at James Island, says: "But for the bravery of three companies of the Massachusetts Fifty-fourth (colored), our whole regiment would have been captured. As it was, we had to double-quick in, to avoid being cut off by the rebel cavalry. *They fought like heroes.*"

But why multiply proof? None but a traitor will now deny it.

COLORED CITIZENS:

The hour you have so long waited for has struck. Your country calls you. Instead of repelling, as hitherto, your patriotic offers, she now invites your services.

To the State of Rhode Island belongs the honor of first recognizing and rewarding your valor in the field.

The First Regiment Rhode Island Heavy Artillery, now organizing there, will consist of eighteen hundred men, all colored soldiers, commanded in part by colored officers. These forces are destined for forts and fortifications on the coast of that State, but liable to be placed by the President where most needed.

This state pays each man a cash bounty of.........$250
Of which you receive $75 as soon as you arrive there, and the remainder in a few days.

You will also get the United States bounty of........$100

Making $350

Also $13 per month, with clothing and rations, the same as white soldiers in every respect. Besides, no man's family will be allowed to want while he is in the service. The wounded will receive pensions for life, and also the families of those who may fall. Above all, you will there be treated with respect, as soldiers and as men. *No other state gives colored men over $50 bounty.* Are you not as patriotic as others? At a numerously attended meeting in Buffalo on the 1st, when nearly every able bodied man present volunteered, the following resolutions were unanimously passed:

Resolved, That we, the colored citizens of Buffalo, not only approve, but we regard the present as the most favorable call for colored soldiers to go as artillerymen, to defend the garrisons and harbors on the coast of the New England States from rebel pirates—those vicegerents of the devil, who, of all the foul creatures which infest and pollute the seas, they, in human shape, are the most loathesome and most to be shunned.

Resolved, That for this purpose we tender Captains Works and Engly, now present with us, our hearty approval, our co-operation, our hearty efforts, our aid and encouragement for enlisting colored soldiers.

Rally then, around the old flag. One and all lend your aid in wiping out the most wicked rebellion that ever polluted the records of heaven. The millions of your brethren still in bondage implore you to strike for their freedom. Will you heed their cry? Go, then, to the State of Rhode Island. She more than welcomes you with her bounties and her honors to enter the service of the Union in her ranks. The rebellion now totters and reels; and hereafter, when traitors will only be remembered to be cursed—with a united country and your brethren free—you will point with just pride to the part you bore, and the place you filled in the Loyal Union Army. Such a record and such deeds, be assured, will be a source of proud remembrance to you and your posterity forever.

VOLUNTEERS!

COME FORWARD AND SIGN THE ROLL.

Let every Man apply in Person, if Possible.

IF NOT, WRITE TO EITHER OF THE PERSONS NAMED BELOW.

Dr. M. R. Delany, Chicago, Ill., Head Quarters for the West, 172 Clark St.
Mr. John Jones, Chicago, Ill., Assistant.

SUB-AGENTS
(The Illinois list is not yet complete.)

Mr. Emanuel Hersey, Quincy, Ill.	Mr. N. D. Thompson, 52 Pine St., Buffalo, N.Y.	Rev. George W. Brodie, Logansport, Ind.
Mr. Johua Highwarden, Indianapolis, Ind.	Rev. Garland H. White, Lafayette, Ind.	Right Rev. Bishop Green
		Lewis Isbell, Traveling Agent

☞ Either of these gentlemen, being fully authorized, will gladly give all further information, furnish you with Railroad Tickets to Rhode Island, and good board and lodging until ready to start.

engage your early notice. All satisfactory References will be given by both of us."

John Jones was a prosperous Chicago tailor and a leader in the fight to repeal Illinois' Black Laws. He and Delany had been on opposite sides in the debate over emigration. Now they were united in their desire to see the Union win with the help of black troops.

Although Stanton never answered his letter, Delany continued recruiting. Hiring subagents in half a dozen cities in Indiana and Illinois, he brought a doctor from Canada to act as examining surgeon. Before long, churches and stores in black communities were plastered with posters calling on BLACK NATIONAL DEFENDERS to APPLY WITHOUT DELAY to DR. M. R. DELANY, and promising EQUAL STATE RIGHTS! AND MONTHLY PAY WITH WHITE MEN! One poster, prepared while he was still recruiting for Rhode Island is illustrated on the preceding pages.

He was overly optimistic when he assured volunteers of equal pay. Although his promise of $13 a month was based on an order of Secretary Stanton's, army paymasters refused to pay black soldiers more than $7 a month, an injustice that was not corrected until June 1864. Nor were blacks accepted as officers, except in the posts of chaplain and surgeon. However, Delany had not exaggerated the size of the bounties being offered to recruits.

Despised and ridiculed a year earlier, black soldiers were now sought after. By the end of 1863, Northern states were clamoring for their services—and not merely because they had proven their ability to fight. A new Conscription Act required districts that could not fill their quotas with volunteers to draft all men of military age. Every black volunteer meant one less white draftee.

A popular song, written in the dialect of the blacks' traditional enemy, the Irish, bluntly expressed the change in sentiment:

> Some tell us 'tis a burnin' shame
>> To make the naygers fight;
> An' that the thrade of bein' kilt
>> Belongs but to the white;
> But as for me, upon my soul!
>> So liberal are we here,
> I'll let Sambo be murthered instead of myself
>> On every day in the year.
> On every day in the year, boys
>> And in every hour of the day;
> The right to be kilt I'll divide wid him,
>> And divil a word I'll say.

The competition for black soldiers became so keen that states bid against each other for their services. The organizers of the Massachusetts 54th had paid a $50 bounty to each man who enlisted. Rhode Island offered $250 to its black artillerymen, Connecticut $300, and New Hampshire was paying bounties of $500 for black volunteers.

These bounties often did not reach black hands. Unscrupulous agents went to refugee camps where numbers of ex-slaves congregated. Paying the freedmen ten dollars or so to enlist, they pocketed the balance of the money themselves. In many instances Negroes, drugged with whiskey and false promises, were shanghaied into the army so that agents could collect their bounties.

Delany and Jones ran an honest recruiting agency. Appealing to black pride as well as patriotism, Delany called for volunteers to strike a blow against slavery. But he also carefully explained to them the regulations governing black regiments and the compensation due to the men and their families. To make sure that they were not swindled after they left their homes he traveled to the army camps with each party of volunteers and supervised their mustering-in.

After supplying soldiers to districts in Pennsylvania and New York, Delany was appointed a state recruiting agent for Western Ohio. With a quota of 2500 men to fill, he went to Nashville, Tennessee, where thousands of slaves from the Mississippi Valley had entered Union lines. Some worked for the army as laborers, teamsters, cooks. Others proved a gold mine for recruiters and substitute brokers.

Substitute brokers were a new species brought into being by a provision of the Conscription Act. The act permitted a draftee to escape service if he could hire a substitute to go to war in his place. By 1864 the price for a substitute had soared to $1000 and brokers were swarming to Nashville to buy up able-bodied black replacements. The brokers became such a nuisance around the camps that field commanders threatened to arrest them on charges of kidnapping.

When Martin Delany arrived he was surrounded by unsavory characters offering him a split of their profits for every man he signed up. He indignantly refused to sell his brothers for a price, but the corrupt atmosphere and the hostility of the army officers left a bad taste in his mouth. Even government agents were not above using strong-arm tactics to "persuade" freedmen to enlist. After making a speech or two, Delany left Nashville.

"I became convinced," he said, "that the business of recruiting had reached such a state of demoralization that no honorable man, except a U.S. commissioned officer, could continue it successfully without jeopardizing his own reputation."

Resigning his state commission, he returned home. "Home" for the Delanys was no longer Chatham. With the Fugitive Slave Law a dead letter, the black communities in Canada were breaking up. The younger men crossed the border to enlist in the army while their parents dreamed of rejoining family and friends in the South after the war was won.

After the signing of the Emancipation Proclamation, Delany had ceased to feel like an expatriate. Even his birthplace, Charles Town, was in the Union—in the new state of West Virginia, formed when old Virginia seceded to join the Confederacy. However, neither Charles Town nor Pittsburgh, where Pati Delany had recently died at the age of ninety-six, offered the kind of environment he and Catherine wanted for their children. There were now seven young Delanys. Rameses Placido had been born in 1862 and Ethiopia Halle, their only daughter, in 1864.

Martin and Catherine decided to move to Wilberforce, a settlement in Green County, Ohio, 3½ miles from the town of Xenia. Originally a summer resort where well-to-do whites came to drink the waters from mineral springs, Wilberforce had been purchased by the AME Church as a college for colored youth. The first black institution of higher learning in the country, it planned to train ex-slaves to become teachers and ministers. Although it was called a "university," its only requirement for admission was good moral character. Its professors taught everything from the ABCs to Latin and Greek.

At Wilberforce the Delany children could grow up in an all-black community where they would never need to face discrimination because of color. In November 1864 Martin purchased a seven-acre lot from the Reverend Daniel A. Payne, the university's president. He planned to build a house there the following spring. Meanwhile he installed his family in a cottage on the college grounds. Facing a spacious lawn with a bubbling fountain in the center, their new home was only a door or two from the main building of the college, an elegant three-story structure left over from watering-place days.

But the peace and beauty of the tree-lined campus was illusory as long as the war continued. With the new year, reports reached Northern newspapers that the Confederate commander in chief, General Robert E. Lee, planned to enroll slaves in his army. The Confederate Congress in Richmond was considering a bill to call up 300,000 additional troops "irrespective of color." If it passed, it would add immeasurably to the strength of the Confederate forces and might prolong the war indefinitely.

Union tacticians had made no systematic effort to bring word of the Emancipation Proclamation to the slaves behind enemy lines. Blinded by their own prejudices, they believed the slaves to be loyal to their masters and doubted their suitability as fighting men anyway. Further, the possibility of encouraging slave uprisings in which blacks might slaughter whites in the style of Nat Turner was as distasteful in Washington as it was in Richmond. To guard against such uprisings, Lincoln had inserted a warning in the Emancipation Proclamation enjoining the freedmen "to abstain from all violence unless in necessary self-defense."

Delany had always believed in the slaves' potential as a fighting force. In *Blake,* he had described a South-wide conspiracy of slaves. Surely now was the time to call on them to rise. The thought that they might be made to fight on the Rebel side, to keep themselves in chains, was intolerable.

"Colored men must organize to prevent so horrible an iniquity," he said. "Why, the whole world would scoff."

For more than a generation, the Underground Railroad

had smuggled slaves to the North. Why not an Underground Railroad in reverse—with blacks going to the South to organize the slaves? As guerrillas fighting behind the enemy lines, they could bring the war to a close in short order.

With a feeling of urgency, Martin Delany took the train to Washington, determined to talk to the President.

In the capital he stayed with Henry Highland Garnet, now pastor of the Fifteenth Street Presbyterian Church. Garnet too had put aside thoughts of Africa and was devoting himself to the struggle for equal rights in the United States.

Soon after his arrival, Delany went to the White House. Curious stares greeted him as he joined the line of people waiting to see the President. Garnet had warned that he would have difficulty obtaining an appointment. To his surprise, after he sent in his card, he was told to come back the following day.

A cold February wind lashed the bare branches of the trees on Pennsylvania Avenue when Martin Delany turned in at the White House gate the next morning. Promptly at eight, a secretary led him up the broad stairway to the President's office.

"On entering the executive chamber, and being introduced to his excellency, a generous grasp and shake of the hand brought me to a seat in front of him," Delany recalled. "No one could mistake the fact that an able and master spirit was before me. Serious without sadness, and pleasant withal, he was soon seated, placing himself at ease, the better to give me a patient audience. He opened the conversation first."

"What can I do for you, sir?" Lincoln inquired.

"Nothing, Mr. President," Delany replied. "I've come to propose something to you which I think will be beneficial to the nation."

Lincoln raised his eyebrows. "Go on," he said.

Reminding the President of the imminent arming of the slaves by the Rebels, Delany explained his plan to have them fight for the Union instead.

"I propose, sir, an army of blacks, commanded by black officers. This army to penetrate the heart of the South, with the banner of Emancipation unfurled, proclaiming freedom as they go. By arming the emancipated, taking them as fresh troops, we could soon have an army of 40,000 blacks in motion. It would be an irresistible force."

"The blacks would go to the interior while the white regiments remained at the front?" Lincoln asked.

"And they would require but little," Delany nodded. "They could subsist on the country as they went along."

"Cavalry and a few light artillery would be all that was necessary," Lincoln mused, "because the siege work would be done by white divisions."

Clearly the President was interested. Delany pressed his advantage by recalling the assistance that slaves had rendered to the army as scouts and guides. Familiar with the terrain of the South, how much more useful they would be with guns. "An army of blacks commanded by blacks," Delany said, "would win every slave for the Union and speedily bring the war to a close."

"Wouldn't that be a grand thing," the President exclaimed. "When I issued my Emancipation Proclamation I had this in mind." He reminded Delany that the preliminary Emancipation Proclamation had forbidden the army to interfere "in any efforts they may make for their actual freedom."

"But Mr. President, these poor people couldn't read your proclamation. Many still don't know anything about it."

For three quarters of an hour, the two men talked. As the interview drew to a close, Lincoln turned in his chair. Abruptly he asked, "Will you take command?"

Delany drew in his breath. For two years black soldiers had been demanding the right to have black commanders. Was the President proposing a change in policy?

"If there be none better qualified than I, sir, I will." He added a modest disclaimer: "As black men we have had no experience in the service as officers."

"That matters but little," the President said. "Some of the finest officers we have never studied tactics till they entered the army. What we require most are men of executive ability."

Delany expressed his thanks and attempted to present some letters of introduction. Lincoln brushed them aside.

"Not now," he said. "I know all about you. There's nothing to be done but to give you a line of introduction to the Secretary of War."

As he reached for a pen, the boom of a cannon shook the room. Lincoln smiled. "Stanton is firing! Listen! He's in his glory!"

"What's the firing about, sir?"

"Haven't you heard the news? Charleston is ours."

Charleston, South Carolina, birthplace of Secession, in Union hands!

Lincoln scrawled a few words on a card:

February 18, 1865

Hon. E. M. Stanton, Secretary of War.

Do not fail to have an interview with this most extraordinary and intelligent black man.

A. LINCOLN

A few minutes later Delany headed for the musty brick building on Seventeenth Street where the War Department was housed. Secretary Stanton was standing behind a high desk in a crowded reception room. For an hour each day he received the general public. When it was Martin's turn he gave Stanton the card that Lincoln had written. Glancing at it quickly, Stanton nodded.

"Come back on Monday," he said.

Delany never knew how he lived through the suspense of the following days. His old mentor, Dr. William Elder, was in Washington, heading the Bureau of Statistics. When Delany sought him out to report on his interview with Lincoln, Elder volunteered to speak to Stanton in his behalf. "You'll get the appointment," Elder was sure.

He did. When he returned to the War Department, Stanton had already made up his mind.

"I propose to commission you at once and send you South to commence raising troops," the Secretary said. "I shall assign you to Charleston, with instructions to Major General Saxton. Do you know him?"

Delany nodded. He knew of General Rufus Saxton, a New England abolitionist, as a friend to black people. In South Carolina since Union forces landed there in 1862, Saxton was currently Superintendent of Recruitment and Organization of Colored Troops, Department of the South.

"You will be given a letter for him," Stanton continued. "But you will also impart to him, in detail, that which will not be written."

After a quick handshake, Stanton turned him over to Colonel Charles W. Foster, chief of the Bureau of Colored Troops.

"Examine him for the position of Major of Infantry," Stanton said.

For the better part of a week, Delany was quizzed by an examining board, thumped by a surgeon, and given endless forms and papers to fill out. On February 26, 1865, Foster brought him back to Stanton's office so that the Secretary could sign the piece of parchment that transformed Martin R. Delany, free black, into a major in the Army of the United States.

"Major Delany, I take great pleasure in handing you this commission," Stanton said. "You are the first of your race who has been thus honored by the government. Therefore much depends and will be expected of you. But I feel assured it is safe in your hands."

With right hand raised, Delany solemnly swore: "I will support and defend the Constitution of the United States against all enemies, foreign and domestic . . . and will well and faithfully discharge the duties of the office on which I am about to enter. So help me God."

What seemed like a routine ceremony to Secretary Stanton, was an extraordinary one for Martin Delany and all black Americans. February had been an extraordinary month. On February 1 John S. Rock, a lawyer from Massachusetts, became the first black man accredited to the Supreme Court which eight years earlier had denied that blacks were citizens. On February 12 Henry Highland Garnet spoke in the House of Representatives. He was the first black man to do so. Sitting in the gallery of the House when Garnet demanded that blacks be given "the well-earned privilege of voting" and be made "in every respect equal before the law," Delany had been profoundly stirred. Now he himself was the first black field officer of high rank in the history of the republic.

"Who shall say we are not on the onward march?" *The Anglo-African* exulted.

Washington's black citizens called at the Garnets' to meet "the black Major." John E. Bruce, a small boy brought there by his uncle, remembered many years later the "awe and reverence" he felt when Delany shook his hand. "He was the *blackest* man I think I had ever seen, with a commanding voice and a confident air. His laugh was full of jollity. He patted me on the head and said he had some boys and girls of his own and that he had named them after great Negroes. He told my uncle that he hoped I'd grow up to become a useful and great man and urged that I be given a good education."

"We rejoice at this appointment of our brother," an editorial in *The Anglo-African* said. "Having devoted the whole of a long life to an unselfish advocacy of our people and their cause, he becomes a fit instrument through which to do them honor." A later issue of the newspaper advertised a portrait of Major Delany "taken in full uniform by the celebrated artist, Bogardus of Broadway. Price per copy, 25 cents."

The New York *Times* carried a front-page story headed A BLACK MAJOR and the Pittsburgh *Dispatch* and Xenia *Sentinel* had kind, if condescending, words to say. The *Sentinel* described Delany as "large, heavy set, vigorous, with a bald, sleek head which shines like a newly-polished boot. And he wears brass buttons and shoulder straps! and is an officer in the army of the Union! These sentences record the history of the progress of the country during the war!"

Martin returned to Wilberforce to arrange his family's finances before leaving for the South. He lingered long enough to speak from the Anti-Slavery Church, just off the Wilberforce campus, on "The Progress of the Government."

"The speaker told his brethren," the Xenia *Sentinel* reported, "that the Government intended to deal justly with them—that it would commission colored officers when they were qualified—that it would treat colored soldiers well—and finally that it intended to make no distinction between white and black soldiers."

Delany was striking a new note here, but he also returned

to familiar themes: "Negroes must have a higher opinion
of themselves. We must declare ourselves to be the equals of
white men, if not their superiors. In no other way can we
attain to our proper position in the body politic."

After his speech several young men in the audience walked
up to the pulpit to enlist in the army. They were followed
by the minister who announced that he was giving up his
church "to fight for my country and my God."

Delany left Wilberforce wearing his new blue uniform,
campaign hat, and tasseled sword. Students and faculty
marched with him to the university gate singing "The Star-
Spangled Banner." There they gave three cheers for the
major, six for Abraham Lincoln and one groan for Jefferson
Davis.

In New York, waiting a week for transportation to South
Carolina, Delany spoke nightly to crowded churches on "The
Progress of the Government" and "The Capacity of the
African Race to the Highest Civilization."

"The Major did not speak like a man who was looking
down from his altitude upon those whom he never expected
to reach him. He spoke like one who was lifting others up
to him. It was an able effort," the Reverend James W. C. Pen-
nington wrote.

It was only human to enjoy the adulation, but Delany did
not lose sight of his objective. The bill to enroll slaves in the
Confederate Army had passed early in March. Recruiting was
already under way in Virginia. There was no time to lose.

Before leaving Washington and in Ohio and New York,
he conferred with black leaders on ways to prevent Rebel en-
listments and to recruit scouts and soldiers for his regiment.
Harriet Tubman, who had served as an army scout earlier
in the war, agreed to meet him in South Carolina. William

Day also promised to join him when his liberation army was organized.

He brought two young men with him to New York—"one an excellent Scout who was born and raised in Charleston and belonged to Major Rhett, rebel officer," he reported in a letter to Colonel Foster. "The other is an intelligent young man who has been an officer and drill-master of a colored volunteer company in Detroit, Michigan for several years. I wish to present them to Brev. Maj. Gen. Saxton, as I know them to be just such persons as we shall want. Would you be pleased to present these facts to the Honorable Secretary of War, and obtain the necessary transportation, sending it on immediately?"

Colonel Foster's reply gave the first intimation that the army way was not always the common-sense way of Martin Delany: "It is not considered expedient to furnish such transportation as the men could not be paid for services as 'Scouts.' It is only by entering the military service that they can be employed and paid for services in connection with the recruitment of colored troops."

Delany reached Beaufort, South Carolina, on April 3. As the army steamer docked, its passengers shouted to the stevedores on the wharf.

"What's the news?"

"Richmond has fallen!"

The capital of the Confederacy was in Union hands. Six days later General Robert E. Lee met General Ulysses S. Grant to negotiate the terms of a surrender.

By then Major Delany was in Charleston enlisting freedmen in the service of the United States. The presence of "the black Major" in Washington was nothing compared to the excitement he caused in Charleston. The once-proud city had been deserted by its white residents. Its blacks flocked to Delany's quarters at all hours of the day or night to enjoy the sight of a black man wearing the shoulder tabs of a United States Army major.

When he spoke in Zion Church, the city's largest black congregation, six thousand people packed the aisles, galleries, and dooryard to hear him. "The freed people could not leave," a Northerner wrote, "until they made a target of the major's head, by aiming at it bouquets, and grasping his hand until it was sore."

President Lincoln had chosen April 14, the fourth anniversary of the fall of Fort Sumter, as the day for a grand victory celebration. Hundreds came from Washington and New York to see the Stars and Stripes raised once again at the fort. The list of honored guests included not only generals, admirals, and Congressmen, but also abolitionists like William Lloyd Garrison.

On the morning of the flag raising, the *Planter,* a Confederate gunboat that black Robert Smalls had liberated in 1862, carried a boatload of freedmen to the fort to watch the ceremonies. Its passengers included Martin and Toussaint Delany. Toussaint's regiment was bivouacked on the outskirts of the city but he had been detailed to assist his father. Standing with them on the quarter-deck was the son of Denmark Vesey, the black carpenter who had led a slave rebellion in Charleston forty years earlier.

As Delany watched the flag of the Union snap in the breeze above the battered walls of the fort, he recalled Garrison's words to the freedmen that morning: "Once I could not feel any gladness at the sight of the American flag, because it was stained with your blood. Now it floats purged of its gory stains. It symbolizes freedom for all, without distinction of race or color."

For another two days Delany shared the spotlight with

Garrison. In Citadel Square they watched a parade of colored school children—boys and girls who had been slaves a month earlier and were now learning to read and write. There were more speeches and songs at Zion Church, more cheers and tossed bouquets at the waterfront when black Charleston turned out to say good-by to their visitors from the North.

The week of jubilation was hardly over when news of President Lincoln's assassination reached Charleston. Delany read and reread the dispatch in the newspaper, trying to understand this staggering event. What would this mean for black people?

The same question echoed along the streets and alleys of Charleston. Zion Church was draped in mourning. Ex-slaves fastened bands of crepe around their arms and nailed black streamers to their doors. The freedmen were overcome with sorrow, but they were frightened and angry too. Would slavery return? Whites who had drifted back to the city remained indoors as blacks talked of setting fire to their homes to avenge Lincoln's death.

In the anxious days that followed, Delany did his best to calm the troubled black Charlestonians. The President was dead, but there was a new President in Washington. The policy of the government would remain the same, he believed.

To assuage their grief as well as his own, he drew up plans for a monument to Abraham Lincoln—"the humane, the benevolent, the philanthropic, the generous, the beloved, the able, the wise, great and good President of the United States"—to be financed by a one-cent contribution from every black man, woman, and child in the country. In letters to *The Anglo-African* he described the monument as he envisaged it: "A female figure, kneeling on the right knee, the face with eyes upturned to Heaven, with distinct tear-drops passing down the face . . . The figure is neither to be

Grecian, Caucasian nor Anglo-Saxon, but African—*very African*—an ideal representative of the race as Brittania or the Goddess of Liberty is to the European race."

A thousand miles to the North, on the night that Lincoln was shot, faculty and students of Wilberforce University had been at a meeting in Xenia celebrating the end of the war. They returned to find the main building a smoldering ruin. Classrooms, dining hall, chapel were destroyed—and with them Delany's correspondence of a lifetime, his manuscripts, and his African collection.

"The destruction of the only University of learning among the colored people on the American Continent was an atrocity of great importance," Delany wrote. "It was the deliberate act of an enemy of the colored people and the Union. The hand which placed the torch was leagued in sentiment with the same dastard-villains who struck down the greatest Chief Magistrate of the present age.

"Wilberforce University must go on. We make an earnest appeal which we know will not be in vain, to the wealthy of the United States, to aid immediately in helping us to rebuild an Institution essential to our elevation as a part of the American people."

As a part of the American people. Despite anger and grief Martin Delany was not giving up his dream of the America that ought to be. For years he had been ending his letters with "For God and Humanity, the redemption of our race and regeneration of Africa." Now his signature read,

In behalf of this great nation,

M. R. Delany

> You do not take a man who, for years, has been hobbled by chains, liberate him, bring him up to the starting line of a race, and then say "You're free to compete with all the others." It is not enough just to open the gates of opportunity.
> —PRESIDENT LYNDON B. JOHNSON, *1967*

22

LET US CRY "GLORY TO GOD"

ATTENTION, CHARLESTONIANS! RALLY ROUND THE FLAG, said the handbill on the wall of the post office:

To the Free Colored Men of Charleston:
The free colored men in this city, between the ages of 18 and 45, are hereby earnestly called upon to come forward to join the
CHARLESTON REGIMENT
It is the duty of every colored man to vindicate his manhood by becoming a soldier. The prospect of your future destiny should be enough to call every man to the ranks. But in addition, you are to have the
PAY, RATIONS AND CLOTHING,
our other soldiers receive.
Let a full Regiment of the Colored Freedmen of

Charleston be under arms, to protect the heritage which
has been promised to your race.

All desired information given at Recruiting Office,
No. 64 St. Philip Street, corner Calhoun.

M. R. Delany
Major 104th United States
Colored Troops

White citizens returning to Charleston read the handbill
with feelings of panic and despair. Their world was in chaos.
Civil government had collapsed. Confederate uniforms were
banned and Confederate money worthless. Shops were shuttered, railroads motionless. Outside of the city, the roads
were clogged with hungry, homeless refugees.

The bitterest of the pills they had to swallow was the
changed status of black people. Men they had owned, body
and soul, were flocking to Major Delany's office on St. Philip
Street to enlist. After a few weeks training, the new recruits
were assigned to the army of occupation that governed the
state.

Most Southerners grudgingly accepted the death of slavery,
but they did not believe, as one told a newspaper man,
"that because the nigger is free he ought to be saucy. He's
helpless and ignorant and dependent and the old masters
will still control him."

Martin Delany did not concern himself with white Charleston's reactions, even when sentinels guarded his quarters at
night after reports of a Rebel plot to assassinate him. He was
confident that the ex-slaves would take part in the rebuilding
of Southern society. Already 4000 black children were attending schools in the city, under the superintendence of James
Redpath, his old adversary in the emigration movement. In
May, Bishop Daniel Payne arrived to organize a branch of

the African Methodist Episcopal Church with the Reverend Richard Cain of Brooklyn as its first minister.

At one public meeting Major Delany urged the establishment of a newspaper "to advocate the interests of the colored population and to show your fitness to be American citizens." General Saxton followed by advising the freedmen to petition the President for the right to vote. "I want you to elect a committee to draft this petition and get every colored man to sign it," he said. "I can get 3000 in Beaufort to sign it, but I want it started here in the City of Charleston, the leading city of the Rebellion."

Delany backed up Saxton with a letter of his own to President Andrew Johnson in which he asked for "the political equality of the blacks with the whites in all of their relations as American citizens." In the hopeful summer of 1865, anything seemed possible.

Two regiments of black South Carolinians were drilling at the race track outside of the city and the ranks of a third were almost filled, when the War Department called a halt to recruiting. Toussaint, who had been working with his father as an acting lieutenant, returned to Boston with the Massachusetts 54th, to be mustered out. Delany was ordered to General Saxton's headquarters in Beaufort for assignment to the Bureau of Refugees, Freedmen and Abandoned Lands, popularly known as the "Freedmen's Bureau."

Created by an act of Congress—one of the last acts signed by President Lincoln before his assassination—the Freedmen's Bureau was intended "to cope with the evils arising from a wicked institution," Senator Charles Sumner said, and to show the freedman "how his new-found liberty shall be made a blessing." Saxton, who had been placed in charge of bureau operations in South Carolina and Georgia, was summoned to Washington just as Delany reached Beaufort.

Finding himself with an unexpected free fortnight on his hands, Martin used it to explore the Sea Islands. Before the war, the chain of islands off the coast between Charleston and Savannah had been the wealthiest and most beautiful agricultural region in the South. Slaves toiled on the plantations to raise Sea Island cotton, a silky long-staple cotton that brought premium prices in the markets of Liverpool and New York. They had little contact with the world beyond Port Royal Sound. The plantations were managed by overseers. Their owners lived in Beaufort on Port Royal Island and spent summers in Charleston or in the mountains.

The beauty was still there: stretches of sandy beach and blue water, profusions of birds and flowers. Stiff palmettos grew at the water's edge. Massive live oaks, their branches dripping with Spanish moss, formed archways above the roads.

The wealth had changed hands. A Union squadron steaming up the Beaufort River in November 1861 brought the region's isolation to an end. Within a day of "the big gun shoot," the whites fled to the mainland. Their slaves—ten thousand of them—remained behind. Freed by the happenstance of war a year before the Emancipation Proclamation, the black Sea Islanders became half-willing guinea pigs in what was known as the "Port Royal Experiment."

The "experiment" consisted of hiring the ex-slaves to raise cotton for the government. Would they work as well as free men as they had as slaves? Would they fight for the Union if black regiments were raised?

While the army and navy used the islands as a staging area for assaults on Confederate strongholds along the coast, volunteers from the North managed the civilian experiment. In the spring of 1862, freedmen's aid societies in Boston and New York dispatched their first boatload of missionaries to the Sea Islands. Plantation superintendents, school teachers, and ministers, they had dedicated themselves to bringing the civilization of New England to the ex-slaves. In the words of a song by John Greenleaf Whittier:

> We go to rear a wall of men
> On Freedom's southern line.
> And plant beside the cotton tree
> The rugged Northern pine!

The experiment had worked, perhaps better than anyone expected. Day and night schools were crowded, the cotton crops were good, and numbers of freedmen fought with the Union Army. However, by 1865, relations between blacks and whites had undergone a significant change. Some of the young white idealists who had come to help their black brothers had become practical businessmen. Buying up plantations when the government sold them for back taxes, they were pocketing substantial profits as a result of the experiment in free labor. The blacks, too, had learned the lessons of New England. They were tired of working on the plantations for wages—and low wages at that. They wanted to raise corn and potatoes on land of their own.

Crossing the Beaufort River on a hot day in July, Martin's first impressions recalled Africa. Like the Kru men of Monrovia, the boatmen sang slow sad songs as they bent to their oars. On St. Helena people spoke a rapid-fire patois that he could scarcely understand, so spiced was it with African words. That night he went to a "praise house," the cabin of the oldest man in a small settlement, to attend a "shout." Men and women, some of them with African tribal marks on their faces, clapped their hands and stamped their feet in unison as they sang spirituals. The New Englanders thought the "shouts" were "the remains of some old idol worship." Delany, whose Christianity was of a quieter sort, doubtless agreed with them.

Cantering down the sandy roads the next day, he passed turbaned women, as handsomely erect as their cousins in the market stalls in Abbeokuta. But here they wore ragged, cast-off garments from the North and wielded heavy hoes in the fields. The crossroads stores were owned by whites and so were all of the large plantations. Yes, this was Africa—in white hands.

Bitterly disappointed in what he saw, Delany sought an opportunity to speak to the people. When he was asked to lecture in the Brick Church on St. Helena where both whites and blacks worshiped on Sundays, he scolded the freedmen for being "too good."

"I am going to tell you what you are worth," he said. "Your master lived in opulence squandering away the wealth you acquired for him. He never earned a single dollar in his life. You men and women, everyone of you around me, supplied the means for your master to lead an idle life and to give his children the education which he denied to you.

"'Oh, the Yankees are smart,' you say. Now tell me, are *you* not worth anything?" Advising them not to trust any of the missionaries, he particularly warned against "those cotton agents who come honey-mouthed unto you, their only intent being to make profit by your inexperience. There *are* good Yankees, but I don't like these fellows who were nothing at home and who now ape the Southerner with his big-brimmed hat. They sit on a fence and say 'Sam, Jim, do this, do that'—as lazy as any Southerner ever was.

"I look around and notice a man, barefooted, covered with rags," he continued. "I hear that he works for thirty cents a task. *That must not be.* These Yankees talk smooth. Their tongues roll like a drum but that's cursed slavery again. I tell you slavery is over. We have 200,000 of our own men well drilled in arms. It's up to you and them to see that slavery never returns.

"Before the South depended on you. Now the whole country will depend on you. Get up a community and get all the lands you can. Grow as much vegetables as you want for your families. On the other part of the land cultivate rice and cotton. One acre of land will grow a crop worth $90. Ten acres will bring $900 every year—and carpets will take the place of bare floors in your cabins."

Essentially this was the same lecture that Delany had been delivering for thirty years. Be proud of your blackness. Work hard. Stand up for your rights. But he was not addressing the Young Men's Literary Society of Pittsburgh. He was speaking to blacks and whites in South Carolina. The time was July 1865. The reverberations from his speech traveled all the way to Washington.

Unknown to him, two young lieutenants were sitting in a back pew making notes of everything he said. Their commanding officer had heard from "a reliable source" that the Major's speech was calculated "to create serious trouble between the Negroes and their employers, for whom they have been quietly and peaceably working up to this time." Their reports confirmed the rumors.

"There is something rotten in Denmark," one lieutenant wrote when he turned in his report the next day. His companion's comments were more extensive: "Major Delany is a thorough hater of the white race and excites the colored people unnecessarily. He says it would be slavery over again if a man should work for an employer . . . The mention of having two hundred thousand men well drilled in arms— does he not hint to them what to do if they should be compelled to work for employers? In my opinion he was trying to encourage them to force their way by insurrection to a position he is ambitious they should attain to."

Their reports traveled from Beaufort to the island of Hilton Head where Quincy Gillmore, commanding general of the Department of South Carolina had his headquarters. Like many regular army men, Gillmore had little use for black soldiers. He had already shipped out the Massachusetts 54th and 55th Regiments because he thought the black troops gave "seditious advice" to the freedmen. Sending the file on Delany's speech to the War Department, he wrote: "The course pursued by Major Delany since his advent into this Department has been calculated to do harm, by inciting the colored people to deeds of violence. The well being of the freed people would be advanced by his removal to some other field of duty."

Gillmore and the two lieutenants had jumped to hasty conclusions—and so had Martin Delany. The land problem was far more complicated than he realized. Its solution lay not with the Sea Islanders but with the President of the United States. Six months earlier General William T. Sherman had issued an order setting aside the islands and coastal lands from Charleston to the St. John's River in Florida for black settlements. Each family was to receive "a plot of not more than 40 acres of tillable ground . . . in the possession of which land the military authorities will afford them protection until such time as they can protect themselves or until Congress shall regulate their title."

Sherman's order was a war measure designed to take care of the tens of thousands of slaves who had left their masters to follow his army. It had been more or less confirmed by Congress, which gave the Freedmen's Bureau authority "to set apart for the use of loyal [white] refugees and freedmen" the abandoned and confiscated lands in the Rebel states. Forty acres were to be assigned to every freedman for a three-year period. At the end of that time, he could purchase the land "and receive such title thereto as the United States can convey."

When Delany spoke at the Brick Church on St. Helena, forty thousand freedmen had already staked out plots in South Carolina's low country and had planted their first crops. General Saxton believed that the freedmen must have land of their own if they were to survive in a hostile world. As rapidly as possible he was distributing the land abandoned by the planters who had run from the Union Army. Now these planters were running to Washington to ask President Andrew Johnson for the return of their lands.

Saxton, who had taken Delany's measure in Charleston, welcomed him as an ally in the coming struggle over the land. Ignoring the reports on the Brick Church speech, he put him in charge of the Freedmen's Bureau office on the island of Hilton Head, with the mouth-filling title of "Assistant Sub-Assistant Commissioner." In addition to Hilton Head, his district would include the neighboring smaller islands of Daufuskie, Bull, Pinckney, and Long Pine.

Before the war, the port of Hilton Head, fifteen miles from Beaufort, had been little more than a boat landing used by planters to ship their cotton to Charleston. As headquarters for the Union Army and Navy in the South Atlantic, it had become a thriving town. Traveling down the river from Beaufort on the *Planter*, Martin saw transports from the North riding at anchor in the broad harbor. Black boatmen rowed passengers to shore and black stevedores unloaded freight on the government wharves. Along the beach were barracks and hospital tents; behind them warehouses where government property was stored. Sutlers—the storekeepers who followed

the army to sell provisions to the soldiers—had built a row
of two-story houses. The sutlers had named their street
"Broadway." Everyone else on the island called it "Robbers'
Row."

The black Major was viewed with considerable suspicion
when he first arrived at Hilton Head. Ignoring his rank, non-
coms ordered him to halt and state his business. The quarter-
master refused transportation for his orderly. He overlooked
these slights, protesting only when General Gillmore issued a
special order that forbade him to "make any speech to, lecture, address, or advise the colored people."

The friction between the army and the black representative of the Freedmen's Bureau disappeared after Gillmore
was replaced by Major General Daniel Sickles and army
headquarters was transferred to Charleston. In a short time
Delany was reporting that the post commandant and the
provost marshal were "liberal and courteous to the Bureau."
They, in turn, discovered that he was as businesslike in his
dealings as he was blunt in his speech.

Assigned to a pleasant cottage on the beach with a view of
Port Royal Sound and the ocean beyond, he soon had his
days organized. Before he finished his breakfast coffee, people were lined up outside of his quarters waiting for him.
Their problems were immediate and local.

A freedman's pig had eaten half a peck of his neighbor's
peanut crop. "You are hereby notified," Major Delany wrote,
"that you must restore the amount of peanuts destroyed or
pay in cash the market value of the same; and henceforth keep
your stock from trespassing on his premises, under penalties
of the law."

Two men were in a dispute over money. "Mr. Wilson Green,
you are hereby summoned to appear at this office on Friday

thirteenth inst. at 2 o'clock, to answer complaint of Mr. Peter Gray for money due him by you."

An employer refused to pay his laborer. "Joshua Johnson claims four days pay for labor done for Mr. Henry Ames. Received only one dollar & thirty cents. Claim $2.70."

A freedman had taken his former mistress' horse, swearing to kill the animal rather than return it. Would Major Delany get back the horse for the lady? He did. And he acted as counsel for seven soldiers who were court-martialed and settled an argument between a tenant and landlord over back rent.

Much of his time was spent in giving out rations and clothing to the needy—whites as well as blacks—and finding them places to stay. Contributions from black soldiers had built a Home for Freedmen on Hilton Head, but its matron— "a nervous sensitive, impatient though otherwise excellent young lady," Delany complained in one of his first reports— turned away people he sent there even when she had room to accommodate them.

At night, when the stream of supplicants slowed to a trickle, he wrote his reports. A weekly report of Rations Issued. An estimate of Rations Required. A weekly report of Issue of Clothing. A Monthly Return of Quarter Master's Stores. A monthly Roster of Commissioned Officers and Civilian Agents on duty in the Bureau (he was the only one). Reports on medicines issued, schools opened, work contracts signed. Seasonal reports on crops, special censuses of black orphans, the aged, and the blind.

As if this were not enough, monthly and quarterly letters summarizing the conditions of the freedmen in his district were required—in duplicate. With each report in his forceful, careless handwriting went a letter beginning "I have the honor to transmit to you herewith" and ending "I am, General, very respectfully, your obed't servant"—a form prescribed in a Special Order to all Bureau officers. And even the Special Orders had to be answered with letters acknowledging their receipt.

Small wonder that in his first quarterly summary of conditions, Martin wrote: "I have been under the necessity of employing at my own private expense, a Clerk and an Errand Boy. The Office needs assistants such as are named in this paragraph." Or that when he was reproved for filing an incomplete report, he explained that the press of business was so great that "derangement is probable"—his wordy way of saying that the paper work was driving him crazy.

Despite the minute-to-minute demands on his time, he quickly found ways to improve conditions in his district. Scarcely anyone had money in South Carolina in 1865. Freedmen and planters alike lived on credit through most of the year, settling up accounts in the fall after the crops were in. Although a few planters were able to pay weekly wages, most plantations were worked on shares. That is, the planter supplied seed, farm tools, and housing for his workers. They raised the cotton and corn and received a share of the crop at the end of the season. Out of their share they repaid the planter or storekeeper who had advanced them food and clothing.

This system worked well for the men who kept the account books. For the freedmen, few of whom were literate, it was often disastrous. After checking the prices on Robbers' Row, Delany discovered that they were being cheated when they bought and when they sold.

"I intend to adopt a Pass-book system," he reported in October, "making it obligatory on all planters and other persons having stores, to enter in a pass-book held by the customer, every item charged against him in the grocery or commissary store. This will be just to both dealer and customer, and more generally satisfactory to the freedmen.

"I intend also to make commissary arrangements whereby the freedmen of the Island may be enabled to obtain their supplies of Rice and grits during the winter at prices far below those now charged, probably from thirty to fifty per cent less.

"I am directing the freedmen to hold their cotton and not dispose of it in the seed to the numerous brokers here at the petty price of ten cents for long staple (Sea Island) but wait for such arrangements as are in contemplation on St. Helena Island. This establishment contemplates the reception, deposit and sale of all freedmen's cotton at the high market prices."

One objective of the Freedmen's Bureau was to restore the economy of the South to normal as quickly as possible. Bureau officers were to persuade freedmen to work, convince planters to treat them fairly, and get the wheels of industry and local government turning.

But what was normal in the fall of 1865? A year earlier the freedmen had been slaves and their owners in rebellion against the United States. Now the former Confederate states were writing new constitutions that recognized the abolition of slavery. Once this was done, according to President Johnson, they would be full-fledged members of the Union again. Northern troops would be withdrawn and Southerners could elect their own officials and send representatives to Congress.

The southern states complied with Johnson's orders, but they had their own version of normality. "This is a white man's government and intended for white men only," Benjamin Perry, South Carolina's provisional governor said at the opening of his state's constitutional convention.

The lawmakers quickly drew up a Black Code which

rigidly limited the freedmen. No person of color could own a business or work at a trade, except as farm laborer or servant, without a special license, which cost up to $100 and was good for only one year. As laborers, their wages were fixed and working hours ran from sunrise to sunset, six days a week, with Sunday work assigned when necessary. Masters could whip servants "moderately" and deduct from their wages losses caused by neglect of duties. Vagrants—defined, among other ways, as those who did not work or who hunted game and fished—could be sentenced to jail or hired out to farmers without pay. Blacks were forbidden to sell liquor or to own pistols, muskets, or swords. They were to be tried in special courts where the crimes punishable by death included stealing a mule or a bale of cotton and assaulting a white woman.

As similar Black Codes were passed in all of the Rebel states, blacks found their voices. In November, Martin was granted leave to attend a Colored Peoples' Convention in Charleston. Meeting in Zion Church, ex-slaves and free blacks appealed to the people of South Carolina and to Congress for "even-handed justice." Their tone was moderate: "We cherish in our hearts no hatred or malice toward those who have held our brethren as slaves. We ask for no special privileges or peculiar favors. We simply desire that the same laws which govern white men shall direct colored men; that we have no obstructions placed in our way."

When Congress met in December it responded to the appeals of the freedmen by refusing to seat the representatives of the new southern governments. For the next year and a half Congress and the President battled over the form that southern Reconstruction should take. In South Carolina General Sickles set aside the Black Code, decreeing that "All laws shall be applicable alike to all inhabitants." Law enforcement remained in the hands of the military until September 1866, when the state legislature revised the Black Code and dropped its most onerous restrictions.

Meanwhile, there was the question of the land. Freedmen's Bureau agents were instructed to supervise work contracts between planters and freedmen to make sure that they were fair. After the 1865 harvest, the planters were eager to sign up laborers for the following year. Some offered the freedmen only a one-quarter or one-fifth share of the crops. Others wanted to pay wages that would not be enough to live on.

In a series of articles in *New South,* a weekly published at Hilton Head, Delany proposed a "triple alliance"—a partnership of capital, land, and labor that would give each an equal share of the profits. He drew up a model contract that specified holidays for the workers, forbade sutlers' stores on the plantations, and insisted that adequate tools and farm animals be supplied. "No labor is to be performed by hand that can better be done by animal labor or machinery," one section of the contract read. In addition to receiving an acre of land on which to raise vegetables for his family, each laborer was guaranteed "one third of all that he or she is able to produce by cultivation."

But the freedmen refused to sign even fair contracts. Some families were already working their own land. Many were waiting for the forty-acre plots that General Sherman had promised them.

The promise was never kept. All summer long planters returned to the islands. Pardoned by the President for their role in the rebellion, they tried to reclaim the plantations that had been given to the freedmen. When the freedmen refused to leave their land, President Johnson sent General Oliver O. Howard, chief of the Freedmen's Bureau, to the South to work out a "mutually satisfactory" arrangement.

At a stormy meeting in a church on Edisto Island, Howard explained to the freedmen the doubtful nature of their land titles. Regretfully, he advised them to sign work contracts with the planters.

"No, no!" people shouted. "General Howard, why do you take away our lands?" a man called from the balcony. "You take away from us who have always been true to the Government! You give them to our all-time enemies! That is not right!"

Right or no, the freedmen were fighting a losing battle. All fall there was turmoil. The freedmen refused to work for their former masters. On Edisto Island they patrolled the beaches with guns and drove off the planters when they attempted to land.

Sympathetic as he was to the freedmen, General Saxton had his orders from Washington. In a circular letter to Bureau officers, he ordered them to correct the "erroneous impression" that the ex-slaves would be given land by the government. "Every proper means will be taken to secure fair written agreements for the coming year; and the freedmen instructed that it is in their best interest to look to the property holders for employment. The Commissioner deprecates hostile action, and wishes every possible exertion made to produce kind feeling and mutual confidence between the blacks and the whites."

In December, Major Delany was called to Charleston by General Sickles "for important special duty for a short time." There were rumors throughout the Sea Islands that a black insurrection was planned for Christmas or New Year's Day. Delany was ordered to make an inspection tour of Port Royal and the islands around Charleston, to convince the freedmen to keep calm. Army officers had accused him of fomenting an insurrection. Now they were calling on him to put one down!

With a detachment of colored troops, he visited Beaufort, Edisto, and the islands near by. The rumors of insurrection were "false and malicious," he wrote Sickles. "I have found things in a much more satisfactory and encouraging state than could have been expected."

On New Year's Day he spoke at an Emancipation celebration on Edisto Island. As an agent of the United States Government, his job was to persuade his listeners to forget the land they had been promised. When he advised them to sign contracts for the coming year, angry men accused him of being in league with the planters. For the first time in his life, he was shouted down by a black audience.

A casual observer might have wondered if he was the same man who had spoken at the Brick Church on St. Helena five months earlier. Basically, he had not changed. For all his black pride, Martin Delany was no revolutionary. He believed firmly in the sanctity of private property. Confiscation of land—even slaveowners' land—was as abhorrent to him as it was to Andrew Johnson. The code that he lived by said that a man must work hard, pull himself up by his bootstraps, and not expect subsidies from the government.

His viewpoint was shared by almost everyone of his generation. The Colored Peoples' Convention in Charleston had not asked for land. Nor had Frederick Douglass or other black spokesmen in the North. Only the former slaves, and a handful of men in Congress, understood that if the big-plantation economy of the South was re-established, the freedmen would not be really free.

Ten years later, after Reconstruction had failed, Frederick Douglass would say, "When the Israelites were emancipated they were told to go and borrow of their neighbors—borrow their coin, borrow their jewels, load themselves down with the means of subsistence. When the Russian serfs had their chains broken and were given their liberty, the government of Russia—aye, the despotic government of Russia—gave to those poor emancipated serfs a few acres of land on which they could live and earn their bread. But when you turned us loose, you gave us no acres, you turned us loose to the sky, to the storm, to the whirlwind, and, worst of all, you turned us loose to the wrath of our infuriated masters."

In 1866 neither Douglass or Delany could see that far ahead. Delany was brimming over with optimism. In a letter to Douglass, John Jones, and others who had had a frustrating interview with Andrew Johnson, he counseled patience: "Since we last met great changes have taken place, and much has been gained. Do not misjudge the President but believe, as I do, that he means to do right; that his intentions are good. Instead of despair, rather let us cry 'Glory to God.'"

On his travels through the islands Delany had talked with the planters. "Everywhere I met them," he wrote Sickles, "I found but one sentiment—a desire to accept the situation, submit to the best terms offered, bending their effort to the restoration of the prosperity of the South." Believing that "a union of whites and blacks" was necessary, they were "willing to enter into any agreement reasonable and just to both parties. . . . The Freedmen will readily enter into arrangements to work," he concluded, as soon as they receive "definite orders from the Government that they cannot obtain the lands they occupy by purchase or otherwise."

The orders were not long in coming. By the time Delany's inspection tour was completed, General Saxton had been dismissed by President Johnson. His place was taken by General Robert K. Scott who had made no promises to the freedmen. Before spring planting began, squads of soldiers traveled from island to island, ordering blacks to sign contracts with the planters. Those who refused were evicted at gunpoint. Scott was able to relocate some who held Sherman land titles, but a year later less than 2000 out of the 100,000 blacks in his district owned their own land.

Back at Hilton Head, Delany heard nothing but praise for his work. "I desire to bear testimony to the efficient and able manner in which Maj. Delany is performing his duties," the Acting Inspector General reported to General Sickles. "I took occasion several times during my stay to go to his Office and hear him talk and explain matters to the Freedmen. Being of their own color they naturally reposed confidence in him. Upon the labor question he entirely reflected the views of the Major-General Commanding and seemed in all things to give them good and sensible advice. In the event of his regiment being mustered out I hope he may be retained as an agent of the Freedmen's Bureau."

Sickles forwarded these comments to the War Department, adding, "I have received the same Satisfactory reports from other sources. I most respectfully recommend that Major M. R. Delany be for the present retained in the military service of the United States."

"The Black Major is now on the right track," the *New South* wrote in February 1866. "He has a wonderful influence for good over the freedmen. He tells them to go to work at once; that labor surely brings its own reward, and that after one more good crop is gathered, they will find their condition much better than at present. And he tells the planters that they must be kind and just to their laborers if they would bring order out of chaos. Our whole community here is taking heart."

Delany was doing what he liked best—bringing order out of chaos. By the summer of 1866 he was able to report "more land under cultivation this year on Hilton Head than was ever known before." But the freedmen were still being cheated out of their pay. "Just at the completion of the crop, some employers, bringing some frivolous charge against the laborer, drive away the employee as though he was a slave, thereby forfeiting his entire season's labor." Other planters deducted so much for food and clothing that "these poor people come out with nothing, absolutely nothing; nay, worse than nothing—in rags and in debt for a 'balance due' on the books."

When the Bureau ignored his request for an inspector to audit accounts and supervise the division of the crops, he badgered the United States Tax Commissioners who still controlled a number of large plantations on the islands. In 1867 when Congress and the President were arguing over the disposition of these lands, he convinced the Commissioners to rent them to the freedmen for one dollar an acre. Under his direction, several hundred blacks pooled their resources and took over fourteen of the best plantations.

This still left them vulnerable when they brought their cotton to market. "A deep laid scheme and system are at work under the name of legitimate trade, to obtain the produce of these simple-minded uneducated people, for little or nothing," he wrote Bureau headquarters in Charleston. "Cotton worth from one to one dollar and forty cents per lb. prepared, are got from the producers at from 12 to 20 cents per lb. in the seed. To prevent this, an Agency under Government auspices should be established to dispose of their cotton for cash to the highest market purchaser."

Going ahead on his own, he found a vacant government warehouse to use as a Freedmen's Cotton Agency. He invited the freedmen to set up their own gins in the building and clean the cotton themselves rather than sell it in the seed for low prices. After it was cleaned, Robert Houston, formerly the purser on the *Planter,* bagged the cotton and sold it in Charleston. He was paid a small percentage of the proceeds for acting as the freedmen's agent. Speaking at freedmen's meetings, Delany urged them not to sell their cotton to the sutlers, but to bring it to the agency instead.

The storekeepers of Robbers' Row, who had been battling him every step of the way, set up a howl. The Major was *forcing* freedmen to dispose of their cotton to *his* agency and was doubtless pocketing a share of the profits. Sent from Charleston to investigate their charges, Brigadier General B. F. Foust found that Delany had no financial interest, direct or indirect, in the agency.

"I think Major Delany has been over-zealous, but his intention has been to benefit the freedmen and not himself," he reported.

However, Delany was ordered to refrain even from suggesting "that the freedmen are not allowed to dispose of their cotton to whom they please." The agency was permitted to continue. At the end of a year, it was so successful that some families were able to buy land with the proceeds of their cotton sales.

Then, after one trip to Charleston, Robert Houston failed to return. With him went $3000 of the freedmen's money—and shreds of Martin Delany's reputation. His enemies on Robbers' Row gleefully helped the freedmen draw up complaints charging him with complicity in the fraud.

"Major Delany's course in recommending the Colored people to place their cotton in the hands of Houston places him in a very unenviable position," General Scott frigidly commented when the complaints reached his desk. "It behooves him to take immediate steps to satisfy the claims held by the freed people against Houston."

No one knew this better than Martin Delany. He had already pursued Houston to Charleston and had him arrested. The freedmen were eventually repaid and Delany escaped with nothing more than a reprimand for "a possible error of judgment."

The Cotton Agency fiasco did not dull his appetite for reform. The year 1867 was a bad year for cotton all over South Carolina. Drought was followed by torrential rains, and rains by a new enemy, the caterpillar.

"It is very evident," he wrote in his annual report, "that the entire system of cultivation will have to be changed to meet the demands of these new possessors of small farms and gardens. Cotton can only be profitably produced by extensive cultivation and large capital. It is a loss of time for the freedmen to plant cotton with their limited means."

On his advice, numbers of freedmen switched from cotton to food crops. The following spring "the yield of corn and sweet potatoes were very good, the latter being greater in quantity and the vegetable larger than known ever before, the people reported."

Nor was he concerned only with bread-and-butter issues. A thousand children in his district were attending school. He begged funds from the Bureau to repair the churches and shanties in which schools were taught and scolded the lady teachers when they whipped their pupils.

"A school house should be made a place of the most pleasurable resort and agreeable associations to children," he wrote. "In no wise can this be the case when the hickory thong, leather strap or bridle rein meets the child as he enters the school house, reminding him of the old plantation overseer, in waiting for his victim."

Another of his innovations was a system of self-government on the big plantations. In slavery days, the planter's word had been law. Now Delany encouraged the people to make their own laws. On each plantation, the workers selected a head man. Given the title of "chief of police" he and his assistants settled all disputes and kept order in their community.

"His duties are similar to those of Captain of Civil Police in a ward or precinct of a City," Delany explained to General Scott. "He is to report all his doings once a month to headquarters. This simple course engenders self-respect, showing them that the new life which they have entered requires more of them than simply obedience to the white man. It engenders confidence and self-reliance and induces them each to seek and respect the counsel of the other."

Nevertheless, the islanders still had a way to go to measure up to Delany's standards of propriety. In his father-knows-best way he arranged for temperance lectures on Sunday afternoons and counseled the freedmen on marriage. Marriages had been forbidden and family relationships discouraged before emancipation. Delany suggested to the Bureau that a "Commissioner of Marriages be sent through this district, who should make it obligatory for all who are living together as husband and wife, to assemble at some church and there receive the Marriage Ceremony, with a certificate."

Another "subject of delicate approach and fearful importance" that he called to the Bureau's attention was the appearance of "Houses of Ill Fame on Hilton Head Island. Some order from Headquarters might not go amiss in checking an evil in the form of the most loathsome diseases which are spreading in the community."

For three years Martin Delany worked with the freedmen on Hilton Head. Life was somewhat as he had imagined it would be if he had brought a party of settlers to Africa. In his island domain he was father, teacher, social worker, lawgiver—with only an occasional rap on the knuckles from his superiors to remind him that they were around.

He never completely conformed to the army way. Time after time he was reprimanded for going ahead on his own without permission from headquarters. He grumbled when the horse he requisitioned was a year in arriving. And he was still complaining after two years because the expenses of his office, including lights and brooms, came out of his own pocket.

But these dissatisfactions were minor. His one regret was that Catherine and the children were not with him. How the boys would have enjoyed the beach in front of his quarters and the tidal creeks that teemed with shrimp and crab!

When he went to Wilberforce on his annual leave, he had tried to persuade Catherine to join him. She was reluctant to go south. Life might be peaceful in the Sea Islands where blacks were in the majority, but in Memphis and New Orleans there had been wholesale massacres of freedmen. In other parts of South Carolina, Bureau agents regularly filed Reports of Outrages—the shooting and whipping of blacks by white vigilante bands.

An equally compelling reason to remain in the North was the children's schooling. It would be years before the hastily organized freedmen's schools could compare with Wilberforce. All the boys except Toussaint were making fine progress in their classes and were looking forward to college.

Toussaint was a problem. Wounded twice while he was in the army, he complained of heart palpitations and spells of blindness that often incapacitated him for weeks. In a later time doctors would probably have diagnosed his condition as shell shock, but in the 1860s his father did not know whether to sympathize with him or accuse him of malingering. When he failed to recover at home, Martin suggested that he come south. He found him a job at Hilton Head and had his eyes treated by a Freedmen's Bureau surgeon. But the sick spells continued and Martin regretfully sent him back to Ohio.

Delany's disappointment with his oldest son made him more determined than ever to keep the others in school. Extraordinary changes were taking place in the country. Barriers were tumbling down faster than anyone could have believed possible before the war.

Late in 1867 there was a new subhead in the Major's quarterly reports: Registration. Blacks still could not vote in Pennsylvania or Ohio, but Congress had passed two Reconstruction Acts that gave them the vote in the South. In September male citizens "of whatever race, color or previous condition" went to the polls to elect delegates who would write a new constitution for South Carolina.

When the constitutional convention met in Charleston, more than half of its members were black. Describing them as "black baboons" and "ring-tailed monkeys," the Charleston *Mercury* labeled the convention "the circus." A New York *Herald* reporter called it "the most incredible, hopeful and yet unbelievable experiment in all the history of mankind."

Prewar South Carolina had been dominated by wealthy slaveowners. A property qualification kept poor whites from voting. As a result, the state had never provided a public school system or the kind of welfare services found in the North. The new constitution established free schools for all children, as well as care for the aged, the blind, and the insane. Imprisonment for debt was abolished. The polling booth, jury box, and state militia were thrown open to all male citizens, regardless of race or class. There was even a motion to enfranchise women, but it was defeated as too radical. The "black baboons" and their white colleagues gave South

Carolina its first democratic constitution and laid the framework for a genuine interracial society.

Would it work? From his island outpost, Martin Delany watched the formation of Republican clubs in Columbia, Charleston, Beaufort. The old South had been controlled by Democrats, but when the voters went to the polls in April 1868 to elect a state government, the Republican Party—the party of Lincoln—won an overwhelming victory. Robert K. Scott, head of the Freedmen's Bureau, was chosen governor and eighty-four black men were elected to the legislature.

"In this District Registration has been general and very highly appreciated by the Freedmen," Delany reported. "On each occasion of voting, the elections passed off with the most commendable propriety, the suffragees deporting themselves like old exemplary citizens."

In July, after the legislature ratified the Fourteenth Amendment, which said that *all* persons born or naturalized in the United States were citizens, South Carolina was formally restored to the Union. The military occupation of the state came to an end and the Freedmen's Bureau began to shut down. On August 10 Martin received a final order from headquarters:

"Major M. R. Delany, 104th USCT, having been mustered out and honorably discharged from the service of the United States on account of his services being no longer required is hereby relieved from duty in this Bureau. He will turn over to Edw. L. Deane, Disbursing Officer, all Government property for which he is responsible, applying to him for bills of lading on which to ship the same to Charleston."

Ever since the Confederacy was reduced to rubble and humiliation by a superior Union war machine, Southern states have embraced the delusion that the South would rise again to its former greatness and walk with white Anglo-Saxon pride across the length of the land, carried faithfully on the backs of contented and loyal black servants. . . . From the smoldering ashes of the Civil War, Southern white families have passed down from generation to generation the unextinguished flame of eternal white supremacy.

—CHUCK STONE, *in* Black Political Power in America, *1968*

23

A WARNING VOICE

Sitting on the platform at a rally in Beaufort, Martin joined the audience in singing a Republican campaign song, to the tune of "Rally Round the Flag":

Oh Reconstruction is the rage
From mountain to the sea.
Let every man at once engage
To help our nominee.

Then rally, boys rally
From mountain, hill and dale.

O, come from every valley
For Grant must not fail.

Oh Reconstruction we demand
And peace and harmony.
Let friend and foe come shake their hand
And help our nominee.

The rally was one of thousands being held across the South as black people looked forward to casting their first vote in a Presidential election. Posters of General Grant were tacked to the walls of the hall. A red-white-and-blue streamer above the speakers' platform said: LET US HAVE PEACE —ULYSSES S. GRANT.

Delany spoke almost perfunctorily, for his mind was on other things. This was his first public appearance in civilian clothes since the war. After three and a half years in uniform, he was now free—to do what?

On the table in front of him lay a stack of books whose gold-embossed spines proclaimed each to be the *Life and Public Services of Martin R. Delany* by Frank A. Rollin. Fugitive slaves had written narratives of their escapes from slavery, but this was the first full-length biography of a black man who had been born free.

"Frank A. Rollin" was the pen name of Frances Rollin, a young woman who had been teaching in a freedmen's school in Beaufort. Born in Santo Domingo and educated at the Institute for Colored Youth in Philadelphia, she was one of four sisters prominent in South Carolina black society. She and Delany had met when he helped her file a complaint against the captain of the *Pilot Boy,* a steamer that carried passengers from Charleston to the Sea Islands. In violation of an order from General Sickles that forbade discrimination on railroads and steamboats, the captain had refused her a first-class ticket. As a result of her complaint, the captain was fined $250 and the staterooms of the *Pilot Boy* were opened to all comers.

To the twenty-year-old schoolteacher Major Delany was the most remarkable black man she had ever met. When she confided to him her ambition to become a writer, he agreed to help her to write the story of his life. She had spent months interviewing him, writing down his not always accurate reminiscences, and plowing through his files of newspaper clippings and army orders. With her research in hand, she had gone to Boston the previous winter to write the book and arrange for its publication. Soon after it went to press, she had married William J. Whipper, a Pennsylvania lawyer who had come South in 1866.

Despite its hero-worshipping tone and an involved style that mirrored the Major's own, the *Life and Public Services* had a moderate success in its day and became a valuable reference for later historians.

"It is decidedly the best book of its kind that has emanated from a colored author in this country, and opens up a vast field of labor and research to coming biographers," a review in the *Christian Recorder* said.

"We are compelled to accord to Maj. Delany a place in the front ranks of American Statesmen and philanthropists. He has for a quarter of a century, battled against the terrible caste-prejudice—which has kept his people under the iron heel of oppression for 200 years. Yet has he succeeded in accomplishing more practical good for his people than any man of his race now living in this country. The highest meed of praise that can be accorded to him is, that Martin R. Delany is now a *poor* man.

"We venture to predict that the end of Martin R. Delany's usefulness is not yet. It is not asking too much of the American people to request that he be permitted to pass the last days of his useful life in some high position of honor and trust in the Republic."

Delany smiled wryly as he read the review. At fifty-six he felt in the prime of life, not yet ready for his "last days." But there was no doubt that he was poor. Almost all of his $200-a-month army salary had gone to Catherine and the children. Aside from his mustering-out pay, his only assets were two house lots—one in Lagos and one in Wilberforce.

Catherine wanted him to return north, to take up the practice of medicine again and build the home they had planned at the edge of the campus. He was reluctant to go. In Ohio he would never be more than a country doctor, as rusty in his knowledge of medicine as the stethoscope and scalpel he had packed away ten years before.

The South was the new land of opportunity for black men. During his years in the service, others had been acquiring property and position in the old Confederate states. In the scant year since they had had the vote, hundreds of blacks had moved into positions of leadership. William Whipper and Robert Smalls, who were seated next to him on the speakers' platform, had bought homes and Sea Island plantations at recent government tax sales. Members of the state legislature, they were both at the beginning of promising political careers.

After General Grant was elected President, Delany made a trip through the former Rebel states, lecturing and writing newspaper articles. He returned to South Carolina filled with enthusiasm. The "incredible, hopeful experiment" was in full swing. Blacks were taking part in state governments, serving on committees, making laws. They were sheriffs, tax collectors, superintendents of schools, policemen, and postmasters. Francis Cardozo, born free in Charleston and educated abroad, was South Carolina's secretary of state. Jonathan Gibbs of Philadelphia was secretary of state in Florida and Oscar J. Dunn, a former slave, was Louisiana's lieutenant governor.

Delany had been able to ride in horsecars and sit in first-class coaches on trains. In New Orleans he visited schools where black and white children attended classes together. Speaking to a crowd of freedmen in Congo Square, he recalled his visit thirty years earlier when a curfew drove black people from the streets at dusk. In Columbia, South Carolina's capital, he attended a reception at the governor's mansion and sat in the State House to watch a black man preside over the Assembly. After more than 200 years of slavery, the South was being reconstructed on the basis of equality for all.

Martin Delany thought of himself as a political economist rather than a politician. He was no back-slapper or hand-shaker. He was used to speaking his mind on every issue. He didn't know if he could play the game of party politics as it was played in the United States. But he would try.

One rule of the game was to reward your friends. The black Republican voters of the South had helped President Grant win the election. Therefore blacks were entitled to a share of federal jobs—as postmasters, collectors of the customs, and the like. Grant had already made the first appointment of a black man to the United States diplomatic service, Ebenezer Bassett as minister to Haiti. Why not also a black minister to Liberia? And who better for this post than Martin Delany?

Throughout 1869 white and black Republicans from South Carolina, Louisiana, Alabama, and Texas sent letters to President Grant and Secretary of State Hamilton Fish, recommending Delany for the post of minister to Liberia. Six bishops of the AME Church representing, they pointed out, "the largest number of Colored Christians in the United States and also the largest number of Colored Voters" also wrote to the President to ask for Delany's appointment.

On a visit to Washington, Delany tried to drum up additional support. He had to wait two years to learn that he had failed. When Grant did send a black man to Liberia, he chose a younger man, from Missouri, who had the backing of leading Western senators.

Delany remained in Washington to attend a National Colored Labor Convention. With political freedom achieved, blacks were organizing to fight job discrimination and low pay. Most of the delegates were young men who had fought in the war. They treated Delany as an elder statesman. After organizing a National Colored Labor Union, they wrote an appeal to Congress that pointed out that Southern farm laborers were paid only $60 a year. To make them independent of the planters who joined together to keep wages down, they urged the formation of a federal land commission which would sell land to the freedmen at low prices.

Returning to South Carolina at the beginning of 1870, Delany wrote a series of articles, "Citizenship," "Civil Rights," and "The Constitution," for the *New National Era,* a weekly in Washington that Frederick Douglass was editing. The articles, later reprinted as a "University Pamphlet" for the students at Wilberforce, were intended "as popular elementary instruction for the new political element in the United States —the freedmen and colored youth."

As he wrote, he could not rid himself of a feeling o‚
uneasiness. Thirty years ago when he first entered politics
black leaders talked of elevation, self-improvement, education‚
Now, in the corridors of the State House in Columbia‚
he heard "Whatever can be done in politics is fair" and "Tc
beat is the duty in a political contest, no matter what mean‚
are used to effect it."

Blacks were in the majority in the legislature, but most o‚
the positions of power and influence were in white hands‚
The wealthy planters who had controlled the state before
the war were sitting on the sidelines, refusing to participat‚
in the government. Their places had been taken by northern‚
ers who had come south during and after the war, and
by a handful of southern-born poor whites. Delany was afraid
that some of the young, inexperienced black lawmakers were
being misled by their white colleagues.

When the legislature established a Bureau of Agricultura‚
Statistics, he went to work as its chief agent. His job wa‚
to advise farm laborers—to supervise their contracts with
employers and to see that the settlements made at the en‚
of the season were fair. Unlike the Freedmen's Bureau, how‚
ever, the new state agency had no power to enforce it‚
decisions.

As he traveled through the state, he found condition‚
far worse than any he had ever seen on the Sea Islands‚
"In thousands of cases, indeed the majority of the rura‚
population, the men and women are in rags, and the smaller
children of both sexes either stark naked or covered with but
a single shirt," he reported. Not only was there widespread
cheating of the families who worked on shares, but many
planters paid their laborers with due bills instead of cash—
IOUs good only at local stores where prices were many
times higher than elsewhere.

At settling-up time as he listened to the freedmen's bitter rhyme:

> Naught's a naught,
> Five's a figger.
> All for the white man
> And none for the nigger.

he felt he could no longer tell them that hard work alone would solve their problems. It would be a long time before they could put carpets on their cabin floors. "The poor, industrious, hard-laboring freedman never will be able to make more than his bread," he wrote. "They must be helped to buy land."

The legislature had set up a state Land Commission, but it lacked the capital for a large-scale program and was soon bogged down in politics. Despairing of assistance from either the federal or state governments, Delany turned to private enterprise—his own.

In 1871 he opened a Land and Real Estate Agency in Charleston, advertising "Lands, plantations and city property bought and sold. All transactions at this office strictly reliable and honorable, as no other will be entertained." Although the agency was primarily a business venture, he tried to put his newly acquired knowledge of land values to work for the benefit of the freedmen.

In a series of open letters to Senator Henry Wilson of Massachusetts and Daniel L. Eaton, an official of the Freedmen's Bank in Washington, he proposed that Northern philanthropists purchase land in the South to sell to the freedmen on reasonable terms. "What the freedman wants is land of his own, with time to pay for it. What the land owner wants is cash for his surplus lands."

With homes of their own, the freedmen would settle down, educate their children, pay taxes. They would become stable citizens, interested in improving their homes and their communities. Land prices were low. The philanthropists would profit from their investment—and so would the whole country.

His letters were published in the Charleston *Republican* in the spring of 1871 and were reprinted in a pamphlet titled "Homes for the Freedmen." The proposal was simple, reasonable, and right for South Carolina that spring—and nobody paid any attention to it. Perhaps that was because little else was simple, reasonable, and right in South Carolina that spring. The whites, who had been waiting for the Reconstruction government to collapse of its own weight, were tired of waiting. They had begun to attack—with guns, whips, and the white-sheeted terror of the Ku Klux Klan.

Reports of violence and murder piled up on Governor Scott's desk. "A. P. Owens, Trial Justice, murdered by about 40 KKK at his home and in the presence of his family . . . James Puler, colored citizen, murdered by unknown parties, evidently Ku Klux . . . A colored man known as Tom Black was killed last Friday night, his throat cut from ear to ear . . . Others in the same vicinity have been found killed since. No offence given except that the murdered men were leading Republicans . . . Volney Powell, elected Judge of Probate, Wade A. Perrin, elected member of the House of Representatives, and eleven others, all leading Republicans, were killed in one day. Fifty men and women taken from their homes and brutally whipped . . . On the night of the 12th, a band of disguised men, numbering about 800, took from the jail ten prisoners, six were shot, two were hung and the remaining two escaped . . . A. Johnson, Trial Justice, was killed, and thirty-two have been whipped, out of which number ten are respectable females . . . A complete organization exists from the Savannah River to Chester, a distance of nearly two hundred miles. Its object is to intimidate Republican voters and if necessary murder leading Republicans . . ."

"There is a fixed purpose among the land holders to kill or drive off every Republican leader so as to gain control of the county," an army officer wrote Scott. "I believe the ulterior objects of the Ku Klux party to be against the U.S. government. Unless thwarted they will finally gain their object. Although not disposed to recommend colored militia, it is remarkable that no Ku Klucking is done in the vicinity of the armed militia."

The state militia, a branch of the National Guard, had been reorganized in 1869. When its ranks were opened to all able-bodied men regardless of color, blacks hastened to volunteer. Rather than serve alongside them in integrated companies, whites boycotted the service. As a result, the state militia had become all black, with a largely black corps of officers. Delany served as an aide-de-camp on the governor's staff, with the rank of lieutenant colonel, and a company called the Delany Rifle Guards had been formed in Charleston.

The militia's duties were largely ceremonial however. They paraded through the streets on the Fourth of July and Emancipation Day in handsome new uniforms. But when the state was faced with an armed rebellion, the white commander-in-chief of the black militia hesitated to call on them.

Fearful of pitting blacks against whites, Scott turned to Congress and the President for help. Similar rebellions were occurring in other Southern states. Congress passed a series of "Ku Klux" laws which empowered the President to send federal troops to the South when the rights of black citizens were endangered. In the fall of 1871 President Grant declared martial law in nine counties of South Carolina. Federal troops jailed almost two thousand men, bringing the reign of terror to an end.

After the Klan rebellion was put down, South Carolina's whites changed their tactics. Aiming a propaganda campaign at public opinion in the North, they charged the state government with extravagance, inefficiency, and corruption. Men of property were being taxed to death, they said, while ignorant blacks and rascally whites squandered or stole millions of dollars of state funds.

There was just enough truth in their statements to disturb Martin Delany. The Republicans had been in power for three years. A black lieutenant governor now presided over the state senate and three black congressmen represented the state in Washington. Yet the majority of the people still lived in dire poverty. Despite high taxes, the state treasury lacked the money to build adequate schools, buy land, or even pay the salaries of its employees.

He blamed most of South Carolina's problems on the Northern politicians who had convinced the blacks that they did not need black leaders. Since the passage of the Fifteenth Amendment, which guaranteed all citizens the right to vote, it had become fashionable to say that the Constitution had abolished color. "We are all one color now," the politicians said. "Republicanism knows no race."

In an open letter to Frederick Douglass, Delany branded this as a "barefaced deception fostered by the demagogues to keep themselves in the best positions. Demagogues and disreputable men must be discarded as leaders, and never more be given opportunity to betray their trust and abuse the interests of the people whom they assume to represent."

He was also sharply critical of the blacks. The Klan terror

had shaken him. Like Scott, he was afraid that an aggressive black militia might provoke open warfare. The blacks had been so misled, he wrote, that "they regularly trained themselves with firearms and marched in companies to political meetings. From a polite, pleasant, agreeable, kindly common people, ever ready and obliging, there is now to be met with an ill mannerly, sullen, disagreeable, unkind, disobliging populace, seemingly filled with hatred and ready for resentment."

"Another shameful evil," he reported, was the drawing of color lines among colored people: "Still adhering to an absurdity, a relic of the degraded past, they cling to the assumption of superiority of white blood and brown complexion."

In *Blake* he had described Charleston's Brown Fellowship Society, whose light-skinned members refused to accept "full-blooded" blacks. The Brown Society had survived slavery— and "fire, military companies, and even churches and graveyards are established on this basis. In one church no blacks are to be seen and in another there is a division between the blacks and browns by different seats."

These distinctions based on complexion were accepted by white society as well, he added. Few "pure black men" were given government jobs. With rare exceptions, these appointments had gone to "those having an admixture of white blood," he wrote. "Under the rallying cry of acting for and representing the 'Negro,' men of every shade of complexion have attained to places of honor, profit, trust and power, except the real Negro himself.

"The colored people must first become reconciled to themselves as a race, and respect each other as do the whites, regardless of complexion," he concluded. "Colored people must have intelligent leaders of their own race, and white people intelligent leaders of theirs; the two combined to compose the leaders of the party. This must be the basis of all future political action."

Douglass recognized the letter as an outpouring from a tired, worried, middle-aged man who felt that his lifetime of experience was being ignored. His reply was warm and friendly.

"Your well-known zeal and ability, and your long devotion to the cause of freedom and equality to all men, will, I am quite sure, obtain for the elaborate letter with which you have honored me a thoughtful perusal by intelligent colored men in all parts of this country. While I heartily concur in much that you say, there are some things in it from which I as heartily dissent. However, even where I dissent, I am compelled to respect your boldness, candor and manly independence in the utterance of your convictions.

"The colored people of the South are just now going to school. It is hardly worth while to lament that the school is not better than it is. I rather think that the colored people have already made considerable progress in political and social knowledge, and that they will soon be able to distinguish between a decent man and a demagogue, no matter what disguises he may assume.

"I hardly think you are quite just in what you say of the changed manners of the colored people of South Carolina. Were you not M. R. Delany, I should say that the man who wrote thus had taken his place with the old planters," he gently chided. "You certainly cannot prefer the lash-inspired manners of the past. I know too well your own proud and independent spirit, to believe the manners of an enslaved people are more to your taste than those which are born of freedom and independence. Have patience, my old friend."

Delany was not alone in his concern. The Reverend Richard

Cain, who had become a state senator, was leading a reform movement in the legislature, and all the black lawmakers were vigorously cleaning house. In 1872 when they met to choose candidates for the fall elections, they determined to get rid of Scott and other Northern politicians who had misgoverned them. Almost all of their slate of candidates was black. Richard Gleaves, a Pennsylvanian whom Delany had known for twenty-five years, was running as lieutenant governor. Francis Cardozo was the candidate for treasurer, and Cain for congressman-at-large. For governor they chose Franklin Moses, Jr., one of the few well-born white South Carolinians who supported Reconstruction.

Urged by Cain, Delany accepted a post on the Republican State Executive Committee and agreed to campaign for the ticket. In October he went to New York to meet with the bankers who handled South Carolina's finances. The state's financial plight was in part caused by its property owners and businessmen. Refusing to pay taxes, they had warned the money men of Wall Street that they would repudiate the state's debts as soon as their party returned to power. As a result, when the state borrowed money to meet its obligations, it had to pay exorbitant interest rates.

Delany's task was to counteract these warnings, to assure the bankers that South Carolina's government was stable and would meet its obligations. He soon had cause to regret his mission.

The Republicans won the election, hands down, giving black men a two-thirds majority in the General Assembly. They carried out many of their promises of reform. They decreased expenses and halved the state debt, but Governor Moses proved to be far more corrupt than Governor Scott. Nor was he the only one.

When the legislature met in December, Delany went to

Columbia to support the candidacy of Robert Brown Elliott for United States senator. South Carolina's senators were
not popularly elected, but were chosen by the Assembly.
Elliott, a lawyer from Massachusetts with a skin as dark
as Martin Delany's, had already served a term in Congress.
He was considered the ablest of the young black politicians
and an orator second only to Frederick Douglass.

Elliott's election seemed a sure thing. Talking with the
legislators as they arrived in the capital, Delany discovered
that it was not. Man after man sheepishly admitted that he
planned to vote for Elliott's rival, John J. Patterson. A white
Pennsylvanian known ironically as "Honest John," Patterson
headed a "railroad ring" that had milked the state treasury
of more than a million dollars.

Shortly before the Assembly vote was taken, Delany and
Elliott were in the offices of the State Executive Committee
when an emissary of Patterson's arrived. Laying an envelope
on the table, he said, "There's $15,000 here. It's yours if you
withdraw from the race."

Elliott, who was young and vigorous, rose in anger. He
threatened to throw the man down the stairs. Only Delany's
intervention prevented the threat from being carried out.

Nevertheless, Honest John Patterson won the election. His
seat in the United States Senate, he later boasted, cost him
$40,000.

South Carolina's lawmakers had no monopoly on bribery
and corruption in 1872–73. There was fraud everywhere.
In New York, Boss Tweed and his cohorts in Tammany
Hall were convicted of stealing $6 million from the people;
the Crédit Mobilier and Whisky Ring scandals touched off
investigations that led all the way to the White House.
But the excuses that "Everybody's doing it," or, "If I don't

take the money, somebody else will," did not satisfy Martin Delany.

He returned to Charleston with a heavy heart. His own affairs were at a low ebb. The real estate agency was bringing only a trickle of income. Some weeks he had no money to send to Catherine. When he entered the campaign, Cain had assured him that Moses would give him a state job after the election.

"Delany's condition is a needy one," Cain wrote to remind the governor. "For heavens sake do not cast him away. He has many strong friends who sympathize with him, and desire to see him placed where he may render the state some services while he makes a living for his wife and children."

But Moses failed to keep his pledge. When Cain went to Washington as congressman-elect, Delany took over the editorship of the *Missionary Record,* a church weekly that Cain had started. In the pages of the newspaper he announced that he was collecting material for a "History of the African Race in America."

He had planned to go North in the summer of 1873 when his son Alexander was graduating from Wilberforce. Instead he finally found work as a U.S. customs inspector in Charleston. The pay was only $1460 a year, little more than half of what he had earned in the Freedmen's Bureau, but it eased his financial burdens. Curiously enough, although the job was a federal appointment, it had come not from Congressman Cain, but through the good offices of Customs Collector H. C. Worthington, a crony of Honest John Patterson's.

Worthington was the first of many strange bedfellows that Delany was to acquire during the next years. As the 1874 elections approached, the propaganda campaign that the state's white supremacy leaders had launched shifted into high gear. A South Carolina Taxpayers' Convention protested to President Grant against the state government's "monstrous oppression" of men of property. Their aim was to convince the country that South Carolina had been "Africanized" and that "depraved Negroes" were engaged in a "saturnalia of corruption."

The Republicans defended themselves by pointing out that most of the money spent had gone for public services that were not available before the war. "We are not ashamed of the fact that our appropriation for schools in 1872–3 is four times greater than in 1859–60 . . . There were no appropriations for the State Lunatic asylum and penitentiary in 1859–60 . . . or for a colored orphan house," they replied.

Certainly the state's printing expenses were higher than they had been in slavery days. "But is it a cause for boastfulness that the people were kept in ignorance and no public information disseminated amongst them for their enlightenment and elevation? We think not."

Individual black spokesmen continued to press for reforms. "Let us drive out the thieves," Robert Brown Elliott said. "With one heart, one aim, one determination, let us move forward to the re-establishment of an honest economical and respectable government in South Carolina."

Reading the northern papers, Delany was afraid that the protestations and promises were too late. Better than his younger colleagues, he knew the extent of race prejudice in the North. Even liberal papers there were sympathetic to the southerners' charges of "Negro domination," "Negro ignorance," and the greatest bugaboo of all, "social equality."

Somehow, the "incredible, hopeful experiment" had gotten

on the wrong track. If it continued as it was going, he
could foresee a collision. Getting rid of men like Moses or
Patterson was not enough. The Rebels who had led the
Secession movement and started the war would not give
up until they regained power. Black men had to come to
terms with them, strike a bargain quickly, before it was too
late.

In an open letter to the young black politicians, he warned
that the sympathies of the country were with South Carolina's
white minority. "The white race is true to itself. It is useless
to conceal the fact that in giving liberty and equality to the
blacks, they had no desire to see them rule over their own
race. There are no white people North nor South who will
submit to see the blacks rule over the whites in America.
We may as well be candid on this point, and let the truth
be known."

Already white laborers were being imported into the state
to take the place of blacks. In five years, he predicted, blacks
would be outnumbered and would lose their power. To prepare for this day, he proposed a system of "cumulative
voting" which would give representation to the minority as
well as the majority. Cumulative voting, later called "propor-
tional representation," was new to American politics. It would
apportion seats in the legislature on a pro-rata basis, irrespective of party, Delany explained.

"Let our Legislature be wise enough now, while it is
in the power of our race to do so, to secure by constitutional
enactment, the right of minority representation." While this
would be of immediate benefit to whites, it would guarantee
representation to the blacks when they were in the minority—
"which they most assuredly will [be], at no distant day."

The Charleston *News and Courier,* the state's most influential paper, reprinted the letter with a headline:

A WARNING VOICE
GOOD ADVICE FROM A BLACK MAN
TO THE BLACKS OF THE STATE

The New York *Times* agreed: "Major Delany has proved himself a sincere and intelligent friend of his race by the advice he has given them on this matter, and we hope he will have the assistance of such enlightened colored men in his state as Mr. Elliott in the task he has undertaken. If the Negroes now having the power will base the government of South Carolina on the whole people, their capacity for public affairs will never be denied in the future."

By the summer of 1874 Delany's concern had changed to alarm. Reconstruction governments were under attack all over the South. In Louisiana, Alabama, Arkansas, blacks and whites were fighting pitched battles in the streets. Organizations calling themselves the "White League," the "Pale Faces," the "Knights of the White Camelia" had joined the Klan in a new reign of terror.

Speaking at a Republican meeting in Columbia, he told his listeners to expect bloodshed in South Carolina too, unless they mended their ways. Nor could they count on help from the federal government. "Don't be misled into believing that Grant, who is a white man, loves the black man better than he does his own race," he said. "A war between the races can only result in the extermination of the black race."

Delany felt that the solution was an alliance with the whites. "The black men of this state are dependent on the whites just as the whites are dependent on them. The black man and the white man must work together. By this mutual cooperation they can bring about the redemption of the state and prosperity and happiness for the whole people."

When the Republicans nominated Daniel Chamberlain, a

white New Englander who had been a member of Patterson's Railroad Ring for governor, Delany and others withdrew to form an Independent Republican Party. The backers of the new organization included black congressmen like Cain and Alonzo Ransier as well as conservative white men. At a convention held in Charleston in October, they chose as their candidate for governor Judge John T. Green, a native of South Carolina who had been mildly pro-Union during the war and mildly pro-Republican afterward. For lieutenant governor, they nominated Martin R. Delany.

Introduced as "the honest exemplar of the honest colored men of South Carolina," Delany's booming voice filled the hall as he pledged "all of the intelligence that I possess, all of the integrity of character to bring about between the two peoples in this state, black and white, those relations that shall tend to the promotion of each others' mutual welfare.

"I do not intend to lower my standard of manhood in regard to the claims of my race one single step. I do not intend to recede from the rights that have been given us by a just Congress one single hairsbreadth; but I do intend to demand the same equal rights and justice to every citizen, black and white, of the state of South Carolina. And upon this line I will fight it out if it takes all winter."

"The band then played the 'Wearing of the Green' and, for fully five minutes, the hall resounded with prolonged and deafening cheers," the News and Courier reported.

The platform of the Independent Republicans agreed plank for plank with that of the regular Republicans. Both supported the national Republican Party. Both promised reform, deprecated violence, and supported the Civil Rights Bill which Congress was then considering. Yet most of the Independent Republicans were Democrats. For six years the

Democratic Party had not been heard from in South Carolina. Realizing that black voters looked on it as the party of slavery, its members had withdrawn from active politics to join local Tax Unions and Honest Government Leagues.

"What we want is to get the State," a leading Democrat had written to a friend. "We can't get it under the name of Democracy, for the nigger has been taught to hate that as he does cold & we must spread our nets to get in all of the disaffected of the Republican Party, white and black."

Martin Delany, who prided himself on his political know-how, was caught in their net. Backed by the Tax Unions and Honest Government Leagues, he stumped the state with Judge Green. Avoiding the counties along the coast where black people had large majorities, they spent their time canvassing in the upcountry where the Klan was strong and whites had vowed that they would never vote for a "nigger." After Judge Green fell ill, Joseph Kershaw, a former Confederate general and South Carolina aristocrat, managed the campaign.

"Major Delany is doing gallant work in the Up Country. It is a surprise and gratification to the whites to hear wise, generous and statesmanlike words from the lips of a black man," the *News and Courier* reported. "Delany's speaking has had great effect on the old hard-shelled Democrats," General Kershaw wrote.

Judge Green died two months after the election. Had the Independent Republicans won, Martin Delany would have been governor of South Carolina. They lost, but the campaign succeeded in bringing out so many white voters that for the first time since Reconstruction began, whites had a small majority in the General Assembly. Delany had helped to win representation for the white minority. Whether his new friends would be equally zealous on behalf of the black majority remained to be seen.

24

THE SPIRIT OF '76

On a blustery night in March 1875 Martin Delany made his way along the snow-covered streets of New York to downtown Irving Hall. A group of eminent New Yorkers had invited him to lecture on "the present political issues of the South." It was ten years since he had last spoken in the city. Then, in his new uniform of Union blue, he had urged black men to fight the Rebels. Now he was addressing an audience of leading white citizens. William Cullen Bryant, white-bearded poet and editor of the New York *Evening Post,* was chairman of the meeting. Flanking him on the platform were Peter Cooper, the inventor, and other notables. Most of them were liberal Republicans.

The North was tired of the strife in the South. Four days

earlier Congress had passed a Civil Rights Bill that banned segregation on trains, in hotels, theaters, and restaurants. With this assurance that Negro rights would be protected, people hoped to forget Reconstruction and get on with business. The South must be brought back into the nation's economy.

Delany told his listeners what they wanted to hear. All of the trouble in the South had been caused by Northerners: "These men stood between the whites and the blacks, with their arms to the elbows in the black man's pocket, and to the armpit in the pocket of the white man—stealing from each." As if carried away by the applause and laughter which greeted this statement, he then described the generosity and courtesy of Southern whites to the freedmen and to him, personally.

"The white people of the South are waiting and willing to take the blacks by the hand and go with them in every measure tending to the common good of both. They don't wish them to lose their position, their manhood or their rights. I want the North to know that there is no animosity between the whites and blacks of the South." ("Cheers," the newspapers reported.)

It was a strange speech for the man about whom Frederick Douglass had once said, "I thank God for making me a man, but Delany always thanks Him for making him a *black man*." Had incorruptible Martin Delany been bought—not with money but with courtesy and kind words? The '74 campaign had brought him in contact with the "best men" of South Carolina. They were charming, these aristocrats of Charleston and the low-country plantations. He could not help admiring their soft cultivated speech and impeccable manners. Had their willingness to work with him, the son of a slave, made him forget his lifelong distrust of slaveowners?

On the train the next day as he headed for Xenia, Ohio, the New York newspapers assured him that he was on the right track. The *Tribune,* the most liberal newspaper in the city, praised him in an editorial: "The address of Major M. R. Delany at Irving Hall last night was notable as the thoughtful utterance of one of the ablest colored men in the South, and one of the few of his class who are in sympathy with the Conservative Party. Major Delany's review of the political situation in the South is worth careful perusal and it would be well if his words of warning to his own race could be heard by every colored voter in the country."

His arrival at Wilberforce called for a grand reunion. The *Tribune* reporter had described him as "about fifty years of age"—he was in fact sixty-two. Catherine, too, looked younger than her years. She had grown plump, but her hair was as shiny black as when she was a girl. She still lived in a rented cottage on the campus, supplementing her income with work as a seamstress. Called "Ma Delany" by the students, she nursed and mothered them as well as her own youngsters. Charlie had dropped out of school, but the others were making splendid progress. Alexander, teaching in a black school in near-by Urbana, came home to see his father. The only one missing was Toussaint who was working in Mississippi.

Returning to Charleston, Delany found Governor Chamberlain surprising everyone with a vigorous program of reform. He had slashed expenses and instituted a more equitable system of collecting taxes. Most reassuring of all to the whites was his order to the black militia in the upcountry to cease drilling and turn in their ammunition and arms.

By summer Charleston's business community and its spokesman, the *News and Courier,* were fulsome in their praise of Chamberlain's "bold and statesmanlike struggle."

When he dismissed incompetent political hacks and began to give jobs to capable men of both parties, Delany's new friends suggested that he apply for an appointment.

He was struggling as usual to make a living. He had resigned from the Customs job to enter the '74 campaign. Now he was trying his hand at general auctioneering. In addition, he had started a weekly newspaper, the Charleston *Independent,* to rally colored men to the standard of good government.

After more than two dozen Broad Street lawyers and businessmen petitioned Governor Chamberlain, Delany was appointed trial justice for Charleston's Third Ward. "Trial justice" was South Carolina's name for a local magistrate or justice of the peace. Sitting informally without a jury, he ruled on minor assault cases and breaches of the peace. A week after the appointment was made, the Charleston *Independent* carried an advertisement:

M. R. Delany
TRIAL JUSTICE
Ward Number 3
ANSON STREET
One door from Market
CIVIL CASES PARTICULARLY
ATTENDED TO
The Rights and Feelings of all persons however
humble, coming into this office, shall be
sacredly respected.

"Col. M. R. Delany, recently appointed trial justice, has inaugurated a happy change in the hitherto unsightly locations of these special Courts," the *News and Courier* said. "He has fitted up for his use an office in Anson St. above the

Market, which far surpasses those of his brother justices. These are six trim settees in the room, 2 chairs especially intended and labeled as 'Constables' Seats,' a long office table furnished with writing materials for the use of reporters and lawyers, besides the private table of the Justice. There is an inner room, suitably furnished, for private conferences. The walls are neatly papered and the whole office is creditable to its use."

In the months that followed the newspaper carried almost daily accounts of the Justice at work:

"W. H. Clagett, colored, was arraigned before Trial Justice Delany yesterday for threatening violence to his brother-in-law. He was put under a peace bond."

"Tobey Bailey, colored, was before the same Justice on the same cause, threatening violence to Jane Ladson. In this case it was thought advisable to discharge the prisoner on his own recognizance, with a few words of good counsel."

"Two young men were brought before the same Justice on a charge of forcible entry into a private residence while under the influence of liquor. They were each fined $4 and made to give bond in the sum of $200 to keep the peace."

"Henry Trebel was up before the same Justice on a charge of receiving goods under false pretenses. He was made to deliver the goods and pay the cost of court."

"John Slawson, colored, was brought before Trial Justice Delany yesterday on the charge of striking a boy named James White in the neighborhood of the artesian well. The evidence was not sufficient to warrant a conviction, so the prisoner was discharged."

"Mr. George F. Habenicht* was brought before Justice

---

* Only when a white man came to court did the *News and Courier* use the prefix "Mr." Even when writing about Martin Delany, the editors called him "Colonel," "Justice," or "Major," but never "Mr."

Delany charged with assaulting April Delany [no relation to Martin] with a deadly weapon. The prosecutor charged that Mr. Habenicht had run a pitchfork almost through his leg. The Justice after hearing both sides of the matter, bound the defendant over to the Court of Sessions under a $300 bond."

Justice Delany was enjoying himself hugely. He was playing "papa" as he had in his Freedmen's Bureau days. But in February 1876 he himself was arrested and brought to trial in the Court of Sessions. The charge was breach of trust and larceny. It was based on the affidavit of a black man who said that five years earlier Delany had taken $212 from the John Wesley Church on John's Island and had fraudulently appropriated the money for his own use.

Delany's version of the story was different. In 1871 when his real estate agency was also engaged in small-scale banking operations, the widow of a trustee of the John's Island church came to him for help. The trustees were quarreling over the church funds that her husband had in his possession at his death. She asked Delany to act as her business agent, holding the money until the quarrel was settled. Delany agreed to invest the money in county warrants, as he did other funds in his keeping.

Throughout South Carolina and in other states as well, municipal governments paid their employees with warrants— promises to pay as soon as sufficient taxes were collected to cover the payments. An employee who needed cash sold his warrant to a broker for less than its face value. When the claim was paid the broker made a profit.

Unfortunately, the claims were not always paid. The county warrants Delany bought proved to be worthless. He had made a bad investment and had lost the church's money. Although he later gave the trustees his note, promising to pay the $212 out of his own pocket, he had never been able to do so. To him $212 was an enormous sum of money. His salary as trial justice was also paid in state warrants that he had to redeem for less than their face value.

The story, an all-too-familiar one in South Carolina in the 1870s, would never have come to light if he had not broken with the Republicans in the '74 elections. Both the man who brought the charge and the prosecuting attorney were members of the state political machine. Although everyone recognized the political nature of the case, it did not ease the situation for Martin Delany.

During a day-long trial, the trustee's widow and other witnesses confirmed his testimony that he had not intended to defraud the church, while the prosecuting attorney "plied the rhetorical lash with vigor and bluster," the *News and Courier* reported. Calling Delany a swindler who stole from widows and church poor boxes, he demanded that he be sent to jail.

Even the judge, also a political appointee, was surprised by the vehemence of the prosecutor's attack. "Your argument to this jury is a most remarkable one," he commented, "considering the tameness with which you acted in that murder trial the other day."

The jury found Delany guilty of grand larceny and fraudulent breach of trust. Martin Delany convicted as a thief, publicly arraigned as a man who stole from a black church! A week later he returned to court to hear his sentence—twelve months in the state penitentiary.

He was paying a terrible price for being a political maverick. The price was so high that all sorts of people began to speak in his behalf. While his lawyer appealed the case to the state Supreme Court, friends lent him the $212 so that he could repay the church. They also petitioned Governor Chamberlain to pardon him.

"We the undersigned Colored Citizens of Charleston

County," one document read, "ask your Excellency's attention to the unfortunate situation of our friend, Brother and Companion, Col. M. R. Delany. M. R. Delany is dear to us, whatever may be his faults, and if we had the money we would willingly pay, *yes* a hundred times over, rather than seeing him go to the Penitentiary. M. R. Delany, Governor, happens to be one of the few of our Race of whom we are proud to claim. We trust you will soon relieve us of our painful anxiety by granting the pardon prayed for by your petitioners."

Their petition was followed by others. Charleston's mayor and chief of police and even the judge and prosecuting attorney asked that Delany be granted "a free and full pardon." The political scene was changing rapidly. For the first time in nine years, the Democratic Party was openly organizing. With the 1876 election approaching, both parties hoped to win Delany's support.

His lawyer, a white Charlestonian of impeccable background, traveled to Columbia to plead his case. But Governor Chamberlain, under pressure from all sides, was in no hurry to act. The summer of 1876 was an anxious time for Martin Delany, for Daniel Chamberlain—and for the whole country.

The United States was celebrating the hundredth anniversary of the Declaration of Independence. The centennial had a special significance in the South. The nation's founders had said, "All men are created equal." Had they meant *all men*— or *all white men?*

Mississippi had already answered the question. Eight months earlier a white minority had captured the state. Captured it literally by using cannons, muskets, squirrel rifles to kill the leaders of the black majority and to drive their followers from the polls on Election Day. After their victory, President Grant said: "Mississippi is governed today by officials chosen through fraud and violence such as would scarcely be accredited to savages, much less to a civilized and Christian people." However, he had made no attempt to stop the fraud and violence or to reverse the result afterward.

Cheered by the success of the Mississippi Plan, men calling themselves "Straightouts" (meaning "no compromise") were organizing in South Carolina. Their goal was to "redeem" the state for white supremacy.

July 4 was a hot humid day across the nation. In the North, government officials and ordinary citizens coverged on Philadelphia to listen to speeches in the old State House and to visit the Centennial Exposition. There, in pavilions in Fairmont Park, they saw the world of the future—Alexander Graham Bell's first telephone, a typewriter, a model of an oil well, a luxurious Pullman car.

In the South, men were still grappling with the world of the past. Since the war's end the Fourth of July had been exclusively the black people's holiday. They cheered the Declaration of Independence; whites saw little to cheer about. Charleston's blacks rose early that day. When the bells of St. Michael's tolled seven, the fire companies and militia men were already in the streets, forming their lines for the big parade. While bands played and flags waved, they marched to the Battery. There city dwellers were joined by boatloads of people from the islands. Hucksters moved through the crowd selling ice cream and lemonade as the speeches started.

Former Congressmen Cain and Ransier, in the style of all Fourth of July orators, praised the great document whose hundredth anniversary they were celebrating. When it was Delany's turn on the rostrum, he scolded his listeners.

"You're not the equals of the white race in many respects," he said. "Men never attain a higher grade of civilization than the women of their race. You will never become the whites' equal until you educate your children and honor and respect your women."

Essentially it was the same lecture he had given since the 1840s, but the reporter from the *News and Courier* had never heard it before. "Col. M. R. Delany made one of those sound, sensible speeches which have always made him so unpopular with his own race," he wrote. He concluded his description of the celebration with words of praise: "It is creditable to the colored people to state that although there was at various times over 10,000 of them on the Battery, there were very few cases of intoxication, and not a single disturbance of any kind."

The Fourth of July was less peaceful in other parts of South Carolina. In Hamburg, a village near the Georgia border, two white men drove their buggy into the midst of a black militia parade. When the militia refused to give way, the whites charged them with obstructing the highway. Four days later two thousand white men arrived in Hamburg to avenge themselves on the forty-man militia company. With cannon brought from Georgia, they killed seven men and drove hundreds more from their homes.

The Hamburg riot was the first pitched battle in the "war of '76." Benjamin Tillman, a leader of the Straightouts, who later became governor, said Hamburg was "like a fire bell in the night." He called on whites "to make one desperate fight to gain their lost liberties." At the suggestion of his brother, the "bloody shirt" became their symbol of defiance.

All during the long hot summer, red-shirted men organized Rifle and Sabre Clubs. Village streets echoed with the sounds of tramping feet. Men on horseback patrolled the roads at night, as they had done during the days of slavery.

Their first targets were the white Republicans who were "respectfully and cordially" invited to join the Democrats.

If a man refused the invitation, night visitors applied sterner measures. Those who survived hastened to switch their allegiance.

Blacks were threatened with economic reprisals as well as whips and guns. In the upcountry, planters drove their laborers from their homes unless they promised to forego voting. "Browbeat and belittle them at all times and in all places," a newspaper suggested.

Martin Delany saw his worst fears coming true. Reconstruction was going to end in a bloodbath unless some sort of compromise could be made.

On August 30 he received the long-awaited pardon from Governor Chamberlain. Writing to thank him "for great and beneficent favors," he volunteered to work for his nomination at the forthcoming Republican convention. Chamberlain was renominated for governor, but Martin Delany shocked his friends and confounded his enemies by announcing his support for General Wade Hampton, the Democratic candidate.

A wealthy slaveowner before the war, Hampton was a Confederate war hero and a Charleston gentleman. Unlike the upcountry Red Shirts who bristled with hatred for blacks, Hampton promised to maintain Negro rights if elected. Privately he had assured his backers, "We can control the black vote."

Here was the compromise Delany had been looking for. No matter that the Democratic ticket, from governor to dogcatcher, was white. He had warned that blacks must be prepared to share their power. It was better to give a little now than to lose everything.

In a long letter to the *News and Courier,* he detailed the reasons for his about-face. Watching "the two races in hostile array" throughout the state, he predicted "political nonentity and race extermination" for his people.

"Shall it be said that at such a crisis the blacks had no statesmen, no men of diplomatic wisdom equal to the demands of the hour? When my race were in bondage, I did not hesitate in using my judgment in aiding to free them. Now that they are free I shall not hesitate in using that judgment in aiding to preserve that freedom.

"I have but one line of duty left me, and that is to aid that effort which best tends to bring about *a union of the two races, white and black, in one common interest in the state.* The present Democratic movement promises this, and asks us, the blacks, simply to try them once; if they do not fulfill their promises, to trust them no more."

He quoted General Hampton's pledge: "We recognize the 13th, 14th and 15th amendments of the Constitution. Not one single right enjoyed by the colored people today shall be taken from them. They shall be the equals, under the law, of any man in South Carolina. And we further pledge that we will give better facilities for education than they have ever had before."

"These are, indeed, most definite, strong, impressive and extraordinary words, and must have been candidly meant, or they never would have been spoken," Delany's letter continued. "I shall hold Gen. Hampton on behalf of my race, before the civilized world, responsible for them.

"Since the Carolinians of the white race did not hesitate to take me at my word and honor me with their support in 1874, I shall not now hesitate to take them at their word, by supporting the State movement and voting the State Democratic ticket for the good of all the people of both races."

Martin Delany was the Democrats' prize catch. South Carolina's population consisted of 415,000 black people and 289,000 whites. The Democrats could not win the election unless they convinced blacks to join them—or forcibly kept them from voting.

In most of the state they chose the latter alternative. The Straightout battle plan, borrowed from Mississippi said: "Every Democrat must feel honor bound to control the vote of at least one Negro, by intimidation, purchase, keeping him away. Never threaten a man individually. If he deserves to be threatened, the necessities of the time require that he should die."

In the upcountry, a thousand grim Red Shirts appeared at a Republican rally, cocking their pistols noisily as the speakers talked. Democratic candidates were escorted from town to town by squadrons of mounted men. After a riot in Ellenton in which thirty-nine blacks and two whites were killed, President Grant declared that a state of insurrection existed in parts of South Carolina. Sending federal troops to the state, he ordered the Rifle Clubs to disband. They disbanded, only to reappear under new names—the Mounted Baseball Club, the Hampton and Tilden Musical Club, Mother's Little Helpers, the First Baptist Sewing Circle—and the bulldozing continued.

The Red Shirts did not try these tactics in the low country where most of the people were black and the black militia was still strong. Here was where Martin Delany was needed. As the only black man of stature to support the Democrats, his job was to persuade his people to vote for Hampton.

It was a tough assignment. Speaking in Charleston where a Colored Democratic Club had been formed, he reminded his hearers that the abolition of slavery had been brought about by the teachings of such Democrats as Thomas Jefferson. "General Hampton and his followers are the first men to restore the principles of Jeffersonian Democracy in South

Carolina. They have made pledges and promises that they would not dare fail to carry out. When a Democrat gives his word, you may trust him," he assured the audience.

Such arguments were useless when he spoke on the Sea Islands. To the islanders, Democrats meant slaveowners, and they would have no part of them. In mid-October, Delany traveled to Edisto Island with a group of Democrat and Republican politicians. As was customary, they were to speak at the same rally, dividing the time. The six hundred people who had gathered at the camp ground listened more or less patiently until Delany climbed onto the wagon that served as a platform.

As if on signal, the audience rose. Members of the band beat their drums to drown out his words while people shouted, "We won't listen to the damned nigger Democrat." The women were the angriest. They crowded around him, shaking their fists, cursing and threatening. A half hour passed before the chairman, a white Republican, was able to restore order.

Tears were close to the surface as Delany looked down at the angry faces of the crowd. Refusing to give the speech he had prepared, he said, "I've been in Europe and Africa. Black as I am, I have never been as insulted as I have today by you, my own people. I'm not your enemy. I came to South Carolina to fight for the freedom of the black man. I'm here today to give you a warning. The Northern white people are altogether in sympathy with the Southern whites." After begging them to see that their only hope lay with the white natives of the state, he climbed down from the wagon.

Two days later he ventured out of Charleston again. The Democrats had chartered a steamer to take them up-river to the village of Cainhoy. The speakers were accompanied by more than a hundred men from the Palmetto and Butler Guards, two of Charleston's Rifle Clubs. Their presence was

intended to impress black audiences with a show of Democratic strength.

The meeting started off peacefully. The band that the Democrats had brought along played patriotic airs. Then a black man walked up to the speakers' stand. Although he was a Republican, the people of Cainhoy mistook him for Martin Delany. A row started. Before anyone realized what was happening, somebody fired a gun.

Both Democrats and Republicans had agreed to leave their weapons at home. Neither side had kept its promise. But the blacks had brought muskets, while the whites had only pistols to protect themselves with.

The audience scattered quickly. A group of whites took refuge in a deserted brick building near by. Martin Delany went with them. Crouching on the floor with his white companions, he watched black men take aim and fire through the windows. They were trying to kill *him*—the fiery abolitionist, the black Major, who had devoted a lifetime to their cause.

What had gone wrong?

Somehow, the Democrats managed to escape and make their way back to the boat landing. During the fighting, six white men and one black lost their lives. The Cainhoy Massacre, as the newspapers called it,* marked one of the few occasions in the bloody centennial year of '76 when more whites than blacks were killed. Martin Delany could take small comfort from the statistic.

He spent the last weeks of the campaign traveling in the "safe" counties of the state with a team of Democratic speakers. "We are getting the darkey splendidly in hand,"

---

* South Carolina historians always refer to the Hamburg and Ellenton *Riots* and the Cainhoy *Massacre*.

General Hampton's principal advisor, General James Conner, wrote to his wife.

"Vote early and often"—the word went out from the headquarters of both parties on Election Day. "The election was one of the greatest farces ever seen," a white Democrat reported. "In counties where the Negroes had terrorized affairs, streams of colored Republicans poured from poll to poll, voting everywhere. In counties terrorized by the whites, white bravoes rode from poll to poll, and voted time and again.

"Hundreds of Georgians and North Carolinians crossed the borders and joined in the work. In Edgefield County the influx of Georgians and the repeating were simply tremendous. The total of voters in that country is 7122, and the county has always gone Republican by one thousand votes; yet, although a thousand Negroes certainly were induced by money or fear of starvation to refrain from voting, the total number of votes cast was 9289 and the Democrats carried the county by the astounding majority of 3225!"

Who had won? No one can yet say positively. The one sure thing is that the black people lost.

More was at stake than the government of South Carolina. For the first time since 1865 the Republican Party was threatened with defeat in a national election. On the day after the voting, Samuel Tilden, Democratic candidate for President appeared to have beaten Republican Rutherford B. Hayes. But Tilden was one vote shy of the majority needed in the Electoral College.

Both parties claimed victory in South Carolina, Louisiana, and Florida. If their electoral votes went to Hayes, as the Republicans said they should, then he would become the President of the United States.

For three confusing months the Presidency was in dispute.

For five months South Carolina had two governors. Governor Chamberlain was inaugurated on December 7, Governor Hampton a week later. The Republican legislature met in the State House with federal troops standing guard. The Democrats convened in Carolina Hall while Red Shirt regiments surrounded the building.

At last the controversy was settled. In a smoke-filled hotel parlor in Washington, northern Republicans and southern Democrats agreed to the most infamous horse-trade in the history of the United States. Hayes was to become President in exchange for "home rule" in South Carolina and Louisiana. As spelled out in a memorandum written by Hayes's backers to the southerners, "home rule" meant "a policy as will give to the people of the states of South Carolina and Louisiana the right to control their own affairs in their own way."

After eight years of Reconstruction, *people* once again meant *white people*. The "incredible, hopeful experiment" was over.

On April 10, 1877, President Hayes announced the withdrawal of federal troops from South Carolina. The next day, Chamberlain turned over the office of governor to Wade Hampton.

Martin Delany had been right when he warned that Northern sympathies were with the whites of the South. But he would soon find that he had been wrong—tragically wrong—to accept the word of the gentlemen of South Carolina.

Across the state in the capital at
Columbia, the Governor and nearly
every legislator had deplored the attack
on black children by 200 men armed
with ax handles, heavy chain links,
screw drivers sharpened to a point and
bricks. But in the courthouse in
Darlington the defendants were
strongly defended by their neighbors.

"Ain't gonna find 12 white men in
this country who'd convict those
fellows," said Tom Smith, a cotton and
tobacco farmer . . .

"Amen," said a younger man. "My
idea of a good nigger is Martin Luther
King." He and the others in his knot
of friends laughed.

Dr. King was assassinated by a
sniper in 1968.

—*New York* Times, *March 6, 1970*

25

TWILIGHT YEARS

"Since the election we have been turned out of house and
home. The Democrats have refused to hire or sell to us and
we are now in a starving condition. They say that they will not
give us any land to work, neither any place to stay because
we voted the Republican ticket. We therefore petition to you
for help," black farm workers in Barnwell County wrote
Daniel Chamberlain on Christmas Day, 1876.

All during the winter and spring of 1877, refugees from

the upcountry streamed into Charleston and Beaufort. From the window of his office on King Street, Martin Delaney could see clusters of men, women, small children standing on the street corners. Ragged and penniless, they had been driven from their homes because of their political views.

Wade Hampton had appointed Delany a trial justice soon after he became governor. Once again Delany had fitted out an office and was engaged in settling disputes, giving advice, collecting fines. To an English visitor who was touring the South he reiterated his support of Hampton. The governor, he said "appoints black men when they really are educated and fit."

Martin Delany was whistling in the dark. He knew his own days in office were numbered. Already the members of the Democratic machine in the city were clamoring for his removal. It was only a question of time before Hampton would give in to them. And aside from his own personal fortunes, the fabric of life for black people in South Carolina was changing.

With the defeat of the Republicans, Democrats ceased to woo black voters. Charleston's Democratic clubs admitted only those who had voted for Hampton in '76. Edgefield County, birthplace of the Straightouters, barred all blacks from Democratic primaries. In little more than a decade, black voting would virtually cease and the *News and Courier* would headline an election story: WHITE MEN CHEAT WHITE MEN IN SOUTH CAROLINA.

As part of its economy drive, the legislature had slashed school appropriations. There was a growing feeling that black children should receive less than their share of school funds on the theory that "to educate a Negro is to spoil a laborer." The University of South Carolina, which had been integrated, now closed its doors. When it reopened, it would no longer accept black students or professors.

Life was hardest for the black sharecroppers and farm laborers. "We have no chance to rise from beggars," a young man from the upcountry complained. "Men own the capital that we work who believe that my race have no more right to any of the profits of their labor than one of their mules. The majority of colored men who work with the heartless Democrats, get just about what the mule gets of the profits of labor. *My God,* the masses of our people, just behind the veil are piteous."

In the winter of 1877 Richard Cain wrote to William Coppinger of the American Colonization Society, to ask when the society planned to send a ship to Liberia. Since emancipation, the attitude of blacks toward the Colonization Society had changed. Many now looked on it as a philanthropic organization—an "African repatriation society"—that would help them return to the land of their fathers. As secretary of the society, Coppinger corresponded with blacks from all parts of the United States.

"There are thousands who are willing and ready to leave South Carolina, Georgia, Florida, and North Carolina but are not able to pay their way," Cain wrote. "The Colored people of the South are tired of the constant struggle for life and liberty and prefer going where no obstacles are in the way of enjoying their liberty."

"You can hear nearly every family crying *Liberia,*" another South Carolinian wrote Coppinger in the spring. "If a ship could be started from Charleston or Beaufort about next January, it would not be able to carry the fifth man that would be ready."

By summer an exodus movement was under way all over the South. Sharecroppers left the plantations of Mississippi and Louisiana to look for land in Kansas and Arkansas. In the coastal states black people who had once dreamed of owning forty acres, ten acres, one acre of American soil looked across the Atlantic Ocean to Africa.

At a rally to celebrate Liberian Independence Day Charleston's black people formed a Liberian Exodus Joint Stock Steamship Company. While the *Missionary Record* ran a standing headline, HO FOR AFRICA! ONE MILLION MEN WANTED FOR AFRICA, the company sold stock at $10 a share. In less than six months it had raised $6000 for the purchase of a ship.

In March 1878 the bark *Azor* sailed from Boston to tie up at Charleston's Atlantic Wharf. Thousands came from the Sea Islands and from Georgia and Florida to see the trim three-masted sailing vessel that their contributions had bought. "The pier at which the *Azor* is lying is covered from morning until night with men, women and children and the little office of the Exodus Association in Exchange St. is made a general rendezvous where the emigrants and their friends daily congregate and talk over their plans, hopes, fears and anticipations," the *News and Courier* reported.

Martin Delany had remained aloof from the movement at its beginning. Not everyone had forgiven him for his support of the Democrats and, on his part, he was not sure that he approved of the young men heading the Exodus Company. But inevitably they came to him for advice and inevitably he gave it. After all, who else in Charleston had actually *been* in Liberia?

The *Azor* was consecrated at a special religious ceremony at White Point Garden. After Delany accepted a Liberian flag made by the ladies of St. Joseph's Union, the Reverend Henry M. Turner, black vice-president of the Colonization Society, explained the ship's mission. It "was not only to bear a load of humanity but to take back the culture, education and religion acquired here" to the continent of Africa.

On April 21, 1878, black Charleston said bon voyage to the *Azor*. From the deck of an excursion steamer in the harbor, Martin watched the "African *Mayflower*" put out to sea. A spanking wind filled her sails, carrying her past the blackened ruins of Fort Sumter. From across the water he could hear the emigrants singing:

> I am bound for the promised land,
> I am bound for the promised land,
> O who will come and go with me?
> I am bound for the promised land.

The *Azor* was scheduled to reach Liberia in twenty-five days. While the emigrants settled on land purchased by the Exodus Company, the captain was to return with a cargo of African goods. The company hoped to realize enough from the sale of this freight to finance a second trip and, eventually, to establish regular sailings between Charleston and Liberia.

After its auspicious start, misfortune dogged the venture. Slowed down by gales and then becalmed, the *Azor* was forced to put in at Sierra Leone at the end of May when its supply of water gave out. From there a British steamer towed it to Liberia. When the captain, unaccountably, returned to Charleston with an empty ship, the Exodus Company was faced with bills of $1680 for supplies and towage and no money to pay them.

Asked to head a Committee on Finance, Delany took charge of the fight to save the *Azor*. He wrote to the president of the American Colonization Society "to enquire whether or not there is to be found among the liberal contributors to the Colonization Movement some one or more gentlemen who would loan us that amount for four months, which would bring us to the midst of our harvest season, when moneys will be coming in plentifully on the sale of stocks. We solicit no money or donations as our movement is intended to be self-sustaining in order to make our people self-reliant. Among the whites here we have no friends to the movement who would aid us by loan, but would rather contribute to prevent success."

His estimate of "the whites here" proved prophetic. With loans from the North and the sale of stock to blacks in the South, the *Azor* was able to go to England on a trading trip. Once again the captain returned with his hold empty and his ledgers loaded with debts. Not until he sued for back pay did Delany realize that the captain had been deliberately pushing the Exodus Company toward bankruptcy in order to secure the ship for himself.

Broadsides headed SAVE OUR SHIP THE AZOR! called people to a mass meeting. More stock was sold, more money borrowed. But it was not enough. On November 8, 1879, the *Azor* was sold at auction. A Charleston merchant bought the ship for half of its original price, with the written understanding that he would sell it back to the Exodus Company if they could raise the money within a year.

Dollar after dollar, they collected the money. But when they went to reclaim their ship, the merchant coolly informed them that the *Azor* was sold. In violation of his contract, he had turned it over to a Boston firm five months earlier.

The black people of South Carolina had invested more than $17,000, along with untold hopes and dreams, in the *Azor*. Now it was gone. A lawsuit dragged through the courts— "But I have no hopes of success, as he has plenty of means and we have none," Delany wrote to William Coppinger. "The transaction has surprised everybody, as this merchant is very wealthy, was commended as being very reliable, and generally reputed to be a gentleman of unswerving integrity."

While struggling to save the *Azor*, Martin Delany had lost his position as trial justice. When Democrats first demanded his removal, a number of white Charlestonians, including the editor of the *News and Courier*, had asked Hampton to keep him on.

"Maj. M. R. Delany is a man of coolness, deliberateness and broad experience, which enabled him to differ widely with many persons of his own race and party and especially with the extravagant and ultra men," they wrote to the governor.

"The colored people are moving in behalf of Delany," General Conner advised Hampton on the same day. "The latter was very much ostracized when he became a Hampton Democrat but the 'panning out' has led the brethren to think that Delany's head was black on top, and they have come back to him so that unless there is good reasons for removal, it would not be politic."

Delany had remained in office until after the election of 1878 when Hampton became a senator. "I lost as soon as they got rid of him by sending him to the U. S. Senate, as he was too liberal for the rank and file of the party leaders," he said.

During his last months as trial justice, Delany had been working on a new book. Putting aside his history of Afro-Americans, he had joined the controversy over Charles Darwin's *Origin of Species*. Darwin's theory, in contradiction to the biblical account of Creation, said that mankind had evolved over a very long period of time from lower species of animals. Most Americans—and Englishmen too—denounced Darwin as an atheist and his book as "an attempt to dethrone God." Even prominent scientists like Louis Agassiz of Harvard ridiculed *Origin of Species* because, he said, "Mr. Darwin affirms the monkey is his brother."

However, some men were quick to seize on Darwin's work to support their belief in inferior and superior races. As long as everyone was descended from Adam and Eve, all men were brothers. But if Darwin were right, it would be easy to say that dark-skinned peoples were at a lower stage of evolution than whites. Perhaps the "struggle for existence" and the "survival of the fittest" which Darwin had observed in the world of plants and animals could be applied to mankind as well. This "Social Darwinism," which "proved" the superiority of the white race, became a popular theme among social scientists during the next half century. Martin Delany was the first man to attempt to refute it.

Pulling together a lifetime of reading and observation he wrote his own account of the origin of races. He disposed of Darwin's theory very simply—by denying it. Quoting the Bible—"And the Lord said, Behold the people is one"—he dated the separation of the races to the period after the Flood when "the Lord scattered them abroad." Most of his book was devoted to following the descendants of Ham as they settled first in Egypt and Ethiopia and then populated all of Africa. From Egyptian sculpture and hieroglyphics and the alphabet of Ethiopia he demonstrated that the "builders of the pyramids, sculptors of the sphinxes, and original god-kings, were blacks of the Negro race." Thus all contemporary civilization stemmed from the black people of antiquity.

In his final chapters he asked: "How do the Africans of the present day compare in morals and social policy with those of ancient times? We answer, that those south of the Sahara, uncontaminated by influences of the coast, especially the Yorubas, are equal in susceptibility and moral integrity to the ancient Africans. Untrammeled in its native purity, the race is a noble one."

The book was an ingenious blend of biblical history, amateur archaeology, and anthropology. Much of it was incorrect by modern standards of scholarship, but it was persuasive in its day. Sending the manuscript to Dr. William Elder, his boyhood advisor, Delany asked for an opinion, adding, "One friend, a professor of a college, writes me, 'I am glad to see the time when a colored person can capture the sciences, and appropriate them to the endowment of his own will.' And this I know to be your feelings. I desire to dare do, what white men have ever dared and done."

Perhaps on Elder's recommendation, the manuscript was published by Harper & Brothers, a printing firm in Philadelphia. Issued in 1879, the book's title page read: "PRINCIPIA OF ETHNOLOGY: THE ORIGIN OF RACES AND COLOR, With an Archaeological Compendium of Ethiopian and Egyptian Civilization from Years of Careful Examination and Enquiry by Martin R. Delany."

But scholarly books did not buy groceries for their authors. After his dismissal as trial justice, Major Delany became Dr. Delany again. Sending to Ohio for his medical books and instruments, he opened a dispensary on Cannon Street. "I am at my old profession of Medicine," he wrote to William Coppinger, "as the best I can do for the present." The "best" was not very good. Medicine had made great strides in recent decades. Men like Louis Pasteur and Robert Koch were discovering the cause of diseases. Although Delany tried to catch up with the new research, his heart was not in medicine any more.

Then, for a few dark weeks, his heart was not in anything. In the summer of 1879, his sons Charles and St. Cyprian had come south looking for jobs. St. Cyprian found work as a postman in Charleston, but Charles went on to Savannah. A week before Christmas a telegram was delivered to Dr. Delany's office. Charles Lenox Remond Delany was dead. While boating with friends on the Savannah River, he had drowned.

Long after the dreary funeral rites were over, Delany was despondent. Charles' death, his meager medical practice, the increasing oppression of black people in the South all contributed to his somber mood. By the summer of 1880 he had made up his mind to leave South Carolina. He had given the American way a good hard try. Now it was time to return to his old love—Africa.

"I am bound for Africa," he wrote to William Coppinger. "My course has been laid out, and my work all fixed and clear before me. If I could get some one of the government favors worth from $2000 to $3000 a year for about two years, this would give me means sufficient to leave my family and children at school and go at once to Africa, the field of my destined labor."

Faustin had graduated from Wilberforce and was teaching mathematics at Lincoln University in Missouri. If he could keep Placido and Ethiopia in school until they finished their studies, then perhaps the whole family would join him in Lagos or Liberia.

"Could I get an appointment such as Superintendent of the Freedmen's Hospital which I suppose pays a reasonable good salary?" he asked Coppinger in one letter. "I should like to obtain the office of Door Keeper of the U. S. Senate," he confided in another.

After the election of 1880, Delany set off for Washington to make the round of government offices. With printed copies of his army record, he called on senators and congressmen. At the State Department he applied for a post as consul to one of the South American countries. At the Treasury he asked for work as a special agent or inspector.

For a while he was hopeful. The Republicans were still giving jobs to black men. After leaving South Carolina both Robert Brown Elliott and Francis Cardozo had found work in the Treasury Department. Frederick Douglass had served as U.S. marshal for the District of Columbia and was now Recorder of Deeds for the District. John M. Langston was minister to Haiti and Henry Highland Garnet had just been appointed to the post of minister to Liberia.

Surely there must be a place for him after his decades of service in the antislavery movement, his years in the army and Freedmen's Bureau. But Delany, away from the national scene, had never managed to play the game. His support of Hampton in '76 was still fresh in politicians' memories. And who recalled the abolitionists' struggles? Who remembered the black Major?

One man did. During his visits to Washington, Delany always stayed at Mrs. Bruce's boardinghouse on Capitol Hill. Her son, John E. Bruce, had been the small boy who went to the Garnets' to meet the black Major. Now a newspaperman, he had not forgotten his boyhood hero. "Martin Delany is decidedly the blackest, jolliest and most brilliant Negro I have ever seen or known," Bruce wrote in 1882. Although Delany had aged "he was still a fighter. He still had the look and voice of command and he bore himself with the old time dignity of other days."

Determined to help, Bruce found him work as a speaker at the campaign headquarters of Congressman John F. Dezendorf. A white Republican and former abolitionist, Dezendorf was running for re-election in a district in Virginia that had a large black population. With something of his old vigor, Delany spoke at meetings in Norfolk. But after a week on the campaign trail, he realized with a stab of fear that he could not keep to the strenuous schedule planned for him. His legs began to tremble after an hour on the platform. And even his voice, the booming voice that had echoed like thunder in so many meeting halls for so many years, was giving way. He had finished one speech in a hoarse whisper while the audience shouted, "Louder! Can't hear you!"

Frightened and humiliated, he withdrew from the campaign. He was seventy years old and the world was in the hands of younger men. During the next year he shuttled back and forth from Washington to Wilberforce to Boston and New York. He was going to Africa as soon as his youngest children finished school. He was going to Africa as soon as he earned the money for passage. There was still that lot in Lagos . . .

For a few happy hours on January 1, 1883, he met with old friends at a banquet in Washington that celebrated the twentieth anniversary of the Emancipation Proclamation. How many faces were missing! William Nell and John Jones were dead. Garnet had died the year before in Liberia and James T. Holly was in Haiti, a bishop of the Protestant Episcopal Church.

After dinner, speakers proposed toasts to the past—to John Brown, William Lloyd Garrison, the Underground Railroad. Then, to the present: "The Colored Man in the South," "The Republican Party." When it was Martin Delany's turn he offered a toast to his future: "The Republic of Liberia."

But he would never see the shores of Africa again. He lived for two more joyless years while the Supreme Court declared the Civil Rights Act of 1875 unconstitutional and the Democratic Party returned to power in Washington. The Court's decision put a final period to the "incredible, hopeful experiment" of Reconstruction and paved the way for a monstrous growth of Jim Crow laws. Three more generations of black Americans were to be condemned to unequal schooling, segregated housing, second-class citizenship from the cradle to the grave.

In the spring of 1884 a Boston firm hired Martin Delany to act as its agent in Central America. He was getting ready to leave the country when he fell ill. At the end of the year he returned to Wilberforce, to Catherine, to the home that had never been his home. He died there on January 24, 1885. After a funeral service in the college chapel, a detachment of Civil War veterans led the procession to the cemetery while a bugler played "Taps."

ACKNOWLEDGMENTS

In spite of the new interest in Black History, researching the story of a nineteenth-century black man still calls for endless digging and detective work. No library has preserved Martin Delany's letters or the files of his newspapers. The historical societies of West Virginia and western Pennsylvania where he lived for more than half of his life are barely aware of his existence. Nor have I been able to locate any Delany descendants, although I have followed innumerable false trails.

This book could not have been completed in the two and a half years it has taken, had it not been for a fortunate encounter with Victor and Louise Ullman. Ullman, journalist and author of *Look to the North Star; A Life of William King*, was also embarking on a biography of Martin Delany. In an arrangement that proved to be personally gratifying as well as productive, we decided to pool our research. I got the best of the bargain. For while I hunted through archives in New York, Boston, and Washington, the Ullmans ranged from Canada to South Carolina, with stopovers in Pittsburgh, Charles Town, and Wilberforce. Louise Ullman, a former librarian, painstakingly deciphered hundreds of pages of handwritten letters and memoranda, as well as articles from old newspapers, and sent me her impeccably typed transcriptions of them. I am deeply in their debt. Victor Ullman's excellent biographical study, *Martin R. Delany: The Beginnings of Black Nationalism,* is published by Beacon Press.

The Ullmans and I were halfway through our research when we were joined by Floyd John Miller. He was then a graduate student in history at the University of Minnesota and was preparing a doctoral dissertation on Martin Delany. In addition to sharing with us a number of letters and newspaper stories by and about Delany, he made an important discovery—the almost-complete text of *Blake,* Delany's novel, which until then had been thought to exist only as a fragment.

Deborah Moore, graduate student in history at Columbia University, turned up several references to Martin Delany when she was working on a master's thesis on Robert Smalls and helped me to learn the fate of San Juan del Norte. Gail Petersen did a thorough study of British newspaper accounts of the Delany-Lord Brougham-George M. Dallas confrontation described in Chapter 19. Dr. Nelson Fausto of Brown University supplied me with information on early nineteenth-century medicine and medical education. For their help, many thanks.

No one can work for long in the field of Black History without being deeply indebted to Jean Hutson and Ernest Kaiser of the Schomburg Collection in New York, to Dorothy Porter of the Moorland-Spingarn Collection at Howard University, and to Sara Jackson of the War Records Office of the National Archives. Other librarians and archivists who have been helpful include Richard J. Wolfe at the Harvard Medical Library, Rachel Tanner of Wilberforce University, R. N. Olsberg of the South Carolina Department of Archives and History, James L. Hupp of the West Virginia Department of Archives and History, Florence Kempter of the Coyle Free Library in Chambersburg, Pennsylvania, and Joanne Kinstman of Old Charles Town Library, Charles Town, West Virginia.

I am deeply grateful to Lila Whipper who permitted me to read the diary kept by her grandmother Frances Rollin Whipper while she was writing the *Life and Public Services of Martin Delany*. I would also like to express my gratitude to Dr. Benjamin Quarles of Morgan State College, Middleton Harris of Negro History Associates, Boyd Stutler and Richard K. MacMaster for helpful suggestions, and above all to Philip Sterling for his perceptive reading and editing of the final draft of my manuscript.

And to all the Delanys who went through family records only to establish that they were *not* descendants of Martin Delany, my hearty appreciation!

Note to Readers

Martin Delany and most of his contemporaries wrote in elaborate sentences and complicated paragraphs, a style characteristic of much nineteenth-century rhetoric. To make their speeches and writings more readable I have taken the liberty of cutting unnecessary passages without always indicating the cuts with the conventional ellipses. In all cases, however, the accuracy and the emphasis of what they intended to say has been preserved.

D.S.

BIBLIOGRAPHY

The most important source of information for this biography of Martin Delany is the *Life and Public Services of Martin R. Delany* by Frank A. Rollin, a pseudonym for Frances Rollin Whipper. Published in Boston in 1868, it was written in close collaboration with its subject. In spite of this—or perhaps because of it—it must be read cautiously. Martin Delany, in 1868, was riding a wave of optimism about black men's chances in the United States. When he told the story of his life to Frances Rollin Whipper, he barely mentioned the years when he had seen no future at all for black Americans and had urged them to emigrate to Africa or Central America. He gave scant notice to his most important book, *The Condition, Elevation, Emigration, and Destiny of the Colored People of the United States,* neglected to tell about his dismissal from Harvard Medical School, and gave an account of the John Brown convention in Chatham that is strangely at variance with all other firsthand accounts of the gathering.

These omissions and deviations, plus several erroneous dates, have been perpetuated in all of the brief biographical notes on Delany written after Mrs. Whipper's book. To correct them and to round out the story of Martin Delany's life, I have consulted the following sources:

Books and Pamphlets by Martin Robison Delany

Blake; or The Huts of America. Published as a serial in *The Anglo-African Magazine* Jan.–July, 1859, and in the *Weekly Anglo-African*, Nov. 23, 1861–Apr., 1862. Reprinted in 1970 by Beacon Press, with an introduction by Floyd J. Miller.

The Condition, Elevation, Emigration, and Destiny of the Colored People of the United States. Philadelphia, 1852. Reprinted in 1968 by Arno Press, with an introduction by Benjamin Quarles.

Eulogy on the Life and Character of the Rev. Fayette Davis. Pittsburgh, 1847.

Introduction to *Four Months in Liberia* by William Nesbit. Pittsburgh, 1855.

Homes for the Freedmen. Charleston, 1871.

Official Report of the Niger Valley Exploring Party. Thomas Hamilton, New York, 1861. Reprinted in *Search for a Place: Black Separatism and Africa, 1860* by University of Michigan Press, 1969, with an introduction by Howard H. Bell.

The Origin and Objects of Ancient Freemasonry: Its Introduction into the United States and Legitimacy among Colored Men. Pittsburgh, 1853.

Political Destiny of the Colored Race on the American Continent in *Proceedings of the National Emigration Convention of Colored People Held at Cleveland Ohio the 24th, 25th and 26th of August, 1854.* Pittsburgh, 1854.

Principia of Ethnology: The Origin of Races and Color with an Archaeological Compendium of Ethiopian and Egyptian Civilization. Harper, 1879.

A Series of Four Tracts on National Polity: The Freedmen. Republican Book and Job Office, Charleston, 1870.

Charles Town Years

Ambler, Charles H. *West Virginia, the Mountain State*. Prentice-Hall, 1958.

Bushong, Millard K. *A History of Jefferson County, West Virginia*. Jefferson Publishing Co., 1941.

Carroll, John, and Mary W. Ashworth. *George Washington*, Vol. VII. Scribner, 1957.

Davis, Julia. *The Shenandoah*. Farrar and Rinehart, 1945.

Dolan, J. R. *The Yankee Peddlers of Early America*. Bramhall House, 1964.

Frazier, E. F. *The Free Negro Family*. Fisk University Press, 1932.

Jackson, Luther P. *Free Negro Labor and Propertyholding in Virginia*. Appleton-Century, 1942.

Jefferson County Historical Society. *Magazine of the Jefferson County Historical Society*, 1934–66.

Russell, John H. *The Free Negro in Virginia*. Johns Hopkins Press, 1913.

Sheeler, John Reuben. "The Spirit of Freedom in Western Virginia," in *West Virginia History*, July 1956.

Thane, Elswyth. *Potomac Squire*. Duell, Sloan and Pearce, 1963.

U. S. Census, Jefferson County, Virginia, 1810, 1820.

Wright, Richardson. *Hawkers and Walkers of Early America*. Lippincott, 1934.

Writers Program of WPA. *The Negro in Virginia*. Hastings House, 1940, *West Virginia*. Oxford University Press, 1941.

Chambersburg Years

Bates, S. P. *History of Franklin County*. Chicago, 1887.

Cooper, John M. *Recollections of Chambersburg, Pa.* Chambersburg, 1900.

Foley, M. A. *A Brief History of the Town of Chambersburg*. Chambersburg, 1877.

BIBLIOGRAPHY 335

Jefferson, Thomas. *The Life and Selected Writings*. Modern Library, 1944.

Hutton, A. J. White. *History of Chambersburg*. Chambersburg, 1930.

McCauley, I. H. *Historical Sketch of Franklin County, Pa.* Pomeroy, 1898.

Wingerd, Edmund. *History of Chambersburg*. Compiled by order of Borough Council, unpublished, 1931.

Woodson, Carter. *Free Negro Heads of Families in the United States in 1830*. Association for the Study of Negro Life and History, 1925.

SCHOOLBOOKS

Dwight, Nathaniel. *A Short But Comprehensive System of the Geography of the World*. Northampton, Mass., 1805.

Morse, Jedidiah. *Elements of Geography*. Boston, 1804.

Olney, J. A. *A Practical System of Modern Geography*. Hartford, 1830.

Smith, Roswell. *Smith's First Book in Geography*. New York, 1839.

Pittsburgh Years

Aptheker, Herbert. *A Documentary History of the Negro People in the United States,* Citadel, 1951.

———— "Militant Abolitionism," in *Journal of Negro History,* Oct. 1941.

Baldwin, Leland. *Pittsburgh: The Story of a City*. University of Pittsburgh Press, 1937.

Boucher, John N., ed. *A Century and a Half of Pittsburg and Her People*. 4 vols. Lewis Publishing Co., 1908.

Craig, Neville. *History of Pittsburg*. Pittsburgh, 1851.

Foner, Philip. *The Life and Writings of Frederick Douglass,* Vol I. International, 1950.

Garrison, William L. *Thoughts on African Colonization*. Boston, 1832.

Harper, Frank C. *Pittsburgh of Today*. 3 vols. American Historical Society, 1931.

Harpster, John W., ed. *Pen Pictures of Early Western Pennsylvania*. University of Pittsburgh Press, 1938.

Hazard's Register. Vol IX, Feb. 1832. "African Education Society."

Johnson, Charles. "The Rise of the Negro Magazine," in *Journal of Negro History*, Jan. 1928.

Killikelly, Sarah. *History of Pittsburgh*. Montgomery Co., 1906.

Litwack, Leon F. *North of Slavery: The Negro in the Free States*. University of Chicago Press, 1961.

Mehlinger, Louis. "The Attitude of the Free Negro Toward African Colonization," in *Journal of Negro History*, July 1916.

Penn, I. G. *The Afro-American Press*. Willey & Co., 1891.

Porter, Dorothy. "The Organized Educational Activities of Negro Literary Societies, 1828–46," in *Journal of Negro Education*, Oct. 1936.

Quarles, Benjamin. *Black Abolitionists*. Oxford University Press, 1969.

―――― *Frederick Douglass*. Atheneum, 1969.

Sherwood, Henry N. "The Formation of the American Colonization Society," in *Journal of Negro History*, July 1917.

Stanton, William. *The Leopard's Spots: Scientific Attitudes Toward Race in America*. University of Chicago Press, 1960.

Turner, Edward. *The Negro in Pennsylvania*. American Historical Association, 1911.

Wilson, Erasmus, ed. *Standard History of Pittsburg, Pa*. Cornell & Co., 1898.

Wright, Richard R. *The Negro in Pennsylvania*. AME Book Concern, n.d.

NEWSPAPERS, MAGAZINES, AND DIRECTORIES

Colored American, 1837–39.
Fahnestock's Pittsburgh Directory for 1850.
Harris' Pittsburgh Business Directory, 1837.
——— *General Business Directory of the Cities of Pittsburgh and Allegheny*, 1847.
National Enquirer and Constitutional Advocate (later *Pennsylvania Freeman*), 1836–53 (incomplete file).
The North Star, 1847–50.
The Mystery, Apr. 16, 1845; Dec. 16, 1846, and exchange articles in *Pennsylvania Freeman, Palladium of Liberty, Pittsburgh Chronicle, Anti-Slavery Bugle, Liberator*, 1843–47.
Pittsburgh *Courier*. Special Supplement, Feb. 24, 1962.
Pittsburgh *Daily Chronicle*, 1843–47.
Pittsburgh *Gazette*, 1833–36.
Pittsburgh *Saturday Visiter*, 1849–53.
Western Pennsylvania Historical Magazine, 1931–68.
Woodward & Rowland's Pittsburgh Directory for 1852.

MANUSCRIPT COLLECTIONS

William Lloyd Garrison Papers. Boston Public Library, Boston, Mass.
Frederick Douglass Papers. National Park Service, Washington, D.C.

Medical Education

Bauer, Edward. *Doctors Made in America.* Lippincott, 1963.
Bowen, Catherine D. *Yankee from Olympus: Oliver Wendell Holmes.* Bantam, 1960.
Cobb, W. Montague. "Martin R. Delany," in *Journal of the National Medical Association*, May 1952.
Harrington, Thomas F. *The Harvard Medical School: A History.* 2 vols., New York, 1905.

Harvard University. *Catalogue of Students Attending Medical Lectures in Boston, 1850–1*. Boston, 1851.

Holmes, Oliver Wendell. *Collected Works*. 10 vols.

Howe, Mark A. De Wolfe. *Holmes of the Breakfast-Table*, Oxford University Press, 1939.

The Liberator, Sept. 27, 1850–May 30, 1851.

Massachusetts Colonization Society. *Annual Reports*. 1848–59.

Mettler, Cecilia. *The History of Medicine*. Blakiston, 1947.

Miller, Kelly. "The Historical Background of Negro Physicians," in *Journal of Negro History*, April 1916.

Morse, John T. *Life and Letters of Oliver Wendell Holmes*, 2 vols. Houghton Mifflin, 1896.

Shyrock, R. H., ed. "The Advent of Modern Medicine in Philadelphia, 1800–50," in *Medicine in America*. Johns Hopkins Press, 1966.

MANUSCRIPT COLLECTIONS

Harvard Medical School Archives, Boston, Mass. Folder of recommendations for Martin R. Delany, 1850.

———— Folder of petitions of students and draft of faculty votes, 1850.

———— Medical Faculty Minutes, Nov. 4, 1850; Dec. 26, 1850.

Central America

The Aliened American, April 9, 1853.

Bard, Samuel. *Waikna: Adventures on the Mosquito Shore*, Harper, 1855.

Frederick Douglass' Paper, May 6, 1852; Aug. 25, 1854.

New York *Herald*, 1852.

New York *Daily Times*, 1852–53.

Peck, Anne Merriman. *The Pageant of Middle American History*. Longmans, Green, 1947.

Squier, E. G. *Notes on Central America*, Harper, 1855.

———— *Nicaragua: Its People, Scenery, Monuments and the Proposed Interoceanic Canal*, Appleton, 1851.

Canada Years

Du Bois, W. E. B. *John Brown.* International, 1962.

Flournoy, H. W., ed. *Calendar of Virginia State Papers,* Vol XI.

Hamilton, James C. "John Brown in Canada," in *Canadian Magazine,* Dec. 1894.

Hinton, Richard. *John Brown and His Men.* Funk & Wagnalls, 1894.

Landon, Fred. "The Anti-Slavery Society of Canada," in *Journal of Negro History,* Jan. 1919.

——— "Canada's Part in Freeing the Slave," in *Ontario Historical Society Magazine,* 1919.

——— "The Negro Migration to Canada after 1850," in *Journal of Negro History,* Jan. 1920.

Lauriston, Victor. *Romantic Kent: The Story of a County.* n.p., 1952.

Tanser, H. S. *Settlement of Negroes in Kent County, Ontario.* University of Toronto Press, 1939.

Villard, Oswald G. *John Brown.* Knopf, 1943.

NEWSPAPERS AND MAGAZINE

The Anglo-African Magazine, 1859.
Chatham *Tri-Weekly Planet,* 1859.
Chatham *Western Planet,* 1853–58.
Frederick Douglass' Paper, 1852–55.
Provincial Freeman, 1853–57.
Voice of the Fugitive, 1851.
Weekly Anglo-African, 1859.

MANUSCRIPT COLLECTIONS

William Lloyd Garrison Papers. Boston Public Library, Boston, Mass.

Memorandum of Deed of Purchase of Property. Book C, Documents No. 21 and 256, County Registry Office, Chatham, Ontario.

Emigration Debates and African Trip

African Civilization Society. Constitution, in Howard Brotz, ed., *Negro Social and Political Thought 1850–1920*. Basic Books, 1966.

Bowen, T. J. *Central Africa*. Southern Baptist Publication Society, 1857.

Bowen, J. W. E., ed. *Africa and the American Negro*. Atlanta, 1896.

Campbell, Robert. *A Pilgrimage to My Motherland*. Reprinted in Howard Bell, ed., *Search For a Place*. University of Michigan Press, 1969.

House of Representatives. *Report of the Select Committee on Emancipation and Colonization*. Washington, 1862.

Kirk-Green, A. H. M. "America in the Niger Valley," in *Phylon*, 3rd quarter, 1962.

Kopytoff, Jean Herskovits. *Preface to Modern Nigeria*. University of Wisconsin Press, 1965.

Livingstone, David. *Perilous Adventures and Extensive Discoveries in the Interior of Africa*. Philadelphia, 1872.

McPherson, James. "Abolitionist and Negro Opposition to Colonization During the Civil War," in *Phylon*, 4th quarter, 1965.

Shepperson, George. "Notes on Negro American Influences on the Emergence of African Nationalism," in *Journal of African History*, Vol. I, No. 2, 1960.

Ullman, Victor. *Look to the North Star: A Life of William King*, Beacon, 1969.

Usher, Roland G. "Lincoln's Plan for Colonizing the Emancipated Negroes," in *Journal of Negro History*, Jan. 1919.

NEWSPAPERS

Cleveland *Morning Leader,* Aug. 25, 1854.
Daily Cleveland Herald, Aug. 25–26, 1854.
The Liberator, May 1, 1863.
Weekly Anglo-African, 1859–62.

MANUSCRIPT COLLECTIONS

African Aid Society Papers. Canadian National Archives, Ottawa,
   Canada.
American Colonization Society Papers. Library of Congress,
   Washington, D.C.

In England

Dallas, Susan, ed. *Diary of George Mifflin Dallas,* Philadelphia,
   1892.
Quarles, Benjamin. "Ministers Without Portfolio," in *Journal of
   Negro History,* Jan. 1954.
Royal Geographical Society of London. *Proceedings,* Vol. IV, pp.
   218–22.
———— *Journal,* 1860.
Wade, John D. *Augustus Baldwin Longstreet,* Macmillan, 1924.

NEWSPAPERS AND MAGAZINES

London *Morning Chronicle,* July 17–23, 1860.
London *Morning Herald,* July 19, 1860.
London *Morning Post,* July 19–23, 1860.
London *Times,* July 17–20, 1860.
Punch, July 25, 1860.
Vanity Fair, Aug. 11, 1860.

MANUSCRIPT COLLECTIONS

National Archives, Washington, D.C. George M. Dallas to Lewis Cass, July 20, 1860; Lewis Cass to George M. Dallas, Sept. 11, 1860.

Civil War Years

Cornish, Dudley. *The Sable Arm.* Norton, 1966.
Emilio, Luis. *History of the Fifty-Fourth Regiment of Massachusetts Volunteer Infantry.* Arno Press, 1969.
McPherson, James. *The Negro's Civil War.* Pantheon, 1965.
Payne, Daniel. *Recollections of Seventy Years.* Arno, 1969.
Quarles, Benjamin. *Lincoln and the Negro.*
────── *The Negro in the Civil War.* Little, Brown, 1953.
Shannon, Fred A. "The Federal Government and the Negro Soldier 1861–65," in *Journal of Negro History*, Oct. 1926.
Stearns, Frank. *The Life and Public Services of George Luther Stearns.* Lippincott, 1907.
Voegeli, V. Jacque. *Free but Not Equal: The Midwest and the Negro during the Civil War.* University of Chicago Press, 1967.
Williams, George A. *A History of Negro Troops in the War of the Rebellion.* Harper, 1888.

NEWSPAPERS

The Anglo-African, 1865.
Christian Recorder, 1866.
Douglass' Monthly, Jan. 1859–Aug. 1862.
New York *Times,* 1864–65.

MANUSCRIPT COLLECTIONS

John E. Bruce Papers. Schomburg Collection, New York Public Library, New York, N.Y.

Martin Delany. Correspondence, recruiting posters, military records in War Records Office, National Archives, Washington, D.C.
Toussaint Delany. Military records in War Records Office, National Archives, Washington, D.C.

Freedmen's Bureau and Reconstruction

Aptheker, Herbert. "South Carolina Negro Conventions, 1865," in *Journal of Negro History,* Jan. 1946.
Abbott, Martin. *The Freedmen's Bureau in South Carolina.* University of North Carolina Press, 1967.
Bennett, Lerone. *Black Power U.S.A.* Johnson Publishing Co., 1967.
Du Bois, W. E. B. *Black Reconstruction.* Harcourt, Brace, 1935.
Hyman, Harold, ed. *The Radical Republicans and Reconstruction.* Bobbs-Merrill, 1967.
Conner, James. *Letters of James Conner.* Bryan Co., 1950.
Jarrell, Hampton M. *Wade Hampton and the Negro.* University of South Carolina Press, 1949.
Reynolds, John. *Reconstruction in South Carolina.* Columbia, 1905.
Simkins, Francis B., and Robert H. Woody. *South Carolina During Reconstruction.* University of North Carolina Press, 1932.
Sterling, Dorothy. *Captain of the* Planter. Doubleday, 1958.
Taylor, A. A. "The Negro in South Carolina During Reconstruction," in *Journal of Negro History,* July 1924.
Williamson, Joel. *After Slavery: The Negro in South Carolina During Reconstruction.* University of North Carolina Press, 1965.

NEWSPAPERS

Beaufort *Republican,* 1872–74.
Charleston *News and Courier,* 1873–85.
Christian Recorder, 1869.

Missionary Record, scattered issues.
New National Era, 1870–74.
New South, 1865–66.
New York *Times,* 1874.
New-York *Daily Tribune,* March 6, 1875.

MANUSCRIPT COLLECTIONS

Martin Delany. Freedmen's Bureau Papers in War Records Office, National Archives, Washington, D.C.
————— Correspondence in General Records of the State Department, National Archives, Washington, D.C.
Papers of Governors Scott, Moses, Chamberlain, Hampton. South Carolina Archives, Columbia, S.C.

Last Years and Family

Arnett, B. W. and S. T. Mitchell, eds. *The Wilberforce Alumnal,* Xenia, Ohio, 1885.
Brown, Hallie Q. *Homespun Heroines and Other Women of Distinction,* Xenia, 1926.
————— *Pen Pictures of Pioneers of Wilberforce,* Aldine, 1937.
Holly, James T. "In Memoriam," in *AME Church Review,* Oct. 1886.
Ransom, Reverdy. *School Days at Wilberforce.* Springfield, Ohio, n.d.
Tindall, George. *South Carolina Negroes 1877–1900,* University of South Carolina Press, 1952.

NEWSPAPERS

Charleston *News and Courier,* 1877–80; Jan. 1885.
Cleveland *Gazette,* Jan. 31, 1885.
Washington *Bee,* 1882–83.
Xenia *Daily Gazette,* Jan. 7, 1885.

MANUSCRIPT COLLECTIONS

John E. Bruce Papers. Schomburg Collection, New York Public Library, New York, N.Y.

Catherine Delany. Pension Application in War Records Office, National Archives, Washington, D.C.

Martin Delany. Correspondence in American Colonization Society Papers, Library of Congress, Washington, D.C.

———— Correspondence in General Records of the Department of the Treasury, National Archives, Washington, D.C.

Toussaint Delany. Pension Applications in War Records Office, National Archives, Washington, D.C.

INDEX

DOROTHY STERLING was educated at Wellesley and Barnard colleges and began her writing career on the Federal Writers Project. After many years as a researcher at Time, Inc., she began writing books for adults and young readers. Mrs. Sterling is well known for her books on black history and culture, including *The Trouble They Seen: The Story of Reconstruction in the Words of African Americans* (available from Da Capo Press); *Ahead of Her Time: Abby Kelley and the Politics of Antislavery; Speak Out in Thunder Tones: Letters and Other Writings by Black Northerners, 1787–1865; We Are Your Sisters: Black Women in the 19th Century; Freedom Train: The Story of Harriet Tubman; Captain of the Planter: The Story of Robert Smalls;* and *Tear Down the Walls.* Mrs. Sterling lives in Wellfleet, Massachusetts, where she is currently at work on a memoir.

Lightning Source UK Ltd.
Milton Keynes UK
UKOW02f2319230616

276964UK00001B/21/P